THE OPIUM SMUGGLERS

A True Story of our Northern Seas

ION IDRIESS

ETT IMPRINT
Exile Bay

This 4th edition published by ETT Imprint, Exile Bay 2022

ETT IMPRINT
PO Box R1906
Royal Exchange NSW 1225 Australia

First published by Angus & Robertson Publishers 1948
Reprinted 1951, 1957.

First electronic edition published by ETT Imprint in 2022

ISBN 978-1-922698-07-0 (pbk)
ISBN 978-1-922698-08-7 (ebk)

Cover: Original cover from the first edition

Designed by Tom Thompson

CONTENTS

Titles available from ETT Imprint

PROSPECTING FOR GOLD
MADMAN'S ISLAND
LASSETER'S LAST RIDE
FLYNN OF THE INLAND
THE DESERT COLUMN
MEN OF THE JUNGLE
GOLD-DUST AND ASHES
DRUMS OF MER
THE YELLOW JOSS
MAN TRACKS
FORTY FATHOMS DEEP
OVER THE RANGE
LIGHTNING RIDGE
SHOOT TO KILL
SNIPING
GUERRILLA TACTICS
TRAPPING THE JAP
LURKING DEATH
THE SCOUT
HEADHUNTERS OF THE CORAL SEA
NEMARLUK; KING OF THE WILDS
HORRIE THE WOG DOG
ISLES OF DESPAIR
THE OPIUM SMUGGLERS
THE WILD WHITE MAN OF BADU
OUTLAWS OF THE LEOPOLDS
THE RED CHIEF
THE SILVER CITY
BACK O' CAIRNS
'GOUGER' OF THE BULLETIN
ION IDRIESS: The Last Interview

OUR FLYING ACES (forthcoming)

Author's Note

This boys' book is for your dad as well as for you. When he was a boy he had mates, and one special mate, just as you have. So I thought I'd write of my adventures with my old mate, Dick.

This is a true story, and dear old Cooktown and Lizard Island with all their historical and pioneer associations, are well on the map. Our great navigator, Captain James Cook, sailed the very waters written of here, put foot upon the very earth Dick and I so humbly trod long afterwards. And the glimpse you will get here of underwater life amongst the coral reefs is exactly as Dick and I saw it, and as anyone who sails to that sunlit sea can see it today.

So come with Dick and me on this voyage of discovery.

If you like this book of our adventures I'll be pleased indeed; and if, in reading it, you learn just a tiny bit about our grand country I'll be more pleased still.

In these pages you will see that I am called "Jack", not Ion. During all my bush life I have been called Jack because, until recently, Ion was an unfamiliar name in the outback. Now there are many Ions and Ians in the back country, but the old hands still call me Jack.

It is a pleasure to thank the Curator of the Brisbane Museum for his courtesy in obtaining for me a photo of the half iron tank in which Mrs Watson made her tragic voyage; and - to thank Mr Poulsen for the' excellent photo which is the frontispiece.

And here I must send a message to two grand friends of mine, A. Standfield Sampson, and A. R. Meldrum, pioneers of Cooktown in my boyhood days. The excellent photos of the life of Cooktown and surrounding waters they sent me to illustrate this book cannot be printed, alas, through circumstances beyond my publisher's control. In future editions, when materials are easier to obtain, we hope to publish these photos. And now, good luck to you all, and I hope you like my old mate Dick.

ION IDRIESS.
1948

A portrait of Mrs Watson.

I

CROSS-EYED JOE

A LOVELY day in which to start a grand adventure - everyone happy, sunlight bathing the hills of Cooktown and shining, too, upon the luggers and ketches, the cutters and canoes and other quaint craft lying in Endeavour Bay.

Our eyes were all for the *Nancy Bell*, the pride and joy of Cross-eyed Joe, the Filipino. Dick and I were sailing on this cruise with him.

Quite a crowd were chatting and laughing as we strolled down the street of the little town, friendly folk come to see us off – Dick's mother and sisters and brothers, of course; Big Charlie Patching, the local solicitor and Mayor, beloved as the "Father of Cooktown"; the girls from the Seaview Hotel, and two score boys and girls who had grown up with Dick; the giant Shipton brothers from the tin-fields away out at Shipton's Hat; good-humoured McIntosh from the Lion's Den in the ranges at Mount Amos; and a dozen prospectors spelling in town from the Batavia River gold diggings in the wild North. Last, but not least in Dick's eyes, half a dozen aboriginal boys from the Mount Cook tribe. For Dick knew many of the abo¬riginal lads from childhood, spent his holidays hunting and fishing with them, doing them many a favour while learning, in return, hardiness and bushcraft.

A very proud lad among those trailing behind us was Little Paddy, almost buried under Dick's swag; he had carried it all the way from Dick's home, would allow no other hand to touch it. The local residents smilingly called him Dick's "Man Friday". Inseparable from Dick in the bush, Little Paddy now staggering along in an old pair of Dick's trousers was nearly breaking his heart that he could not sail with us. His father, Big Paddy, was one of the crew, and had asked that Little Paddy should be signed on. But Cross-eyed Joe, with a cross-eyed smile, shook his head.

A sandalwood team was lumbering into town, the packhorses heavy-laden with the rich yellow wood from the wild west coast away up the Peninsula. The last team to come into town from the Lukin had reported two men speared by the blacks. We strolled past dimly lighted shops fronting the warren of Chinatown. Solemn-faced men and Smiling women in quaint trousers and sandals farewelled us from the doorways, for everyone in Cooktown knows everyone else.

Down the main street our chattering little company dawdled, with the good-humoured folk calling greeting from footpath, home, and shop. A crowd of tin-scratchers and gold-seekers from the veranda of the West Coast Hotel gave us a rousing farewell, for Dick's folk were very popular. To a clatter of hooves and a piercing yell all hands stood and gazed up the street. Here came Wild Ned at full gallop and bareback, spanking his horse with his hat. He passed us with a yell that echoed out across the waterway. Hell for leather, Ned would gallop defiantly down the street past the police station to the wharf where, in a cloud of dust, he must wheel round to run the gauntlet back again. Wild Ned, one of the back-country's great horsemen, had come to town "on the jag" again.

"I'll bet it's not his own horse he's riding," said Dick, laughing.

"You bet it's not," drawled a tin-scratcher. "He's lifted it from some cattleman up north."

"Just like Ned," said Long Andy, "to gallop a borrowed horse past the police station."

"It's an ill wind – " remarked Mr Patching, the solicitor.

"Looks like another case for you, Charlie," added Dick's elder brother.

"I am grateful for what the good Lord provides," answered the "Father of Cooktown".

"You'll lose a paying client when Wild Ned breaks his neck," said Billy Sleep.

"The devil looks after his own," replied Mr Patching confidently. "Wild Ned is good for many a good case yet."

With a laugh, we carried on past B.P's where the bank manager, together with the old warden, both good blokes, strolled across from the bank opposite. We greeted them, watching Wild Ned now come galloping back up the street. He had been too quick for the police this time and signalled his triumph with piercing yells. Next time, after he galloped past the station, the Law would run out with a rope and stretch it across the street. But in this quiet little town of lots of time, no one cared much. A regiment of soldiers could have galloped down the street without hurting anyone.

With a glance at Mrs Watson's monument (seldom did anyone pass without glancing at it), we strolled along the embankment past Captain Cook's monument. breathing the clean, sweet breeze. At the water's edge before us was a little crowd of coloured folk and aboriginals. The flashing eyes of our dark-skinned skipper's wife were smilingly bright as she lorded it in a new dress that set off a slim figure. Alor San's and Ah Matt's brown-eyed girl friends were there, all smiles and chatter as is the way of the coloured folk at the least excuse. There, too, were wives, youngsters, and hosts of "relations" of Big Paddy and

Billy, not to mention their dogs. The *Nancy Bell* was to receive a royal send-off. As if to give it an official touch the old Sergeant and the Customs Officer strolled across from the steamer wharf.

"All the heads of the town have turned up," murmured Dick bashfully. "You'd think we were the king or something."

From the veranda of the Seaview Hotel folk waved to us as, with laughing chatter, we crowded round Captain Cook's tree. At that time the big old stump was still standing, and the Town Council kept it fenced in. It was to this tree that Captain Cook had moored the brave little Endeavour when he careened and repaired her after striking a coral reef. Here the Endeavour River empties into the bay. And now, from this very spot where Britain's greatest navigator and his lion-hearted men had refitted their vessel for the unknown seas again, Dick and I were about to sail.

Surely a voyage from this historic spot must be destined for adventure.

Out on the *Nancy Bell,* Cross-eyed Joe stood up and waved. Big Paddy stepped into the dinghy astern and came rowing towards us, for Skipper Joe was keen to be away' with the tide. I nodded, "Be seeing you", as friends crowded round; and Dick bashfully stepped towards the dinghy at the water's edge, waving a hand to the last farewells from his mother. Already he had said good-bye to his people and' hated doing it again before all this crowd. But I noticed he quietly smiled into Little Paddy's eyes as Big Paddy and my own Aboriginal boy chum put the swags in the dinghy. Little Paddy was nearly howling.

Dick stepped into the dinghy, I followed, and father Paddy, ignoring his family, bent over to fondly pat the head of his hunting dog. The aboriginal boys pushed the dinghy into deeper water, Big Paddy settled down at the oars. A chorus of laughing farewells, calls of advice – "Look after yourselves! Be sure and bring back plenty of shell, boys" – followed us from the shore as Big Paddy's dog lifted his head and howled dismally.

We pulled alongside the cutter, threw the swags aboard and climbed up on deck.

"Where Little Paddy?" asked Cross-eyed Joe in his soft voice.

"Longa shore," growled Big Paddy.

"Little Paddy like come, too, Dicky?" asked Joe, Smiling.

"Too right!" answered Dick eagerly. "I wish you could find room for him, skipper – he's only the size of a mouse, and I'm sure he'd earn his keep.

"Arright," nodded Joe. "Big Paddy bring him aboard." A happy smile on Dick's boyish face, broad grins from our two Malays and aboriginal shipmates. Big Paddy bent to the oars again.

Excitement ashore, then shrill cries from women and girls and boys calling out for Little Paddy. He had vanished.

At Big Paddy's guttural shout, a little black monkey with tear-stained face popped out from behind a tree. He came running like a deer and jumped straight into the dinghy, to a chorus of laughter.

Big Paddy came rowing back again. Little Paddy in the stern quaintly seemed to have grown into one huge grin from which two big shining eyes stared up at Dick. They jumped aboard. The two Malay seamen leaned over and, with an expert heave, lifted the dinghy aboard and lashed it down.

"Up jib!" ordered Joe.

"Up anchor!" and the crew stepped to the windlass while we stowed our swags below.

"We're aboard," said Dick happily as the winch pawls clanked. "Smell the sea in her! Wasn't it great of Joe to let Little Paddy come at the last moment? He's not a bad old bloke, old Cross-eyed Joe. Let's hurry up top, Jack, and we'll give them a hand."

"Up mainsail!" called Joe, and as the big sail billowed up with squeak of blocks the *Nancy Bell* made way. With Joe at the tiller, we went heading for the open sea.

We waved towards shore, from where the shouts grew fainter. From pearling luggers and trochus cutters came, sweetly over the water the farewell shouts in good old Australian, in Malay and Aboriginal and pidgin English. We were gliding past the steamer wharf, and lazy waves came splashing, inviting the *Nancy Bell* to dance saucily. Hugging the low line of hills, the little town on the waterfront looked very pretty in the bright sunlight. Soon it looked but a toy town, the white Signal Station standing boldly above it on top of Grassy Hill. We were at sea. We turned to make the cutter snug and shipshape, Little Paddy falling over himself to help.

With Cross-eyed Joe we were off to seek trochus shell. It was bringing £80 a ton in Cooktown, where the merchants shipped it to China and Japan to be made into "pearl" buttons.

Beside Cross-eyed Joe, Dick and his "Man Friday" and me, there were four in the crew: the Malays Alor San and Ah Matt, and the aboriginals Big Paddy and Billy.

Our dark-skinned skipper, Cross-eyed Joe, was a tall, sinewy Filipino with a shadowy smile. Few would guess that he was by no means the quiet, inoffensive gentleman he appeared to be. Alor San and Ah Matt were broad-faced, quick-eyed, nuggety little fellows, cheery mates, both tough Macassar men with the blood from centuries of pirate forefathers running hotly in their veins, but ever ready with a joke and a smile, and quick and expert at a job. Big Paddy and Billy were Mount Cook aboriginals, known to Dick ever since he could remember. Like most coastal aboriginals they were good seamen, at such times as they felt inclined to forsake their hunting-grounds for a cruise. Dick and I were aboard on Cross-eyed Joe's invitation to a "working holiday". We were to lend a hand and make ourselves generally useful. We would receive no wage, but a small share of any shell won. The more shell, the more money. We had jumped at the opportunity.

Dick was familiar with the small craft that made Cooktown their home port, and I had already sailed once before the mast. So that, although we both were boys, old Cross-eyed Joe knew we would more than pay our way.

Our skipper of the iron-grey hair was by no means an old man. He was old to the ways of his world though, and perhaps this made him seem old to us.

With Dick at the tiller we were rounding Cape Bedford when Big Paddy shouted and painted out over the starboard bow. Some furious commotion appeared in the water away out there, a splashing as of monsters under a cloud of shrieking sea-birds.

"Killers," grunted Joe. "They fight him whale." Presently the waters quietened, except for the disappointed birds.

"He's sounded," said Joe. "He dives, try dodge devils away below. They chase him right down deep. Tigers, those killers, devils. He lucky whale suppose he shake them off."

Little Paddy was staring longingly out where the whale had been.

"Plenty big-feller tucker that one," laughed Dick.

"Sposem he bin come close up, I bin spear 'im!", declared Little Paddy boastfully.

While boiling the sea kettle I almost tumbled overboard as, with a startled shout Joe shoved the tiller hard over. The deck seemed to buck away from underfoot as almost at our bows a black "island" broke surface while a torpedo-thing shot up and landed "Smack!" upon it.

The whale had been harried from the depths to breathe.

We gaped at the enormous thing, its little eyes staring at us as, with a gasping roar, it blew a fountain of vapour. The cross-eyed half of Joe's face was startling as he pressed hard on the tiller, and Little Paddy turned ashen green as we glided past that glistening bulk now attacked on all sides by leaping, snapping killer whales lunging at the whale's massive jaws in a terrible striving to tear out its tongue. For one awful moment the tormented monster seemed about to hurl itself upon us, to crush its foes against the *Nancy Bell.* A gleaming body shot straight out of the water across the bows to smack down on the whale's head then bury its fangs in its jaws; That killer saved us at the critical moment, and now a dozen killers were lunging at the whale with flashing ivory fangs, wrenching away great mouthfuls of blubber. The air was a swishing and shrieking bedlam of sea birds diving to snatch at scraps of skin and blubber. And those birds somehow scared me the most with their piercing shrieks, the vicious hiss of their hurtling bodies as, taking no faintest notice of us, they dived straight past and down amongst those clashing jaws to snatch a scrap from the living prey.

It was a frightening sight indeed as we steered through the turmoil. The killers, nearly as long as the *Nancy Bell,* Hashed black and white as the long black fins sheared through the water and the big flippers thrashed the foam. Like wolves they attacked their prey, tearing the whale to pieces in an orgy of ferocious teamwork. The agonized beast rolled beside us to keep with us, as if some dim thing in its tortured mind whispered to it that this strange creature might give it help. In a wallow of foam and blood it now rolled over, and Joe's eyes nearly started from his head as the mighty tail with those massive flukes rose up like the side of a house and thundered down upon the dodging killers, drenching us with spray. Dick's face was white, Big Paddy's and Billy's Sickly grey. With the *Nancy Bell* fairly bouncing in the cauldron we splashed past, staring back as the great black tail heaved up again to crash in a thunderous wall of spray. Killers shot into the air, spinning down upon the whale to rip and tear ceaselessly.

"Close up we finish that time!" sighed Alor San with a sickly grin.

"S'pose whale he hit Nancy Bell that one time," said Ah Matt, "we splinters an' sausage meat now!"

"By cripe!" gasped Big Paddy. "Belly belong me all water."

"Lucky man you not in killer's belly!" declared Joe grimly.

And so thought all of us. Especially me, for I'd so nearly slipped overboard.

2

THE COCKROACHES

WE anchored that evening in a sheltered little bay between Cape Flattery and Lookout Point. While the cutter was being made snug, Dick at the galley was stirring the curry, and it smelt good. Little Paddy couldn't keep his goggly eyes off the pot, nor his tongue from licking expectant lips. That curry, besides its spuds and onions and chillies was tasty with chopped up fish and preserved Chinese shrimps and noodles and appetizing herbs. Alor San had enlivened it with Indian curry and soy sauce. It would taste good.

Squatting on the washed down deck, we ate with the appetite that only work at sea can give. Little Paddy finished his third helping, but still gazed longingly at the pot.

"You like him curry?" grinned Cross-eyed Joe. "Good-feller, too right!" Sighed Little Paddy. "That one tucker burn 'im up belly belonga me!"

"Ou ai!" agreed Billy, and grunted a fiery breath.

The washing-up was simple: we each rinsed our plate and pannikin over the side.

The stars shone out over a sea quiet as a river; a fish sped by in a whirl of phosphorus.

The coast near by was blackness of cliff and hill, dark mystery vanishing back into the interior. With the boys sprawled on their blankets for'ard, Dick was smoking. Eager as usual for information about the wild Cape York Peninsula that held our dreams, he was asking Big Paddy and Billy about the natives inland; they were replying in uneasy tones, telling tales of myall tribes of wild men only a little farther north. Neither Big Paddy nor Billy would care to land on the coast now, for already they were out of their own country.

"No good go longa shore," growled Billy. 'Wild black man spear 'im."

Little Paddy looked fearful at the very thought, certain that to go ashore would mean being killed and eaten.

"You'd be no good," said Dick teasingly. "You're too tough. Anyway, you'd hardly make a decent mouthful for a warrior."

"Warrior got 'im big-feller mouth," murmured Little Paddy.

"You no fright longa warrior?" queried Ah Matt. "You spear 'im?"

"Maybe warrior spear 'im me," mumbled Little Paddy dubiously.

Cross-eyed Joe and I were smoking aft. The Filipino was a silent man, even-tempered but not given to speaking unless he was giving an order or answering a question. I would rather have been with Dick and the boys for'ard, yarning, but you can't leave a man entirely alone when at sea, even if he is the skipper. I could hear the soft voice, the low laughs of Alor telling stories of his grandfather's and his father's pirate days, when they sailed from Macassar to raid the seas, to plunder and cut throats and seize slaves from any ships or villages not strong enough to fight them off. Then Ah Matt joined in with tales of some blood-thirsty sultan and his grim forays against rival sultans and the Dutch. Dick's eyes were shining in the starlight; he loved such stories.

Little Paddy curled up like a monkey beside Dick when he could keep awake no longer. Gradually the voices died away. Big Paddy yawned cavernously and stretched out. Billy coiled up beside him.

Joe smiled. "Talk finish – they sleep now. Me turn in, Jacky."

And with a glance at sea and sky he stepped noiselessly below.

I followed him down past the engine into the tiny, stuffy cabin: from the cockpit we had to crawl into the humid, smelly place. Joe struck a match, and his sombre face stood out like the head on a copper penny as he stooped to light the hurricane lamp. Yawning, he pulled off his singlet and unbuckled his belt. His trousers fell down, and with slow, easy movement he wrapped a sarong around his waist. Being constantly in and out of the water, we would generally wear the comfortable sarong while at sea now. Joe hunched forward on the edge of his bunk, rolled a last cigarette, lit it, seemed to slide back into his bunk, and puffed at the cabin top so close to his head. The smoke dawdled there, eddying its way to escape. I crawled into the other bunk, glad to undress, for it was almost suffocatingly hot in this dim-lit cubby-hole. Up above was coolness and starlight and space, but in this stagnant hole the hurricane lamp seemed a slow-burning fire.

Joe stubbed out his cigarette butt, turned the lamp down low, smiled through wisps of smoke.

"Good night, Jacky," he murmured, and in a few moments was asleep.

All was deathly quiet. Then, from away up for'ard came Big Paddy's snore, harsh as a dugong breaking surface.

I rolled another cigarette – there seemed no one in the world but me.

There came a whispering-then a musical gurgle-the tide was beginning to turn, slipping along the bows, sighing in soft gurglings along the sides within inches of my head. Beads of sweat were now glistening on Joe's dark-skinned body. His face looked sinister in the dim light, for the cross-eyed lid was all screwed up as if to ward off the blow that had made the deep scar that cut down along his forehead and cheek. I wondered whether it was slash of knife or cut of axe that had once so nearly split his face in half. Perhaps he got it during a brawl in a gambling dive in Chinatown, perhaps in a fight with some coloured crew at sea.

I grew aware of the faintest, whispering rustle, like insect feet through deathly quietness creeping over stiff tissue paper. Again it came, again, growing from the murk, all the cabin faintly hissing in the eeriest of rustling scratchings.

Then it came definitely – urgently. Lots and lots of rustling "somethings".

Something was crawling about.

In the dull glow of the hurricane lamp, a gigantic cockroach appeared on the cabin roof. Its crawly-legged, gingery body was nearly six inches long. Its wriggling "whiskers" seemed longer, stretching out and waggling inquisitively in a ghoulish seeking. It was spying out what was doing, staring down at all in the cabin and at Joe and me at the same time-particularly at Joe and me. The beastly thing decided on. Joe: it knew he was asleep – I was awake.

Another appeared on the cabin side, then three more, yellowish ones these, very lively. With sight attuned to the murky light, I distinguished countless whiskers reaching out from everywhere around and above and below; then dozens of cockroach heads, then scores and scores, came peeping from places where there seemed no join of timber, no crack, no slightest crevice from which they could come. Then the bodies came as if being squeezed out from the very timbers. And the cabin was alive with cockroaches, spying 'roaches, moving 'roaches, fluttering 'roaches, running 'roaches, wingy 'roaches, the eerie murmur of their moving now a sharp rustling of countless feet and claws and legs and wing-things.

A horrid form of life – they knew things, they planned things.

The first big fellow dropped straight on to Joe's thick, iron-grey hair. It slithered down his temple, began to nibble the hair just above his ear. Three more scuttled over his chest, others started racing along his bare legs. The floor was alive with them, others rustling up the bunk and now in speedy eagerness swarming upon Joe.

Other brutes resented that I was awake. These were manoeuvring for action so as to avoid risk, but they were determined on action. The cabin roof above my bunk was now a ginger mass of them, with ginger whiskers wriggling and probing and pointing and spearing down, watching me. One dropped, but I hit the beastly thing from my chest. The others slithered back then surged round again; two dropped on my feet and hurriedly I kicked them off. They waited then and manoeuvred a bit; they knew I must fall asleep some time.

A new sound broke into these urgent rustlings, an arresting sound, crisp and gritty like the tiniest, sharpest teeth determinedly biting into some hard substance.

A massive ginger 'roach with arched back was chewing into Joe's big toenail, wolfing it, gnawing away like a miniature fiery vampire under the lamp glow. As I listened the sound magnified itself through the rustling until I thought of Dick's old dog crunching a bone, only this sound was more horribly mechanical, like the steely teeth-bites of a cross-cut saw.

The first big old fellow was still busy trimming Joe's hair, he was gnawing a distinct ridge through it; and now a big yellow fellow slid to the other ear. His broad back was a light, watery yellow, and the way the lamp glow fell on it it appeared to be semi-transparent, I thought I could see part of its beastly insides pulsing within it. I wondered why they always prefer the hair round a man's temples, between his ear and his head. Perhaps because he sweats a lot there, which salts the tasty morsel. Another hefty fellow was chewing into the other big toenail now, the sound of his teeth gathering intensity to rival the hunched up brute opposite. I lay there awhile wondering and wondering why men's toenails are a real delicacy to deep-sea cockroaches, especially such horn as grows on the feet of men who make their living from the waters of the Great Barrier Reef. They rarely wear boots, and perhaps the water in which they spend so much of their time soaks in, making their toenails salty. I felt quite pleased to believe I'd reasoned it out; the deep-sea 'roaches must relish salt. Though why they like to chew it from men's hair and toenails, what nourishment they get from such food I could not imagine. But it certainly makes them lively and tough and aggressive and hefty, for these deep-sea 'roaches are enormous fellows. And what they can and do eat is unbelievable,

There was a brute at each of Joe's other toenails now, several were in holts battling to get a chew at a nail. But though there was a lot of savage pushing the battle was being fought out with gloved tooth and claw, probably because if they had fought outright the scrimmage would have awakened the victim. And they cunningly guarded against that. He moved-they "froze" like cautious mice. When he breathed evenly again the harsh chewing broke out with renewed vigour.

Joe lay there slumbering uneasily, only a protesting quiver of his fingers, jerky breath and lips, convulsive movement of hand or toes when they swarmed too thickly upon him.

There he would lie until those clever fellows at his toes made a slip and gnawed into the quick. Then he would kick and snarl, and the 'roaches would scuttle aside until he relapsed into sleep again.

But they would feast tonight, for Joe had been six weeks with his family ashore and his hair and nails had grown a lot in that time. Meantime the 'roaches aboard had grown hungry.

When the 'roaches aboard such a craft increase to unbearable numbers, the master angrily empties his vessel of everything and beaches her in a creek where the high tide will flood over her decks. Only the mast or masts then stand above water. I have seen a mast such a swarming mass of brown and red and yellow 'roaches that not one spot of it was visible. They are knocked off with bags and leafy branches while the crew stand by with spears, awaiting the fish that generally come ravenously to the feast. Strange, even horrifying, to think how everything lives on everything else. Sea 'roaches, apart from other tucker, will live upon toenails. Fish gobble 'roaches. Man eats fish.

In these days the larger boats are fumigated. But it is so much trouble either to flood or to fumigate that some owners of small boats delay cleansing them until either the 'roaches or crew must leave. And the 'roaches won't leave until forced to.

Five of the beastly things dropped off the cabin roof on me at once – I must have dozed off. I climbed out of the bunk to a rustling scurry, grabbed my blankets and clothes and tobacco, determined to climb up to the cool, sweet air.

At the tiny companionway I glanced back. In a bath of sweat Cross-eyed Joe lay there breathing heavily, his temples and his toenails a mass of russet, ginger, and yellow feasting cockroaches. A busy, ceaseless gnawing emphasized by silence.

The quick of his toes would be tender tomorrow or the next day – or the next at latest. The slightest touch on his toes then and he'd squirm. At the kiss of salt spray he would smart.

I was only a boy, he was a man to which this life meant home. Still, I could not leave him like this, although he was so used to it. I stepped back, bent over him. The 'roaches on the roof rustled aside, those on his toes merely "stepped back".

"Skipper!" I murmured, and shook him.

In an instant he sat up and startled me as the 'roaches scuttled back. His good eye was blazing. It is a fool thing to wake abruptly any man used to a dangerous life.

"The cockroaches," I murmured. "They are eating your toes off!"

His face dropped back to its half-smiling mask.

"Roaches," he murmured softly. "Oh, he not too bad, Jacky. They trouble you?"

"Too much."

He smiled from one eye.

"Soon get used to them," he murmured.

He yawned, and reached under his bunk with a grunt.

Pulling out two empty bags, he grunted as he thrust his feet into them, bound them around, then tied them with cord.

Yawning, he lay back. "Goo' night, Jacky," he murmured, and closed his eyes.

I'd done my job, been matey with the skipper. But I could not stand the 'roaches' as well. He was welcome to them.

Up on deck the sweet night was all beauty. I spread my blankets, lay down, and rolled a cigarette. It would be a heavenly smoke and sleep after the sweating heat of that insect inferno below.

The cigarette half-smoked, I was falling asleep when in a flash the truth struck me.

Cross-eyed Joe, the Filipino, had two faces.

I'd seen them both. The kindly, deeply-gashed cross-eyed face of everyday. That other face when he was asleep then suddenly awakened, that half of a face that flashed out so momentarily you forgot the cross-eyed half. That alert-eyed, shrewd, tight-lipped second half.

Cross-eyed Joe was two men.

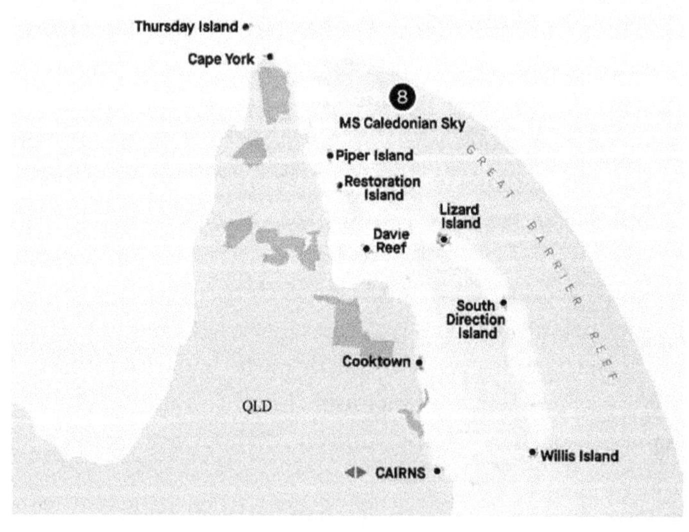

3

LAZILY SAILING ALONG

I AWOKE to the chattering of the boys. It was chilly and quite dark, a fire blazed in the galley illuminating Alor San and Ah Matt squatting beside the cooking pots. Dick woke and yawned, threw aside his blanket, pulled the blanket from Little Paddy - and rolled him across the deck.

"Shake a leg, Man Friday," laughed Dick. "The ship's on fire!"

But it takes more than that to wake an aboriginal boy to the day's work.

"All right," said Dick unfeelingly. "Stay there, then. We're hauling up the anchor – you've missed your breakfast!"

Two eyes opened wide in an alarmed black face. Little Paddy sat up and gazed anxiously towards the galley, saw the preparations there 'and grinned his relief. Dick gave Big Paddy and Billy a toe awakener in the ribs, then joined the gossipers at the galley. Joe came yawning up from below, threw a bucket overboard with an expert twist on the rope, hauled it up and plunged his head in it. I wondered how far his toenails were pared down.

The smell of ship and sea was distinct through the chilly coldness.

"What say you, Ah Matt?" said Dick. "You like this new day better than yesterday?"

"Maybe." Ah Matt smiled philosophically. "No can tell yet. No matter, plenty more day."

"You like this-feller day?" Alor San was grinning at Little Paddy.

"Breakfus more better!" muttered Little Paddy, and shivered.

Only to the rattle of plates and an appetizing smell did I "wake up". Who wakes first must generally be cook! With gusto we attacked breakfast as the sky lightened to a pearly grey. Soon the sun shot straight up out of the sea, a golden ball. And the shoreline beside us was white beaches and red cliffs, and a thousand hills of green and brown and grey.

"Up jib!" called Joe. "Up anchor!"

"Up main-sail!" and to a wisp of breeze we were gliding on our way enlivened by a laugh at Little Paddy, who in his anxiety to lend a hand had nearly fallen overboard.

"What for you want to make him breakfus for shark?" laughed Alor San. "Jacky try jump down whale's mouth yesterday, now you jump overboard for shark."

"Well use him for bait later on," promised Dick. "First time we grow hungry-feller." But little Man Friday grinned at his hero from adoring eyes.

A sparkling sea, porpoises racing round the *Nancy Bell* in effortless motion of graceful speed. Gulls white as snow, wheeling low to ,starboard in noisy divings upon a shoal of silver herrings. The *Nancy Bell* beginning to rise saucily to a playful sea, now and then shaking spray from her bows like a lively colt shaking a summer shower from his mane. Alor San squatting for'ard splicing a rope while Dick washed down the deck, Man Friday lending him a hand as usual.

Ah Matt with squat, intent brown face was carving a pretty comb from tortoiseshell. With soft words he'd try it on some brown-skinned maid when he returned to port. Big Paddy and Billy were sprawled out on deck smoking their beloved pipes, otherwise doing nothing in particular – and, like me, doing it well. Cross-eyed Joe sat quietly at the tiller.

Life aboard those tiny vessels is rough and strenuous while working at shell, but pleasantly easy while cruising on a lazy sea.

We had the towline out, and at a yell from Ah Matt we made a dive for it We had the towline out, and at a yell from Ah Matt we made a dive for it-first man to grab the line enjoys the fun of hauling in the fish. This was a fourteen-pounder kingfish by guess, a lithe silver thing that fought like a demon. He was a streak through the water as he surfaced and leapt high in a bowspring, trying to shake away the hook. Then he sped to the depths with a hiss of line. He fought for his life to the last gasp, fought even after we'd landed him gasping aboard. They nearly always do. Strangely enough, you can catch far larger fellows than this one with a white rag or the shiny lid of a cigarette tin for bait. That bait when towed behind a vessel spins round and looks like a speeding fish. It's great sport when sailing through a school of these beauties to see the big fellows fighting for the bait.

The little bit of excitement was hardly over when, to another yell, Alor San seemed to fly over the deck and snatch at the towline. And this time it was a fight. All Alor's strength and cunning were taxed to the utmost to land this monster-twenty minutes' lively battling between man and fish, Alor's face all laughing excitement as, braced against the stern, his clenched hands and taut arms took the strain. The big beauty struggled furiously, and Alor was gasping when he landed it, a monstrous silver body crashing up on the deck to leap and bound and thump with clashing jaws of frightful teeth, snapping viciously while we battered it to death. A Spanish mackeral this, born to fight throughout his savage life. Tremendously powerful and dangerous monsters, the excitement they bring to the deck of a small vessel is hectic while it lasts. We had no means of weighing this palpitating fellow, but we measured him and he taped five feet ten inches, just as "long" as

Cross-eyed Joe.

The little bit of excitement awoke the work instinct in Big Paddy, and he began to make his eager offspring a fish-spear. Man Friday disdained fishing-lines, as most aboriginals do. Not knowing he was coming aboard he'd left his trusted spear in camp, and the fish-spears lying round the deck or propped against the rigging were three times as long as himself. So Big Paddy and Billy squatted down and put in a pleasant day fashioning a handy-sized, four-pronged spear while Little Paddy looked on with shining eyes. Solemn father Paddy cut the haft from a bamboo rod to the little fellow's right length and balance. Then he cut four prongs from a piece of fencing wire, straightened and sharpened them, then bound them to the spearhead with cord and a mixture of powdered bloodwood gum and beeswax. By mid-afternoon it was finished. Little Paddy proudly flourished his new fish-spear, testing its weight and balance, keen to try it.

No aboriginal, whether boy or warrior, considers himself dressed without his spear. He is naked without it.

We merely lazed along that day, or, as Billy expressed it, "No more work 'im this-feller day – we ony play about."

"What say you, Paddy?" inquired Alor San, grinning.

"More better we work?"

"What for work 'im?" grunted Big Paddy. "Plenty tucker longa ship!"

Cross-eyed Joe smiled tolerantly. He did not seem to be making for anywhere in particular. And the *Nancy Bell* reacted like a bird to his hand on the tiller. That evening we anchored by the Turtle group. Only mud and sandbanks, thick with mangrove; several of the islands are partly under water at high tide. Out of curiosity Dick and I rowed to one as the sun was setting, Little Paddy of course with us, to tryout his spear.

"Only sand and mud and mangroves," said Dick disappointedly. "The mangroves are so thick there's barely a chance to step ashore and stretch our legs. Hold her!" he called suddenly.

I rested on the oars. Dick was pointing towards the mangrove edge and there, barely distinguishable against the muddy roots, lay a sixteen-foot crocodile.

"Just where we were going to land!" exclaimed Dick. 'What a surprise we'd have got. And we haven't brought a gun."

There was intense longing in Dick's voice. He was a good shot. I'd seen him hit a scrub turkey in flight with a rifle shot, and many a time he'd shot wild pigs when hunting with his aboriginal friends. But on this trip to sea we never dreamt we might need firearms.

As if he knew we were unarmed, the lurking brute lay there motionless as an old log. Which was just what he looked like, his eyes mere slits in his wrinkled snout.

"How I'd love to send a bullet fair into that ugly head!" sighed Dick. "He might have got one of us if we'd stepped ashore."

"You mean he certainly would have!" I replied. 'We were going to run the dinghy right up beside him."

"Why you no more spear 'im 'gator?" demanded Dick.

"You pright [fright] longa him?"

"No more," answered Man Friday dubiously. "Him bad-feller too much. More better you shoot 'im."

"No got gun!" snapped Dick. "You spear 'im."

"No more," answered Little Paddy uneasily. "S'pose me-feller spear 'im he pight [fight] longa us-me lose 'im spear. More better we go back longa cutter. Dinner time he come soon," he added persuasively.

"You'd rather eat than be eaten by the crocodile," laughed Dick. "But your advice is good this time. I do wish we had a rifle, though," he said longingly as we turned about for the *Nancy Bell.*

Our next breakfast we ate to a sight never seen in town or city or inland. The water dark as plush, still as a sheet of steel. Just to the east the sea-line growing dimly visible, imperceptibly lightening to quiver in pearly grey. Then behind it rose a reflection as of a distant bushfire. Suddenly, it seemed only a few miles east of us, the Great Barrier Reef itself caught fire. Rapidly the blaze fanned out to right and left along the sea-line in rippling, growing, quivering arms of fire, reaching swiftly away to south and north. Its centre now burst into a Hush of crimson from which streams of flame darted up; lighting dim blackness that was the sky. A sea-bird shrieked. Then, from down in that hidden furnace up popped the tip of a crimson rim that leapt into a perfect disc of raging fire, all a-quivering, within itself, huge and glorious. The little *Nancy Bell,* every man in her and every strand in every rope shone in rosy reflection.

The great disc poised a moment, beautifully balanced on the Reef. Then it shot up just above the sea and remained there, a moment, as if to allow its raging furnaces time to cool into a disc of molten gold. Sea birds came gliding over the *Nancy Bell.* Majestically the sun began to climb. To all things came light-another day was born.

"That one proper-feller fire," nodded Joe towards the sky's wonder-furnace. "He boil billy belonga you all right."

"No more," frowned Little Paddy at the sun. "'Spose me catch 'im what time he wake up, me no more put billy on longa 'im, 'im burn 'im me!"

The dawn breeze came gently, it was up with the mud-hook then, and the bow turned east into the sun, the Great Barrier, and the bulk of

Lizard Island looming from the sea not twenty miles away. Within an hour or so we were quite close to the Lizard group, and then began only to crawl along. But it did not matter now, we were "prospecting", seeking likely bottom on which might 'browse" a patch of trochus shell – or should I say a "colony of trochus shellfish"? When the breeze freshened we would furl the main-sail and just drift along under the jib. Dick was gazing longingly towards the big, bold hill of Lizard Island, presently so close. We could see plainly the grey of its granite rocks, the scrubby trees, the grey bushes and brown grass upon the smaller hill-slopes. Cross-eyed Joe stood at the helm, Alor San in the bows keeping a sharp look-out for reefs, Paddy and Billy and Little Paddy by the rail with fish-spears in hand, intently gazing down into the quiet water. Ah Matt, like a big brown monkey, was clinging easily to the masthead, now and then with a lazy wave of the hand signalling Joe to port or starboard. He was gazing away out over the moveless sea, at the blue of the deep water, the green of the "ordinary" depth, the pale green of the shallow patches, the lighter green of the shallower and the yellow-green of the very shallow, betraying bottom or reef almost visible. While keeping a sharp lookout lest we run upon a reef, it was the shallower areas of water we were seeking; and among these, only particular areas, those which grow a certain tasty weed upon the reefs. For it is on this weed that the fish within the trochus shell lives. It crawls over the reef, finds a tasty patch of weed and clings to it and eats, nibbling away at its leisure. Then again, this particular weed, for some climatic or tidal reason, grows mostly on the south-eastern side of the reefs, so that we were seeking not only shallow water, but those areas of it that had reefs and would grow the weed, and of those reefs we had to find the south-eastern portion. And when we should find an area of water in which all conditions were favourable, there probably would be one vital thing missing – the trochus shell.

"It's like prospecting for gold or tin," said Dick. "First, you must find the right country. Then the right rocks. Then the right place. Then – the goldl"

"You no like Turtle group for mineral, Dicky?" asked Cross-eyed Joe.

"No, skipper. They are only mudbanks, or coral-sand and coral. There is no real rock there; there can be no mineral."

"Plenty of gold in the Peninsula, Dicky?" inquired Alor San.

"Yes, for those lucky enough to drop on it. There's been some good nuggets found on the Batavia lately, beauties, as large as your fist. The Great Northern has put through another rich crushing at the Coen, too. And the Mountain Maid is on rich stone at Ebagoolah."

Cross-eyed Joe and Alor San and Ah Matt looked dreamy.

All men are attentive at the talk of gold, and Dick loved to talk of the goldfields – just in case.

"Dicky, maybe you an' Jacky like to try some island perhaps we land on," he suggested.

The suggestion suited Dick and me down to the ground. Presently we were cruising across the deep blue water of Cook's Channel, the channel the great navigator had found to enable him to sail the Endeavour safely amongst these countless reefs, then out through his "Cook's Passage" in the Great Barrier Reef to the open sea. With what relief must he and all his jack tars have breathed when at last they emerged safely through the last reef – only to again escape disaster by a miracle! Rough weather almost smashed them upon the great Reef itself. They were even more thankful to creep back to the calm water inside than they had been to escape from its dangers.

By what slender threads did the great navigator and his men escape disaster again and again! I wonder who at last would have claimed Australia if Cook and his men had perished and never been heard of again?

Sawn-off iron tank, in which Mrs Watson escaped from Lizard Island with the wounded Chinaman and her baby.

4

FORTUNE SMILES ON THE *NANCY BELL*

WE cruised past Lizard Island so close we could see the ruined hut down on the flat that had known the tragedy of Mrs Watson when she was attacked by the blacks. Lonely, forlorn indeed looked the hut on this lovely morning, drooping pandanus palms outlined in the tiny valley behind it.

The island was barren and desolate-looking, hills of grey granite relieved only by scanty shrubbery. The blue of water faded into lighter blue, the. dark green then into lighter green. We had crossed the channel and were drifting over reefs again. Presently we were gazing down through pale-green water at white patches of sand vivid against grey-green masses of corals and grasses and gardens of the sea. Big Paddy's spear sped down, the haft vanishing only to bob up and wobble along the surface as the impaled fish sped away.

"Hurray!" shouted Dick. "That's a beauty, Paddy!" Big Paddy grinned with pleasure.

Ah Matt climbed down from the masthead and Joe turned the bows head on to the light breeze; the jib flapped idly once, and we became stationary, except for the tide. We lifted the dinghies overboard, and Dick and both Paddys and Billy jumped into one and rowed away after the fish-spear, the haft of which was now travelling in drunken, ever-slowing circles as the fish became exhausted. I took the oars in the other dinghy and rowed slowly away with Alor San and Ah Matt, who gazed overside, studying the bottom.

It appeared lovely down there, brilliant sunlight made the water so clear that shellfish crawling over the bottom gave me the quaint impression that they were "undressed". If at the surface, then only their many-shaped, variously-coloured shells would have been visible. But down there their moving heads stuck out as they sampled the plants, or their different-coloured tails were visible, or you could see the fleshy part creeping out from under the shell as they crawled along about their business. They were out to eat something – or be eaten!

A bright blue starfish was hobbling along on energetic legs, going somewhere in a hurry, in a sort of tumbling run. If he could find a shellfish weaker than himself he would attack it in fury until he wrenched open its shell and devoured the fish inside. For starfish are by no means the quiet, peaceful little things they appear to be.

Fish of brilliant colours sped in and out of coral gardens that were a maze of weird plants and sea flowers. Alor grunted and I ceased rowing. Alor and Ah Matt slipped overside, took a deep breath, sank, then gracefully turned over and with one kick sped down. The soles of their feet flashed startlingly white through the water. Plain to see now how the movement of those white soles and white palms of hands may attract the eye of a cruising shark. The brown-skinned men were fairy forms moving amongst the waving plants and turrets of coloured corals, to glide across glistening white sand. They turned upward, and their magnified eyes were big and brown and beautiful as they came swiftly up. They broke surface and grasped the dinghy side, grunting and smiling as they drew deep breaths. I paddled slowly on.

Again they went down, and again. An hour later Alor San broke surface with a fistful of the weed on which the trochus shell lives. So we were getting on to the right track. "We catch him soon maybe, Jacky," Alor smiled. "Trochus like eat this one grass."

I shouted the good news to Dick.

Three hundred yards away Dick was manning the other dinghy, while Big Paddy and Billy went down, also prospecting the sea floor for trochus shell.

"We're on colours, too!" shouted Dick with a laugh.

He was thinking of our prospecting trips to come-on land. When searching for gold or tin you nearly always find "colours" first. Follow them up, and if you're lucky you find the mineral. We had found the trochus weed, by following it up we might find the trochus. We all hoped so.

These shellfish are really a marine snail, the large ones the size of a man's fist. The shells are cone-shaped. The outer covering of the shell is sometimes dark grey or dull green, not easy to distinguish when the fish inside remains, stationary, or moves slowly about the coral garden. The great majority, though, are prettily banded in red and white. Apart from this thin outer covering, the inner shell is all of mother-of-pearl, and this makes the shell valuable. The main markets are in China and Japan. There the dull outer covering is ground off (it can be done on an emery wheel) and the inner mother-of-pearl is cut and polished into buttons and ornaments. Your dad used to buy them for his shirt, as "genuine pearl-shell" buttons.

Alor San and Ah Matt, with Big Paddy and Billy further along, were now "skin" diving; that is, diving in their bare skins. It is the pearl-shell diver, working mostly in much deeper water, who wears the diving dress. Our men generally wore watertight goggles. These not only keep a man's eyes from becoming sore from many hours in the water, but enable him to see far more distinctly when down below. In the dinghy we also had what we called "the glass". It was a wooden box about two feet long and six inches square. One end had a window of ordinary glass fitted to it and as we drifted along one man studied the ocean floor through this box. Leaning over the side of the dinghy, which stopped, he put the glass end to the water, and gazed down through the box.

The glass prevented vision being blurred by ripples. The sea bottom could then be seen with uncanny distinctness – sand and mud, pebble and shingle, those portions covered with grasses, or bare of either plant life or coral, and the reefs – all the fascinating variety that was there below the dinghy could be seen plainly.

By means of this glass we saved time and unnecessary work, for the Malays only dived when they could see that the bottom might be favourable for trochus shell.

The setting sun was painting the sea rosy when Alor San kicked the bottom, and I thrilled to the triumph in his eyes as he sped up. He broke surface. with a snort and, holding up a big shell in each hand, threw them into the boat.

"A patch, Jackyl" he cried, laughing excitedly. "Me see plenty!" And a moment later up bobbed Ah Matt, also with two shells.

My heart leapt as I shouted to Cross-eyed Joe watching from the cutter, then waved to Dick. For a patch of pearl-shell, of *beche-de-mer* or trochus means much the same to the fisher as a patch of gold or tin or wolfram means to the prospector. We thrilled to this wonderful news, shouted excitedly from dinghy to dinghy and across to the *Nancy Bell*. We had expected to win, after considerable time and hard work, perhaps two or three tons of trochus. But to strike a patch of the shellfish in our very first day of prospecting was almost unbelievable good fortune.

A wave from Cross-eyed Joe, a cheer from Dick, echoed by a war-cry from Little Paddy, and we were racing back to the cutter to discuss the great find. Apprehensively we gazed round, immensely relieved that there was no ship in sight but our own.

It was too dark to begin diving in earnest now. We would talk, and eat, and plan; the evening meal would be sauced by the knowledge that we had struck a patch of trochus. The dawn could not come quickly enough. We would be working that trochus in our sleep.'

As we leapt aboard the Nancy Bell the skipper stared questioningly at Alor San and Ah Matt. They answered swiftly in English and Malay, expressive-faced, laughing, handing him the shells. Yes, they were certain it was a patch. The shellfish were clustered along the bottom, thick under the ledges and loose blocks of coral. They had only come on them at the last dive, but the shell was so plentiful that both men were certain they had struck the edge of a patch.

Cross-eyed Joe smiled with a half-puzzled, half-quizzical expression.

"Kismet!" he murmured, and glanced at Alor San. "That news makes you feel good, skipper," declared Dick, laughing.

"Very good, Dicky," grinned Cross-eye Joe. "We all plenty pleased. Just the same like you and Jacky strike gold mine, eh?"

"Too right," agreed Dick enthusiastically. "That's just how we do feel. And Jack and I will strike that gold mine, too, some day."

"Good luck," smiled Joe. "Now we eat. You plenty hungry?"

Big and Little Paddy and Billy grinned for answer.

"No need to ask them," said Dick cheerfully. "Anyway, I could eat a horse myself."

We all enjoyed that curried fish and what-nots seasoned with spices, flavoured with soy sauce, curried as only the Eastern people can curry, with big helpings of rice cooked as only the Oriental can cook rice. We finished off with the last of our town bread, washed down with tasty pannikins of tea.

A Long Tom skipped the water in quivering leaps; velvet darkness spread over the moveless sea now specked with star beams as a myriad stars came twinkling out above.

Just about too full to move, lazily we congratulated Cross-eyed Joe on his cooking.

"Must keep you all strong men," replied Joe with a pleased smile. "Man no can work, row, dive all day long without good food in stomach."

And many a good meal he cooked for us in the long, active days ahead. A popular shipboard cook was Cross-eyed Joe.

"I believe he could make a sea-snake taste like curried chicken," declared Dick.

Alor San and Ah Matt grinned as at some quiet joke.

The *Nancy Bell* was only a cutter of five tons burthen.

If a fifteen- or twenty-ton lugger breezed along she could be manned by perhaps a dozen men. With that number diving as against our four, and her hold able to stow twenty tons of shell, she would win three times and more the amount of shell we could. If the patch proved to be small, then a well-manned lugger could clean up three parts of the shell and we'd get only the leavings.

And if that vessel should be cruising within touch of a sister ship! The very last thing we wanted to see now was a sail upon the sea.

"We keep sharp look-out now," murmured the skipper. "Be ready to up anchor and run before they see us."

Cunning subterfuge, ingenious and sometimes cruel schemes have been worked throughout the years in the Coral Sea to keep a trespassing vessel off the scent of a find.

"It would be crook to have anyone jump our claim now," mused Dick. "I'd feel like those gold-diggers who've pulled guns when the claim-jumpers came around."

Tragedies have occurred in the Coral Sea and along the Great Barrier Reef, in some cases due to bitter rivalries. It is unbelievable how quickly news of a find gets around, the very breeze seems to carry it. And, once on the scent, the prowlers of the sea cling like leeches.

Grouped together on the deck we began to plan what we would do at first sign of an unwelcome sail.

"We beat them," broke in Cross-eyed Joe's quiet voice.

"I have good plan – think him out proper tonight."

"Good on you, skipper," cried Dick enthusiastically.

"They'll have to be pretty wide awake to catch you napping." We warmed with a glow of confidence in our skipper. Then, for a fleeting second, I imagined that Cross-eye smiled with that "other half" of his face, the shrewd, deep-down part of him.

Sprawled on our blankets, smoking, we listened to tales told by Alor San and Ah Matt of other voyages when their ships had "struck" a fabulous bed of pearl-shell, or a rich patch of trochus or trepang. And Cross-eyed Joe, quietly smoking, would nod his head and grunt approval at episodes concerning rich finds or disaster, of the outwitting of rivals and enemies, of intrigue and revenge, of the perils and disappointments and often unexpected rewards of the sea. A colourful book the experiences and hidden lives of these three men would have made.

Big Paddy and Billy, laughing and joking with shining eyes, were already spending their extra pay, the extra blankets and s tores, tobacco and presents that now would be theirs when we sailed back to Cooktown with the *Nancy Bell* loaded with trochus. Big men indeed would they be to their families and tribes-people awaiting them far away, round the camp-fires at Mount Cook.

"Little Paddy get his share, too," stated Cross-eyed Joe, with a grin. "Man Friday belonga Dicky work plenty hard feller now."

Little Paddy nearly fell over himself with delight.

"Me work plenty-feller too much," he gurgled. "Me work plenty-feller hard all a time!"

And he did.

Dick and I fell asleep dreaming of the *Nancy Bell* loaded up again and again with trochus shell, dreaming of a rising market, dreaming of the greatly enriched share that would be ours if results proved that we really had struck a patch. There might be enough to buy three horses each, a new rifle and gun, and stores enough to go bush on a six months prospecting trip. Oh, if only the sea proved kindly.

A musical gurgle from the anchor chain told that the tide was on the turn; a splash and swirl betrayed the nearness of a big fish. A pleasant coolness was in the air, and above was the everlasting beauty of the stars.

Happy dreams made sleep pleasant for all aboard the *Nancy Bell* that night.

5

WE GUARD AGAINST TRESPASSERS

WE were at work when dawn's fiery glow made diving possible, Dick with the aboriginals in one dinghy, the Malays and I in the other. Our job was to attend the divers, to watch them at work and regulate the dinghy to their movements, to keep the dinghy from drifting away, and to have it handy as each man rose up to the surface. Again and again they went down, to bob up, "blow", throw half a dozen shells and sometimes more into the dinghy, rest a few moments with hand on thwart, smile and say, "Good luck, Jacky" ... then dive again.

A hundred yards further along the reef Dick was similarly tending Big Paddy, Billy, and Little Paddy. For Little Paddy proved to be an eel in the water and was working like a Trojan under direction of father Paddy, who was teaching him where to look for the shell. Shooting up with his shells, he was all eyes for Dick's encouraging face, and gloried in Dick's boisterous congratulations. Now and then Dick would yell out to me, hold up a particularly good shell, and bend to pat Man Friday on the head. I'd see the kid's grin as down he'd dive again, sometimes acting "flash", showing off his little black tail for a second, like a playful porpoise.

Joe stayed aboard the cutter to attend to the vessel and the cooking, and to prepare the boiler for cleaning the shell. He had also to get the bags and sewing-tackle all ready, and, as it turned out, to bring up a lot of stores and gear on deck. There was plenty to do aboard. Meanwhile he could drift down to us on the tide should we draw too far away, or, if against the tide, he could use the small but surprisingly good engine he had recently installed.

For the *Nancy Bell* had been made "real modern". One of the dinghies had been fitted for an outboard motor, and this enabled us to tow the other and, if necessary, work a good distance from our tiny mother ship. We could also work in water too dangerously shallow even for her. At the same time, should a blow suddenly threaten, we could quickly make back for the *Nancy Bell.*

"He moves with the times, does shrewd old Cross-eyed Joe," remarked Dick. Yes, we were modernized all right

The weather set in to a dead calm and soon the sea was glistening like polished glass. Joe dropped a tin on the cutter's deck and the sound rolled out like a thunderclap; the occasional call of a sea-bird sounded piercingly. No other sound but the pop-up of a diver's head through the surface, his gasp for breath, the thud of the heavy shells thrown into the dinghy.

There's a distinct knack in bringing up more than one shell in each hand. Every now and then Alor San or Ah Matt would break surface with a broad grin, carrying ten good shells. I'd "hurrah" in delight, not only at the expert workmanship but at the further proof that we really were on a patch of shell. For they must be plentiful indeed for a man to find, snatch the shells, then surface with ten in his arms in the one dive. When snatching shell like that down below the diver Swiftly works with both hands, holding his upper arms close to his side, and gripping the shells between upper arms and side. Then, "throwing" other shells between forearms and chest he finally holds all by pressing his hands across his shoulder blades. A thoroughly experienced swimmer can come to the surface with twelve shells that way. But he must be a good man, and the shellfish, of course, must be plentiful and easy of access. In a patch you sometimes find them clustered together like giant snails gripping the under part of a leaf. In this way they often cling to coral boulders.

Some divers use a little netted bag slung round the neck and fastened round the chest in . which to carry the shell, but others prefer the skilful use of their arms.

Among our long but easy duties Dick and I had a particular one: to keep a sharp look-out for sharks. Only the tiger and grey nurse are feared; these are terrors of the sea. It is commonly believed that coloured divers do not fear sharks, but this is not so. The divers, to their sorrow, know so much about the grey nurse and tiger shark that they treat them with the greatest respect. So Dick in his dinghy some little distance away, and I in mine, kept a sharp look-out. Any ominous fin cleaving this moveless water would be instantly visible a long way away. But we had to watch away below, and all round the swimmers, too. It was surprising how far we could see through the shallow water, under brilliant sunlight. Coral grottoes and gardens of fantastic plant life lay clearly displayed; battlements of corals like dwarfs' castles, and clear patches of sand with quaint things distinctly wriggling, crawling, or floating over them; brilliant parrot fish and ugly porcupine fish, with here and there a dark red sea-slug, side by side with a spiky sea-urchin. And through it all the coppery bodies of Alar San and Ah Matt gliding in beautiful movement, with, further away, the glistening black bodies of Paddy and Billy, like porpoises speeding under water. And ever and again quick to catch the eye, the white flash that was the sales of their feet.

There came no ominous grey shadow. Had it come, then whoever saw it would instantly have leant over and clapped hands under water.

Dick could do it as well as an aboriginal, while I was not too bad at it. There is a peculiar way with a downward stroke, to clap cupped hands together underwater. Do it properly and the noise reverberates under water like a thunderclap, giving the swimmers on the sea bottom instant warning that a shark is coming.

In two days we'd fished half a ton of shell, a great catch.

But they'd soon begin to "hum" on board and so, that evening, Cross-eyed Joe gave his orders.

"Tomorrow, early morning time we sail Lizard Island. Make shore station there. Boil fish there. Keep look-out."

So that was his plan. As simple as that. And we had not thought of it.

The island would be our fishing station. There we would I clean and bag the shell, and keep a look out. The *Nancy Bell* could fish in security, for at sign of a strange sail we would signal her. She would sail away until the stranger vanished on her business. Even if a sail came right to the island there would be nothing unusual in finding it occupied as a fishing station. As to where our fishing grounds were, well they could be a hundred miles away – two hundred. They would not dream of a rich patch of trochus just close to the island shore.

A shore station suited Dick and me down to the ground.

Before dawn we were quietly steaming towards the great black shadow of the island. Not a breath of wind stirred. The Lizard would make an ideal base besides affording pleasant variety for life aboard a tiny, cramped cutter.

We found sheltered anchorage in a little cove on the nor-west side. Dawn burst up over the Great Barrier as we dropped the hook. Beside us the cliff, with, further along, sloping walls of granite running to the sea-edge gleamed suddenly in rosy light. A bird chirped from the shore trees.

Dick's eyes were all for the land as we ate a hearty breakfast. I knew he was thinking of mineral, and wishing the island was larger. Cross-eyed Joe and Alor San and Ah Matt were gazing at the island, seeing it in a new light. They, too, were thinking about mineral. I was eager to be ashore also, for those rocks were granite and we well knew that granite can indicate mineral country.

"You like try prospect, Dicky?"

Dick was surprised, for Cross-eyed Joe had read his thoughts.

"Yes, skipper, I'll give it a go in our spare time."

"Good. What you think?"

'Well," said Dick doubtfully, "it's good-looking granite, judging from here – there may be a chance of a bit of tin there. But I don't see any quartz."

"You think no gold then?"

"I'm very doubtful, skipper. If there was a splash of quartz and ironstone and slate about there'd be a chance. But it looks more like possible tin country to me."

Little Paddy was keen to go ashore with his fish-spear.

A ton of tin would be of no use to him, but he knew what he could do with fish.

Eagerly we loaded the dinghies, pulling ashore to a tiny beach at the base of the Big Hill. Above high-water mark the country levelled off, to form a plain on the inland side of the Big Hill and the ridge. On the grass by a small clump of trees we dumped the boiler and provisions, while Alor San and Ah Matt rowed back to the *Nancy Bell* for another load.

"Catch 'im fish belonga dinner," ordered Dick, and Little Paddy gleefully took himself to the water's edge.

Dick and I and the aboriginals started to rig a tent back from the beach. Cross-eyed Joe was climbing the big Hill.

"There's a bonzer look-out away up there," said Dick, pointing. "I'm anxious to have a look-see .. It's the very look-out that Captain Cook used, I've heard it called 'Cook's Look-out'. From up there old Cross-eye will be able to look out all over the sea."

Just as well he did so! When he came down he told us there was a lugger cruising on a slow drift, prospecting for shell directly north. She would have seen us had we been on our fishing grounds, though she was a good way away.

We congratulated ourselves on our luck, finding toil a pleasure in building a bush shed, and a galley for use just outside the tent. We would make this a permanent fishing station, there was plenty of water and enough wood. Here we would boil, clean, bag and stack the shell. Dick and I and Little Paddy would work ashore when necessary, and keep a look-out. We'd store a few weeks' provisions in the tent so that should the *Nancy Bell* have to run for it if a trespasser came nosing about then we'd be quite all right, even if bad weather prevented our ship returning for a few weeks. For that matter we could have lasted for months on the island, for we had fish-spears and knew how to use them. Better still, we knew something of the habits and haunts of those fish, and edible shellfish, and big crabs that frequent most northern island-shores; that live in the inlets or creeks or salt-water arms of the sea. For it's not much use knowing how to use fishing-line and trap and spear unless you know where to look for the fish. There were quail on this island, too.

"Suppose storm come and blow us away from island, you no starve, Jacky," Cross-eyed Joe smiled.

"Not on your life. But Little Paddy might."

"No go hungry-feller," protested Little Paddy boastfully. "Plenty tucker longa islan'."

"Yes," growled Dick. "And you'll look for it in the camp." "No more," grinned Man Friday. "Me walkabout, gettem own tucker."

"You're telling me," replied Dick derisively.

6

MRS WATSON'S TRAGEDY

IT was late afternoon before the camp was snug and ship-shape with the tent, bush-shed, galley and iron boiler in place. Bunks were rigged, provisions stowed under cover, the shell. brought on shore and wood gathered for the boiler. While Dick knocked up a few johnnies on the coals for the evening meal, we started to boil the water and tip the shell in. It only requires about ten minutes' boiling, This cooks and loosens the fish inside so that it can be withdrawn from its spiral home. If not properly cleaned the shell attracts myriads of tiny flies, and these make life almost unbearable aboard. In a small vessel infested with cockroaches, not 'to mention a lively colony of bugs, a swarm of trochus fly is just about enough to drive all hands crazy. You've no idea of the misery these awful insect pests can cause, especially in an atmosphere reeking with engine smells, cooking odours, oil, and bilge, "humming" with trochus and fishy smells from the shell.

Besides, the merchants who buy the shell most definitely object to the trochus fly. A bad shipment may not only drive all hands from the storage shed, but also cause uproar all along the waterfront. For the pest, in devilish delight, spreads to other luggers. If there happens to be a steamer at the wharf the flies invade it. And the nice, clean, tender crew and passengers quickly say things about that dirty little tub that brought the fly. They just "don't know what's bit 'em"! This brings the unsympathetic port authorities into the fray, and they promptly fine the skipper whose vessel has brought the fly into port.

"Merchant angry with me," grinned Cross-eyed Joe, "all luggers angry with me, steamer angry with me, port officers angry with me. Little fly, that trochus fly, you hardly see him but he make plenty big trouble."

So for good reasons we must clean the shell as soon as possible, and clean it properly.

Salt water does a better job than fresh.

After boiling, the shell is tipped out to cool. The fish inside is then a withered "corkscrew" strip of meat, a "coil". It can be shaken out by a sharp, peculiar twist of the wrist, or pulled out with finger or wire aided by a twist of the shell. If the "tail" end of the fish, the last spiral, breaks and is left in the shell, this will bring the Hies. If that little spiral snaps off, then it is very difficult to drag it out from the bottom of the shell.

The most "stick fast" fish can be hooked out with a thin piece of wire. Little Paddy liked this job for he could all the time be stuffing himself with the cooked fish. All folk like it. This dried shellfish meat brings £60 a ton at Thursday Island for the Easter markets. It takes a great amount to make up a ton weight, and time is spent in drying and curing it. We were not going to bother, for time was too valuable; we would use it in winning all the shell we could from the patch.

When the shells are cleaned they are bagged and stacked. As time went on we found that our shell averaged sixteen bags to the ton. Apart from the diving, there was going to be quite a lot of work while we were "on "shell", which pleased Dick and me.

"Whatever money we make out of this cruise we'll earn," said Dick in satisfied tones.

"That's so, Dick. Old Cross-eye won't be sorry he asked us to come along."

We were a tired crowd that evening when all was ship-shape. Night came with a dreamy quietness. The still water was velvet black where the hill rose up beside it. But our camp-fire shot out a rosy finger right to the *Nancy Bell*. After the evening yarn Cross-eyed Joe and his crew gave us a quiet "good-night", and rowed out to the Nancy Bell. Little Paddy was already sound asleep, his fish-spear lying beside him. Dick and I rolled ourselves in our blankets and fell fast asleep.

After breakfast next morning, Cross-eyed Joe and Alor San came ashore to climb the hill and see if all was clear. Dick was in charge of the shore camp, so he ordered Little Paddy to spear enough fish for dinner.

"I'll tan your hide if you don't," he warned. But Man Friday grinned impishly to this often-heard threat. Proudly he picked up his spear and stepped down to the beach, sea-snipe running along the sand before him.

Big Paddy and Billy came ashore and Were ordered· to collect wood for the boiler, and good cooking wood for the galley.

The shore party, while on shore, must cook for themselves. How I hated cooking! And I had an idea that whichever unfortunate ones had to eat my dampers would hate my cooking, too.

Dick and I walked across the grassy Hat behind the camp to the old hut, which Dick was itching to inspect. It looked exactly like a little blockhouse, which was what it had been built for. It was roofless now, but three walls and part of the other were still standing, roughly built of coral lime, mud, and stone. Within those walls, behind the barred door; the woman and the wounded Chinaman had put up a heroic fight for life.

Fronting the place was a long strip of flat, then the sea. Behind and around it were a few small clumps of pandanus palm, crooked, gnarly-rooted relics of a primitive age.

"Down towards the beach was the vegetable garden," said Dick, pointing. It was there the Chinamen were surprised. One was killed, the other badly wounded.

Like the story of Cook's Endeavour, this story was familiar to all Cooktown boys. Dick knew it by heart. I'm afraid Dick had not shone while at school, except in the history of exploration by sea of the Great Barrier Reef, and by land of Cape York Peninsula. Dick delighted in the stories of the great navigators and explorers, and of our own local pioneers, and the lion-hearted prospectors who had opened up so much unknown country. Every Cooktown lad was deeply proud of Cooktown's back¬country, and particularly of the romance of his own wild Cape York Peninsula. And here on this lonely little island, where the great navigator had left his footprints in the sands of time, we now stood on the very earth stained by the blood of a great pioneer tragedy, with its heart-breaking remorse and suspense, and loneliness, and utter desperation, relieved, although in death, by sublime heroism.

Captain Watson in his *beche-de-mer* lugger, with wife and baby and crew, had sailed from Cooktown, and landed on Lizard Island to make a home-base and station for *beche-de-mer* and pearl-shell fishing. A hut was built with an eye to possible defence. The heavy door was well barred and loopholed, and rough benches built inside for the storage of provisions. A big vegetable garden was dug and planted, and the signal cairn rebuilt up on Captain Cook's Look-out. When the home was made all snug Captain Watson fished the waters near by until the garden was well towards production, for its produce was to go a long way towards feeding his crew as well as his home. Even-tually he left on a cruise two hundred miles further nor'-west to Knight Island, to form an advanced station. Mrs Watson with her baby and the two Chinese gardeners, Ah Leong and Ah Sam, remained on this home-station on Lizard Island.

Lonely days passed. All went well for a time.

Then, one night, ten canoes loaded with natives paddled across the sea from the mainland, and landed before dawn, hiding their dugouts, then hiding themselves at the lower end of the garden. At dawn, smoke rose from the hut chimney. Presently the two Chinese, chattering as they carried their tools, came walking down towards the garden. But Ah Sam stayed to work within two hundred yards of the hut, clearing grass from between some pandanus palms. It was only Ah Leong who came right down to the end of the garden.

He began work. The sun shone warmly. Ah Sam still worked away up the other end of the garden, visible as he dug out the tall grass. The woman in the hut was bathing the baby. The natives were disappointed that Ah Sam did not come down to the garden end as usual.

They speared Ah Leong – with one swift volley so that he fell riddled, without a sound. Then they dragged his body away, and waited.

Ah Leong did not come up to the hut for early morning tea, so Ah Sam walked down to call him. He became uneasy, then suspicious. Finally he halted and called out. No answer .... He looked round. In the tall grass he saw Ah Leong's hat.

He started back towards the hut, and then the natives were after him. He stumbled and screamed when the first spear struck him – screamed loudly to warn Missy. They howled after him in pursuit. Mrs Watson seized a gun and fired from the hut door and, as Ah Sam staggered into the hut, she slammed the heavy door and barricaded it. Then she fired through the loophole.

Ah Sam, who to the last was to prove a brave and gallant gentleman, loaded the guns for the woman. Blood was welling from seven spear wounds, but none was fatal.

The woman could shoot straight, so the natives surrounded the hut and lay low. She dressed Ah Sam's wounds while he kept watch as best he could through the loophole.

For some days and nights the nerve-racking siege went on; utter silence outside, sleepless suspense in the hut. Then to Mrs Watson suddenly came the heart-breaking realization that it was only a matter of time – water! There was only half a kerosene tin of water in the hut, and it was the dry season. The hut, with the door closed was soon stifling.

The natives' plans had been well laid. Had both Chinamen gone as usual to the further end of the garden they would both have been killed, and the woman would have been taken by surprise.

The hut had been well prepared for defence, and there were a number of large tins inside to hold a good supply of water. But – those in the hut had forgotten to keep the tins refilled. They must perish of thirst.

Ah Sam begged to be allowed to creep away to the swamp, and try to bring back water. Mrs Watson knew this was the very thing the natives were waiting for. They must not venture from the hut. The natives did not know they were short of water.

Eventually the attackers tried subterfuge. They launched their canoes and paddled away. But Mrs Watson guessed that several might be hidden near the water, while those in the canoes would paddle out of Sight, then double back, away behind the island. They would hide in the ridge and attack again in a few days, creeping up in the night behind the hut and waiting for the door to open.

To remain in the hut meant to perish, so she decided to take one desperate chance-to attempt escape by sea in the half of an iron tank.

With their remaining water and a few provisions the brave woman with her child and the faithful Ah Sam crept from the hut and away through the long grass, in fear lest the sleeping baby should whimper.

On the beach, drawn up above high-tide mark, was the half of an ordinary iron tank. The original square-built iron tank had been sawn in half. Each half of a tank makes an excellent boiler in which the trepang men boil their *beche-de-mer*, in preparation for market.

Inch by inch, with noiseless haste, they dragged this half-tank across the beach to the water. It was high tide, just on the turn. They climbed into the tank, and pushed off with a stick. Slowly the tide carried them out from the island.

It was a time of calms, the sea shimmering with heat from the blazing sun. The nights were breathless. The wounded Chinaman did all he could to comfort "Missy", but nothing but death could beat Mrs Watson – she was living for her baby. Day by terrible day she kept a pathetic little diary. And not once did she complain.

They drifted to Howick Island, nearly forty miles away, and the Chinaman crawled away to see if he could find water. He could not, and stared affrighted at the tracks of natives.

The pity of it! If only he could have found the water!

There is a tiny native well on that small island, but it is just within the edge of the dense forest of mangroves, very difficult to locate. If only Ah Sam had been a bushman! the little birds would have saved them. For all day long, on hot days, many small birds keep up a constant chattering round the well as they cool off, and bathe in the shallow water. I have seen and heard them there many a time.

The native tracks may have been old ones, for they visit the Howicks but seldom.

Wearily the fugitives drifted away again, until at last they grounded on one of the mud banks of the Turtle group. Ah Sam, with drawn smile, mumbled, "Farewell", to Missy, and crawled away among the mangroves. He wished to spare her from seeing him die.

Vale to Ah Sam – gentlelman.

The diary commenced on 2 October. It ended on the eleventh: "Nearly dead with thirst."

Captain Bremner of the schooner Kate Kearney found the pitiful remains long afterwards, the baby clasped in its mother's arms.

Copy of Mrs Watson's diary, as found by Captain Bremner:

DIARY

No. 1. Found at Lizard Island:-

September 27 – Blowing gale of wind 'S.E. Ah Sam saw smoke in S. direction, supposed to be from native camp. Steamer bound north very close about 6 p.m.; Corea, I think.

September 28 – Blowing strong S.E. breeze.

September 29 – Blowing strong breeze S.E. although not so hard as yesterday. No eggs. Ah Leong killed by the blacks over at the farm (a quarter of a mile from her cottage). Ah Sam found his hat, which is the only proof.

September 30 – Natives down on the beach at 7 p.m. Fired off rifle and revolver and they went away.

October 1 – Natives (four) speared Ah Sam; four places in the right side, and three on the shoulder., Got three spears from the natives. Saw ten men altogether---

DIARY

No.2. Found in the tank near her body at No.5 Howick:-

Left Lizard Island October 2nd (Sunday afternoon) in tank (or the pot in which *beche-de-mer* is boiled). Got about three miles or four from the Lizards.

October 4 – Made for the sand bank off the Lizards, but could not reach it. Got on a reef.

October 5 – Remained on the reef all day on the look-out for a boat, but saw none.

October 6 – Very calm morning. Able to pull the tank up to an island with three small mountains on it. Ah Sam went ashore to try and get water, as ours was done. There were natives camped there, so we were afraid to go far away. We had to wait return of tide. Anchored on the reef. Very calm.

October 7 – Made for another Island four or five miles from the one spoken of yesterday. Ashore, but could not find any water. Cooked some rice and clam-fish. Moderate S.E. breeze. Stayed there all night. Saw a steamer bound north, Hoisted Ferrier's (her baby boy) white and pink wrap but did not answer us.

October 8 – Changed anchorage of boat as the wind was freshening. Went down to a kind of little lake on the same island (this done last night). Remained here all day looking out for a boat; did not see any. Very cold night; blowing very hard. No water.

October 9 – Brought the tank ashore as far as possible with this morning's tide. Made camp all day under, the trees. Blowing very hard. No water. Gave Ferrier a dip in the sea; he is showing symptoms of thirst, and

and I took a dip myself. Ah Sam and self very parched with thirst. Ferrier is showing symptoms.

October 10 – Ferrier very bad with inflammation; very much alarmed. No fresh water, and no milk, but condensed. Self very weak; really thought I would have died last night (Sunday).

October ll – Still all alive. Ferrier very much better this morning. Self feeling very weak. I think it will rain to-day; clouds very heavy; wind not quite so hard. No rain. Morning fine weather. Ah Sam preparing to die. Have not seen him since 9. Ferrier more cheerful. Self not feeling at all well. Have not seen any boat of any description. No water. Nearly dead with thirst.

These verses describing the tragedy were written for the Sydney *Bulletin*:

DEAD WITH THIRST

The drama's over, and we know the end,
The bitter worst:
In droughty agony, with none to tend,
But with a fortitude that scorned to bend,
She died of thirst!

For ever menaced by the savage spears,
By night and day,
With nameless horrors threatened, nameless fears,
No time for grieving, fainting, or for tears,
But aye at bay.

She kept them off – the black and devilish band,
The fiends accurst;
And in her iron craft escaped the land –
Alas! upon the cruel, parching sand
To die of thirst!

At death's worst anguish she could firmly look,
And never quail:
Though wan and weak, her fingers never shook,
As day by day she entered in the book
Her piteous tale.

From first to last, there is not one complaint;
No useless cry;
No sign of heroine's heart-strength waxing faint,
The while she watched-with pains no pen can paint –
Her baby die.

Five fearful days beneath the scorching glare,
Her babe she nursed,
God knows the pangs that woman had to bear,
Whose last sad entry showed a mother's care,
Then – nearly dead with thirst!"

A.F.

Mrs Watson's *beche-de-mer* tank, Queensland Museum.

7

WE INSPECT OUR ISLAND

WE strolled back towards the hill, Dick boyishly eager to climb the 1100 feet and stand where Captain Cook had stood, and gaze upon the scene just as the famous navigator had done.

"I wonder why it was named Lizard Island," I said. "Captain Cook named it Lizard Island because he found plenty of lizards here," answered Dick. "And do you see those two rocky little islets just off the shore there?"

'Yes."

"They are called Iguana and Newt."

A hero-worshipper of the men who had done things was my mate Dick; of Kennedy, and Leichhardt, and the Jardine brothers, of the famous prospectors who had found the gold- and tinfields from the Palmer to the Batavia River. He knew all their adventurous stories. And I knew more of his secret dreams than he guessed. He was burningly eager to go through unexplored country in the Peninsula, to find a new goldfield, and to open up new country, as Bill Baird and the blackboy Romeo had done. While on a trip to Mount Romeo Dick had shown me the very place in the creek where Romeo, sent to the creek for a billy of water, had returned to camp in laughing excitement, the billycan filled with stream tin. Mount Romeo proved to be a very rich tinfield, still producing today.

Bill Baird, still with the faithful Romeo, later travelled right up through the Peninsula to the Batavia, ever restless, as all true prospectors are, seeking distant fields. of gold.

He found his goldfield, and they named it Bairdsville after him. He was speared by the blacks while working it, Romeo galloping up too late to save him.

Dick wanted to blaze new tracks, to find new mineral fields as these men had done. And, like Bill Baird, he had his "Man Friday".

"I'll bet old Cross-eye is anxious to see us busy with the prospecting dish," he remarked, with an eye to the granite.

"Yes. The granite looks kindly, too."

"Just what I was thinking. It would be funny if we came out here looking for trochus and found a tin show."

"It would do me."

It would do the skipper and his mates, too. For we had come prepared, to "try" any islands on which we might land. It was an unusual, but very practical way in which we two boys could yet again "pay our way" with the shrewd Filipino. We both knew mineral country when we saw it, knew how to prospect for gold, tin, and wolfram. Little Cooktown really lived two lives, the life of its waterfront, and the life of the town with its main interest in the back-country mineral fields to north, west, and south. In the town most of the talk was of gold, tin, wolfram, and sandalwood; along the waterfront it was of pearl-shell, trochus, *beche-de-mer*, tortoise-shell, and sandalwood. But the dream of many of the seafaring men was to find a gold, or tin, or wolfram mine on some island away up the coast. On the rare occasions when such finds had been made they had fallen to the lot of venturesome prospectors who left their horses for the time being to prospect island or coast by boat. Although the seafaring men were constantly landing on the many scattered islands to form fishing stations, or cure their beche-de-mer, they knew nothing about prospecting. They could not even tell whether an island was worth "looking at" or not, let alone know one rock formation from another. As to prospecting for actual mineral, they were helpless as fish out of water.

And so, when Cross-eyed Joe had invited Dick and me on this cruise, we knew he had two strings to his bow: the possible discovery of a patch of trochus shell, and the possible discovery of mineral, through Dick and me.

We were pleased this was so, and now we were both itching to get to work with pick and dish. As we climbed, I was noting the "kindly" look of the granite rocks, keeping a sharp eye open and hoping very much to see the milky white of a "likely" quartz reef.

From the seeming flatness surrounding us we climbed up towards the immensity of a deep blue sky, with round us, to furthest horizons, the blue of sea.

"Even the air seems to have a bluish tinge," said Dick.

"We are like ants climbing up a needle into a blue world."

A sweet smell of grass in the air, with just a tang of the sea, came on the faint breeze as we stepped up on the summit of the Hill.

The skipper and Alor San were sitting there, idly gazing out to sea.

"She still there, Dicky," called Cross-eyed Joe, and nodded to the far north .

Without the glasses, from this height, a strange lugger appeared like a toy painted upon limitless blue.

She was prospecting for shell, which meant we must keep away from our fishing grounds until she vanished. 'What you think of island, Dicky?" asked Joe. "Tin countree maybe?"

"It's good-looking granite," admitted Dick. 'I've seen the same sort out on the tinfields."

A pleasurable thrill ran through all of us as Dick climbed a big cairn of rocks' on the very summit. From here, ships at sea would be visible many miles away. With sparkling eyes and a rapt look on his face Dick was gazing far out over the treacherous loveliness to north and nor'-east.

I lit a cigarette, knowing what was in Dick's mind. He was gazing exactly as Captain Cook had gazed, was standing where Captain Cook had stood – except that when Cook stood there, there was no cairn of rocks.

A surveying party from H.M.S. *Fly* in 1843 had first erected the cairn as a survey mark to aid their ships while miles away out to sea, charting passages and reefs. Perhaps other surveying ships had added to the cairn. Captain Watson had, when he formed his home and station here. His wife used to signal him from a flagstaff when his vessel was miles at sea.

I climbed up beside Dick. It was a marvellous view. "There's Cook's Passage!" cried Dick excitedly. "I'd swear to it. Fancy being able to see it like this!"

To the nor'-east, brilliant sunlight made the sea like glass, and in its transparency we could trace for miles the green of deeper water, the light green of shallow, the yellow-green of very shallow, the straw colour of sandbanks under shallow water, and the dark patches of many reefs. Reefs, shallows, sandbanks everywhere – and winding away out through the frightening maze was a dark-blue line, like a river twisting and flowing through the green.

That dark blue was deep water. Cook guessed and hoped it, though the sight of those countless "reefs of rocks" (they were coral) filled him with trepidation. He must have blessed this hill whence he saw a chance of escape through those thousand reefs.

"See the Great Barrier Reef," said Dick, pointing. "That winding channel runs right to it, and out through Cook's Passage."

Away to the east was a low, lazily forming line of white "smoke", stretching as far north and south as we could see. It was not smoke, it was foam and spray from the rollers billowing in from the vast Pacific to thunder and break upon the Great Barrier Reef, the mighty rampart guarding Australia's north-eastern coast.

Cross-eyed Joe and Alor San were standing at the foot of the cairn, earnestly gazing to the south, then to the nor-west, We thought they were reassuring themselves that at least there was no "bushranger" sail out there.

Far to the nor-west we could see, hazily, the peak of Howick Island.

"That's where Ah Sam crept ashore for water, and couldn't find it," said Dick, "and there –" he pointed west to what appeared like clouds upon the water – "is the Turtle group, where Mrs Watson and the baby and Ah

Sam perished.

Further still to the west was the now hazy outline of coast. Away south were specks of islands. We were gazing along that "inner sea" which runs north and south, hemmed in on the west by the Peninsula mainland, on the east by that line of smoky foam that marks the Great Barrier Reef. A lonely land, a lonely sea.

We glanced down, then, at our own island spread out so solidly at our feet. Looking southward, our big Hill joined a much smaller hill, which was connected to a smaller still, until they ended in mere mounds stretching along the shoreline in the form of a small ridge. In places the bare rock bases sloped right down into the water, but. here and there the rock was broken by a tiny beach, or portion of shore. From the few scattered trees a chattering of birds came up plainly through the clear air. Just off-shore were the little islands of Iguana and Newt, and not far away were Saddle Island and North Direction Island.

Close by where we stood, topped by granite boulders, one face of our Hill was a precipice sloping sheer down to the sea.

"What a great place for a look-out camp," said Dick; "in nearly all weathers."

He was pointing to a little hollow sheltered by big boulders on the summit of the Hill. With the aid of a tarpaulin or tent-fly a cosy look-out camp could be formed there, protected against nearly all weathers. Joe and Alar San took in the position at a glance.

When is the *Changte* due, I wonder?" mused Dick. "We could see her or the *Taiping* plainly from here on a clear day, see their lights at night, too. I' d like to see either of them pass by from here."

Momentarily, I imagined a strange expression Hit across the face of Cross-eyed Joe, as he gazed fixedly at Dick. On Alor San's square, good-humoured face there seemed a shade of wonderment.

The *Changte* and *Taiping* and other China boats were well known in the north. We'd seen them loading up with pearl-shell and trochus, *beche-de-mer* and sandalwood for China.

We turned towards the east, and there the island was spread out like a shallow basin, hemmed in between two ridges, the ridge on which we stood and an apology for a ridge running along part of the eastern shore. But that "ridge" was only a few bush-covered mounds. The grass-covered valley, with here and there a small, thin grove of pandanus palm, ran from end to end of the island.

Towards its northern end a thicker grove of pandanus palm, only a few hundred yards behind our camp, clustered round the ruined hut, now bathed in sunshine.

"See," pointed Dick. "That's strange. Through the grass, even at this date, you can plainly see the furrows that were the Chinamen's garden."

And it was so, I suppose because we were looking down from a height. It was remarkable, though, that those old furrows should have shown up through the thick grass like that.

From the inland base of the ridge a few springs seeped out and formed a little green swamp near the hut. And from here a tiny rivulet welled its way through green palms to a beach, past the hut.

"Well," said Dick, "here we are. There's not much to see; it's not a big island."

"That's so. And there's not much on it, either, and what there is you can see in one eyeful. How big do you think it is?"

"Just about three miles long, and about two wide," answered Dick. "How about if we try a few dishes?"

Eagerly we hurried down from the Hill to prospect the tiny, gullies for tin, or any ordinary mineral the island might contain.

8

CORAL GARDENS

WITH all hands at our heels, with dish, pick, and shovel we tried the little gullies running from the Hill. These men could teach us about the sea, and had a wealth of knowledge of what lay under the water. But we could teach them what the earth might contain.

Not that Big Paddy and Billy and Little Paddy were impressed. They looked on with amused grins, very different from the doubting, hopeful expectancy on the faces of the Filipino and Malays.

But to describe the next few days, with their quick hopes and slow disappointments, would take too long. Suffice it to say that, to our great surprise, Dick and I actually found some small prospects of tin.

At night we built castles in the air, because for a couple of days it actually appeared as if we might have found a tin mine. Cross-eyed Joe and Alor San and Ah Matt watched breathlessly as we washed the prospects. But a few days proved to us that the tin was not payable. At least, we could not trace either payable reef or alluvial.

Joe and Alor San and Ah Matt were very disappointed, but Big Paddy and Billy and Man Friday were barely interested. If we had been digging holes in the ground for something good to eat they could have understood it, but toiling in the hope of finding pieces of black stone left them bored.

One afternoon the lugger that had been hovering about vanished into the misty north.

'We start work early-morning time," said Cross-eyed Joe.

We did, putting to sea when the mists had lifted, and Dick from away up on the Look-out had signalled "all clear". For one of us must always be on look-out duty now; either Dick, Little, Paddy, or me. Dick was training Little Paddy today, and 'he already could use the glasses. Dick would explain to him that trouble could be expected from the nor'-west in particular for it was from that direction that the Thursday Island fleets cruised down the "Inner Sea". There was just a chance of trouble from the north, and a fair chance from the south. Dick emphasized the fact that no alarm must be given unless a vessel was tacking directly for the island, and not then till she approached within a certain distance. The danger Signal, which would allow the dinghies plenty of time to collect their divers and rejoin the *Nancy Bell* must then be given. Joe would land all shore hands, then either steam away in the opposite direction to the oncoming vessel, or hide round the back of the island, depending on whether the skipper should think the stranger meant real business, or was only nosing around. When she finally sailed away, whether in hours or days, we at the shore station would signal the *Nancy Bell* from the Look-out.

Our little venture was well planned and well organized.

We congratulated ourselves and the skipper. Even if a trespasser, or trespassers came we could outwit them and win all the shell.

'I'll bet old Cross-eye is jolly glad he asked us to come now," Dick chuckled. "And I'll bet he's jolly glad he brought Little Paddy along."

"That's so," I mused. "I hadn't thought of it. We can just manage to keep both dinghies working full time, and keep a daily look-out, too."

"Yes," said Dick. "One man short, even Man Friday, would have made a big difference."

The weather was so calm Joe had to use the little engine to chug us out to the fishing grounds. The rising sun turned the sea all golden, as its rays pierced a low bank of clouds and seemed to set them on fire. Cross-eyed Joe was squinting back at the Hill; he would have loved to find a tin mine there. So would all of us. Little spirals of mist, risen from the plain, had drifted to the base of the Hill and, gathering in wraith-like clouds now began to roll up it effortlessly. Up on the peak, Dick and Little Paddy stood sharply outlined; but even as we watched they were blotted out as the mists rolled up over the top of the Hill and enveloped them. A few minutes later wreathy vapour dissolved upward, leaving Dick and Man Friday statues in brilliant sunlight. Joe shut off the engine, we lifted the dinghies overboard, rowed across the shallows until above the reef, then commenced diving.

The trochus were still there, to our delight, and there were plenty of them. We secured a ton of shell that week, and the trochus seemed to be growing more plentiful. Everyone was happy.

Occasionally, when Alor San or Ah Matt needed a spell, I would go down and bring up a few shells, if I was not on look-out duty. Dick and Little Paddy would do the same to relieve Big Paddy or Billy. Not that Dick and I brought up much shell, but it gave the divers a chance for a smoke and a breather, and a joke at our expense. Little Paddy could swim like a fish. The way he used to twist and glide amongst the water grasses and pinnacles of corals often reminded me of an eel. Since he'd learnt where to look for the trochus he brought up shell with surprising speed.

To me, it always seemed like swimming down into a living fairyland, for those coral gardens were so mysterious and lovely, more fascinating by far when seen under water than from the surface. And the water was so clear on a bright day that even grains of sand were distinct.

Sometimes those sands sparkled as if they were powder of diamonds.

One thing amazed me, the tracks. I knew the importance of tracks in the bush, but had never dreamt of tracks on the sea floor. Yet here they were distinctly, wherever there was a patch of sand. The long groove made by a wandering *beche-de-mer* reminded me somewhat of a snake's track. I gazed down at the tracks of crabs, the "furrow" of a browsing turtle, the numerous and different tracks of shellfish large and small, tracks from pinpoint size to that of a dinner plate. Here, plainly, were the tracks of Alor San and Ah Matt, even my own track, where I had stood a moment upon the sea floor.

It was glorious to swim down to the mazes of queer plant life, amongst the differently shaped and coloured grasses growing up from the sea bed or overhanging the coral ledges and caverns. These were sometimes like trellised vines, with ferns and long fronds of things like groping arms amongst them. The tiniest of baby trees, perfect in shape, sometimes no taller than a blade of grass rose from the sand. Corals of innumerable shapes and colours entrancing. One of bright orange, shaped like fern leaves, with tiny lights like pinheads of colour blinking and glowing on the tip of each frond was particularly lovely. These lights probably were living phosphorescent insects; I do not know. In this ghastly yet vivid world of green twilight I would hardly have been dismayed if a mermaid or mischievous sea-gnome had come floating towards me. In the deathly silence the Feather Stars gliding over the bottom appear like lovely fancies, imagined only in dreams. Their graceful, tendril-like arms fringed with fine silks pulse gently as they glide along, collecting food that must be delicate as a breath. These Feather Stars shone in scarlet or bright purple, sometimes in vivid yellow. Occasionally one of the smaller crabs was uncannily beautiful, its shell glowing like opal. It was a shadow world of countless weird things, amazing things, too, of beauty in sometimes lovely, sometimes simple, and sometimes grotesque shapes. I'm afraid that very often I came gasping to the surface empty handed, suddenly to remember that I'd really gone down to gather trochus shell.

"I think we ask skipper sign on Jack again nex' cruise," Alor would innocently murmur to Ah Matt. "He make good diver – bring up plenty trochus shell."

"Yes," Ah Matt would reply dreamily, "he make good money – we all make good money with Jack for diver."

And I'd grin and take it.

There are many areas within the Great Reef where the sea bottom is quite ordinary, sometimes disappointingly uninteresting. But everywhere we worked the sea bed in these Lizard Island waters was a fairyland. Even the fish were brighter, more "alive", and often quite "tame", as if they knew that we were in their world and there was no need to be afraid of us. Occasionally they would come swimming up to me with magnified eyes quivering in rainbow colours. The scales of many were beautiful, in scarlet and green and gold, while some Hashed tails of the quaintest shapes, brilliantly coloured. Some, too, were unusually marked. One had a line of "portholes" along his side, another patterned with diamonds like those on a playing card. Yet others were marked with narrow or broad stripes, either horizontal or vertical, or patterned with spots or circles of different colours, some startlingly vivid.

I'll never forget my first "Eye" fish. Quite a big fellow, fat and self confident, he Came leisurely swimming towards me with his thick lips quietly opening and shutting, funnily reminiscent of an invitation to kiss. His eyes were balls of liquid gold. Leisurely he swam round and round my head, and my eyes were staring into eyes, eyes, eyes. Along his sides, in bright colours, glowed painted eyes, vivid eyes all staring at me as round and round he went. A queer experience, but a lovely one.

When I surfaced I described the fish.

"He Eye-fish, Jacky," grinned Alor San. "He sees you all ways, but you only see him one way. Why you no put salt on his tail? He good to eat." But I knew that I could not have eaten such a lovely thing.

One afternoon I went down, and the bottom "came up" to me like a grassy paddock, vividly green after rain. I brought a handful of the grass to the surface. It had leaves shaped something like a fingernail, each leaf of the same queer pattern. Alor San noted my curiosity, and when next he went down he brought up a fistful of the grass and handed it to me.

"What you think Jacky?" he asked. "See anything?"

I examined the grass and then its leaves, having already learnt that many things on the sea bottom are not always what they seem. They may hold the most unexpected surprises. But this grass was exactly like the grass I had brought up.

"It's just the same," I declared.

Alor San with his finger-tip smartly flicked a leaf off the grass. It dropped to the bottom of the dinghy, hurriedly unfolded the daintiest legs, and swiftly crawled under the bailing tin.

It was a wee green crab, exactly the same colour, and exactly the same shape as those leaves of grass. Alor San grinned his pleasure at my surprise. "Crab he live longa that grass Jacky," he explained. "You touch grass, crab make himself a leaf."

Although we were only a few weeks actually fishing in those fascinating waters, I could write many, many pages telling of the wonderful life we saw there in that submarine world But we must get on with the story.

9

THE SHARK

ONE beautiful morning Alor San and I were diving. The water was so clear that objects below seemed magnified plainer than if they had been in the sunshine above. Alar San Hashed past like a living bronze as we glided down, I into a tall shrubbery of brown and yellow and russet leaves like broad ribbons slowly pulsing with the tide. Among them, upon a circle of snowy sand, lay the vivid, scarlet bands of a trochus. Alor glided to deeper bottom, between pinnacles of pink corals, as my hand clutched the shellfish. Then came a thunder clap like the clang of doom. Instantly wheeling, I was gazing into the startled eyes of Alor, barely twelve feet away. Big eyes stared swiftly up and around then Hashed me a terrible warning as his body sank belly-first between the corals to the bottom. As I desperately gripped the sea-bed and pulled myself down the grasses closed over and around me like entwining snakes. Through them I could just distinguish that Alor San was striving to squeeze his belly deep into the very bottom. Icy fear gripped me, for the sales of his wriggling feet were shining white as a snowy shell. Then the shark was gliding between us, his baleful eye brilliant as the coldest emerald. A tiger! That huge, flattened head with the great bluff snout, the body so terrifyingly, so lithely beautiful, were so close that I stared at beads of phosphorus like dewdrops of coloured oils clinging to the hide. In the deathly silence he glided by. Like a flash he was back, glaring down at those tell-tale white feet, his tail brushing the leaves before my face. Then his snout edged down as his tail rose up, and with wavy movement of snout and tail he tried to reach down to Alor San. But the enormous head, that great rounded snout, could not reach down into the narrow space between the coral pinnacles in which the victim was wedged. I only had leaves to cover me, while Alor San had the protection of those narrow coral walls. But-they had not hidden the wliite soles of his feet.

In a second the shark was "standing on his head", effortlessly, smelling down upon Alor San. Fortunate was Alor that the Tiger has such an enormous head, and that he was wedged down in such a narrow space. Then, in a flash, the shark vanished.

I knew he would come again. He would come three times. The third time he would go away for good, or he would fairly worry Alor San from his grip on the bottom, would keep worrying him until Alor's last breath must go. Now he would travel a little further away, then wheel back to see whether his prey had fallen into the trap and exposed himself. The next time, the third and last time he would cruise still further away.

I knew that for me there would be no third time, my lungs were bursting now. When he came again and worried Alor San and vanished again, then I must let go, and cry to God to speed me up to the dinghy.

Now came the sound of clapping blows from the surface.

Clap upon clap mingled with the heartening thump of racing rowlocks as Dick's dinghy approached, all aboard clapping frantically under water, in the faint hope of scaring the shark. I gazed up in agonized hope. Both dinghies were so close it seemed I only had to reach up to touch the keels. I could see stars in the brilliant blue far above, and the faces of Ah Matt and Dick and Big Paddy, their mouths wide with shouting.

I could see, too, the thrashing oars and the quick whites of their hands, furiously clapping just below the surface.

And then – he was back again. Butting down with his snout, wrenching and heaving with it between the corals, using his great weight with brutish ferocity to crush downwards in an effort to reach Alor and lever him over. That was a sickening sound, that crunching murmur as the massive, leathery snout' wedged down past the brittle, feathery coral. With the sharp snap of a coral branch he got a partial purchase. Then, bending his body like a giant spring, he tried to lever Alor over and out.

I could feel the movement of the water, imagine the quivering strength with which Alor was clinging to the bottom, burrowing his tautened body right into it while a murky smoke of disturbed sand and powdered vegetation rose slowly over man and shark. In a flash he was gone, and I was half way to the surface, unconscious that I had even kicked out. In my imagination the feeling of shark's teeth ripping my stomach filled the seconds with an eternity. Hands grabbed me as I snatched the dinghy and fairly leaped over into it, coming into violent and happy collision with Alor San plunging in over the opposite side. He, too, had not waited for the third coming!

To a shout from Ah Matt and the vicious smack of paddles there came a crash against the dinghy as the infuriated shark lashed out and slewed away. He had returned just too late. Alor San and I were gasping in the dinghy-bottom, too paralysed with relief to move.

There would be no more fishing that day, nor for three days afterwards. For the shark had smelt human flesh. And when a shark does that he may hang about for three days, returning every now and then-so the coloured divers believe.

We rowed to the *Nancy Bell*, where Joe ordered up the anchor, and we sailed for the island. There we would do a few camp and shipboard jobs while Alor San and I got over the shock, and our fishing ground became safe again.

"Maybe shark he like you, Jacky," said Cross-eyed Joe quietly. "You near fall in mouth killer shark – now shark near gobble you on sea bottom. Be careful next time, Jacky."

I shuddered. The others were silent. The third time! These coloured people are deeply superstitious.

Little olive-green honey birds were flitting about happily in the shore trees; an oyster-catcher very smart in his black coat with scarlet legs and beak was stalking the tide edge on business bent. It was good to be alive. Dick and I climbed up to the Look-out, welcomed by a wonderful grin from Little Paddy.

"A fat lot he cares about sharks," scowled Dick. "He's going to have company on his look-out duty now." But Man Friday's grin only broadened as he gazed at his hero.

The calm blue of sea and sky was beautiful and the outline of mainland and distant inlets sharply distinct. Not a sail in Sight.

"What great luck we're having," said Dick. 'We must have nearly three tons of shell by now, and, except at the very start, there's not been a sail to worry us. I wonder if our luck will hold."

"I hope so. Two or three trips as successful as this one to town and back and we'll earn enough money to buy half a dozen horses."

"That's right, Jack. We'll get a real good outfit together."

And my mate and I indulged in dreams. More than anything else in the world we desired a good outfit to go bush, prospecting for gold together. We felt that our dreams were coming true.

"It's a strange thing," mused. Dick. "Our luck with this trochus fishing. Often we've planned and hoped that we'd strike a few bags of tin, or a few Ounces of gold to enable us to buy an outfit. But we never dreamt that we'd get our chance from the sea."

"The money's good, wherever it comes from."

"Yes," agreed Dick. But 1 knew he would rather it had come from the wild ranges of the Peninsula.

Dick and 1 with Man Friday camped ashore, while Cross-eyed Joe with Alor and Ah Matt, Big Paddy and Billy, slept aboard. One night after we'd turned in Dick continued to toss restlessly.

"What's the matter?" I asked, yawning.

"Can't sleep," he growled, and sat up to roll a cigarette. So did I.

"What say we take a walk up the Hill?" he suggested.

"We might see a ship go by. I'd like to see the *Taiping* or *Changte* from Captain Cook's Look-out."

"*Changte, Taiping,* my eyel" I retorted. "They might be a thousand miles away."

"And they mightn't. They must be just about due now." "Oh, all right," I grumbled, and pulled on trousers and boots.

I know Dick had only made an excuse. It would be lucky coincidence if on this particular night either of these ships sailed past. But to climb to the Look-out appealed to me.

The night was dark, but brilliant starlight made a silhouette feather edge of the grass along the sides and crown of the Hill. As we climbed higher up through the blackness amongst the rocks every bush, every tuft of grass on the summit became distinct, outlined against the stars. As we reached the summit we halted in amazement as the shadow of a man glided over a crest of the ridge, and vanished.

"Did you see it?" exclaimed Dick. "Yes, a man!"

"I thought I was seeing things," frowned Dick. 'Who on earth can he be?"

I shook my head. Sorely puzzled, we gazed down at the shadowy camp, then at the Nancy Bell, motionless at anchor under the stars. There was no sound, no sign of life except the dull glow of the fire down by the camp.

'We can't both have been mistaken," murmured Dick.

"Yet there's not a soul on this island except ourselves."

He was staring towards the blackness of the little hollow, shielded by big boulders on the summit of the Hill; the place he had once said would be a bonzer look-out, sheltered from all weathers. Picking his way among the rocks he walked down towards it, with me close behind.

Dick stared around. Sheltered by the big boulders we stood in a little pit of darkness, the starlit sea a dull velvet pond away below. In the quietness I heard Dick sniffing. Then he bent down, sniffing, slowly groping.

Gradually I detected a faint smell of tobacco smoke. Dick stood up with an exclamation of triumph. He held the stub of a cigarette, just smouldering.

"Do you see it?" he whispered. "Yes."

"No you don't – I mean the end of the butt! See how it is chewed! That's just the way that Alor San smokes his cigarettes."

"Alor San?" I said, puzzled. "But Alor is asleep on the *Nancy Bell.*"

"He is not," replied Dick emphatically. "I have seen him smoke too many cigarettes not to recognize a stub he has smoked. Alor San was sitting in this little hide-out, watching out to sea – in the night! And he slipped away when he heard us coming up over the crown of the Hill."

"Why did he run?" I asked doubtfully.

"How should I know?" answered Dick. "Tell me why he should have been here at all, secretly in the night-gazing out to sea?"

We stared at one another.

10

THE SECRET VIGIL OF ALOR SAN

NEXT morning after breakfast we were bagging shells when Alor San and Ah Matt came ashore with cheery greeting. They settled down to lend us a hand, chatting amiably. But not a word of the night before.

Like a statue, spear in hand, Big Paddy balanced in the dinghy off shore, Billy at the oars. Just keeping the dinghy drifting. From the corner of my eye I saw Man Friday vanishing behind the camp, he winked impishly when he saw I'd noticed him. Not a stitch of clothes was on the little blackboy, but he was fully. dressed for he grasped his beloved spear.

"Where's Little Paddy?" asked Dick as I began to sew up a bag.

"I've an idea he's gone to the mangroves after crabs."

"Oh, has he! Sneaked away again when there's a spot of work to do!"

"There's not much to do."

"I know," growled Dick, "but if all hands got to it then I'd be able to go fishing all the sooner."

Two little birds commenced a lively twittering on a tree by the camp.

"That fellow will break his neck," muttered Dick, nodding.

"That fellow" was obviously the Romeo bird, showing off to his lady friend by clinging upside down to a twig, whistling his throat out at the earth below. Suddenly he let go and fell like a stone to the grass tops, only to scoot upward like a shot, fluttering above his lady-love, twittering triumphantly.

"That boy can do his stuff," said Dick admiringly. "Yes, his lady friend's beginning to sit up and take notice."

Out on the anchorage Cross-eyed Joe was tinkering with the engine of the Nancy Bell. Very keen, now, were we on our natty little ship, confident we could fight out any storm with her, even a cyclone, maybe, and get away with it.

The skipper, as every skipper should be, was immensely pleased when we praised his little ship. She certainly was seaworthy, and could sail like a bird under a stiff breeze. He and Alor San and Ah Matt kept her in apple-pie order. But they did not bother about the livestock she carried. They had lived amongst cockroaches in all manner of ships for so many years that they recognized them as pests, but part of the ship.

"How about knocking up a few johnnies, Jack?" suggested Dick. "It looks as if we're going to have this hungry crowd ashore for dinner."

I "knocked 'em up" all right, mixed the flour, forgot to put the cream of tartar in, punched 'em up, raked out the coals, and threw the wretched things on. They didn't seem to rise much, but when they were burnt a bit I turned them over with a stick. When they seemed to be done I scraped them off the fire, knocked off the biggest pieces of charcoal, and they were ready. Some distance away, Dick was frying platefuls of very appetizing fish, three four-pounders that had fallen to Little Paddy's spear, with half a dozen big mangrove crabs. Big Paddy and Billy were roasting their own catch on the coals. When the billy was boiled we gathered round.

"What the blazes are these?" Dick demanded, staring. «Johnnies," I answered.

"Heavens!" snorted Dick, and dished out the tucker. They tried my johnnies, only tried them. The aboriginals, though, ate and liked them. Dick merely growled his disgust, but Alor San and Ah Matt laughed hilariously with unseemly mirth. Cross-eyed Joe was quietly sympathetic, though with a cross-eyed grin.

"You better diver than cook, Jack," he murmured. "Never mind. We teach you cook, too."

I was pretty certain they would not, and also was fairly sure I wouldn't be called upon to cook on state occasions again-or on any other, I hoped!

After the midday meal Alor San and Ah Matt stretched out under the shade of the bush-shed, smoking. A lazy, dreamy feeling enveloped the island.

'What about a peep from the Look-out?" suggested Dick.

"See if anything is doing."

"There's nothing doing," I growled. I was just snoozing off.

"How do you know?" persisted Dick. "There might be a ship coming our way."

"Let her. We're here ashore. The *Nancy Bell* is, at anchorage. They wouldn't find out anything."

"Oh, come on, Jack – you'll have plenty of time to sleep tonight."

"You'll be fishing tonight."

"Ye-es, I suppose so. Oh, come on, you lazy coot!"

"Oh, all right," I growled, and stood up. 'What you want to climb that blooming hill for when there's nothing to do beats me."

With the hum of insects in our ears we climbed the Hill to the Look-out. Coarse was the grass, rough the granite rocks, hot under the sun. We stepped up into space, and gazed out.

Dick pointed far out towards the mainland. "A sail!" he said.

She looked like a pocket handkerchief, miles away, nearer the mainland than we were. Just a white speck motionless on the water, for the breeze was the faintest.

"We needn't worry about her," said Dick. "She's sailing south, and much too far away to see us, even if the *Nancy Bell* was out fishing."

"What is she?" I asked. Dick studied her through the glasses.

"The dead spit of one of Tommy Farquhar's luggers from Thursday Island," he replied.

"The *Pearl King*," I suggested.

"Yes," answered Dick, "maybe. He's a great battler, a good bloke. He deserves his luck."

"They say his fleet have found some lovely pearls this season already."

"Yes," answered Dick. "One gem cost him one of his best divers, though – paralysis."

"The woman who wears that pearl will never know that it cost the life of a man."

We gazed, to the north, but saw no sign of a sail. To the east stretched the mighty ramparts of the Barrier Reef; we were safe from that quarter. A frigate bird, majestic visitor from the high seas, came sailing down low over us, his legs tucked well in beneath him, staring down from bright, beady eyes.

"How wonderful it would be to glide through the air like him," sighed Dick.

"He's a pirate," I answered. "Grabs other birds' fish."

"There's other pirates besides frigate birds," Dick grinned.

"I suppose so," I said. "Two-legged ones. Though he's got two legs-like most pirates. Anyway, I'd love to swim like a porpoise."

"If I could swim and dive and stay under water like Alor San or Ah Matt or Big Paddy or Billy it would do me," replied Dick, enviously.

"I wouldn't mind being able to swim like Little Paddy," I admitted.

"Yes," mused Dick. "They can put it all over us-in their own way. But I suppose there's some compensation."

He led the way along the slope, to the tiny hollow among the boulders. Bending down, he began carefully to pull the tufted grasses aside. As I walked to him his fingers burrowed down, then he held up something with a triumphant "Ah!"

It was an old cigarette butt, long since cold. The dried end was all chewed up, just as Alor San always chewed his butts.

"He's been here before," declared Dick. "Every time we're ashore, by the look of things. As we keep the Look-out by day, he must come in the night. Now why does he sit here night after night?"

But we could think of no explanation. We sat down, gazing out to sea.

"The boulders would shelter a man from cold or wind or rain; mused Dick, "while the brow of the Hill folds round him like the back of a, chair, and the strongest blow from the Great Barrier would not trouble him. He can see south to his left, north and nor'-west to his right, while straight ahead he gazes towards the mainland. And between us and the mainland are the passages along which the ships steam north and south. On dark nights no sail would be visible, and, as the luggers and cutters carry no lights, he could not see one even if it was coming this way, whereas we would see it when we climbed the Look-out at dawn. Now why does Alor San keep watch on this hill by night, when there's no need to, and when he could not see a lugger even if it was coming our way?"

"He'd only be able to see a ship if it passed by," I ventured. "He'd see the lights of a steamer easily enough."

"That's just it," said Dick quietly. "From this height, on a dark night, he could see the lights of a steamer passing by as plainly as if it were a comet gliding between us and the mainland."

"But why would. he want to see a steamer?" I asked, puzzled. "They don't interest us."

"Ask me!" answered Dick thoughtfully. "He must watch out for something. And the only thing he could see at night would be a passing steamer."

"Oh, well, let him," I yawned lazily, and lay back on the grass. 'Whatever he comes here for doesn't matter to us. He may come here to say his prayers for all we know," I added, grinning, "to be nearer Mohammed or something. I've known white men do that. And when you come to think of it, what better place could a man find than this lonely hill-top above the sea, by night? And remember, these Malays are much more conscientious about their religion than we are."

"He could see the *Changte* steaming north, or the *Taiping* steaming south," murmured Dick.

"What?"

"Any of us would recognize either ship by night, as well as by day," he droned on.

"But why on earth should he want to see the *Taiping* or *Changte*?" I asked irritably.

"Ask me!" replied Dick. "Big Paddy's got a fish."

Lazily I rolled up on my arm and gazed away below to where Billy was swiftly paddling the dinghy in pursuit of a spear haft speeding through the water.

"It's a big one," I said.

"Yes," answered Dick gloatingly. "Fish for tea."

From this height we could see the bottom quite plainly, while further out every well known line in the deck of the *Nancy Bell* was perfectly distinct. The skipper stood up and waved. I waved my hat in reply.

"A cunning old fox is Cross-eyed Joe," remarked Dick, smiling.

"He's not a bad bloke," I answered. 'What a lucky chance it was that 'he asked us to come on this cruise!"

"You bet it was!" Dick declared enthusiastically. "And he's glad he asked us, too. We're doing our bit with the rest of them. I do hope no other luggers find us here. If the patch only holds out long enough we'll be able to buy those horses!" And the thought was a thrill.

We commenced diving again, delighted to find the trochus were still there, they seemed to be thicker than ever.

"You two boys bring us luck," smiled Alor San.

"Plenty luck," agreed Ah Matt. "Skipper think that a way, too! You come too next cruise – maybe we go further north look for pearl-shell – suppose you still bring luck maybe we find plenty pearls."

"That so," agreed Alor San with shining eyes. "Maybe we find gold-tin, too. Plenty island up north."

Dick and I were pleased that the ship's company regarded us as mascots. We knew a little of what store Filipinos and Malays set on lucky charms and portents, both for good and evil, in anything they undertake.

Little Paddy, proud of managing a dinghy, was now an expert at finding shell. When giving his shaggy-browed father or the easy-going Billy a breather he'd pop overside, do a little flash stuff for Dick's especial benefit, then streak to the bottom like an eel. He'd squirm about with amazing swiftness down in the coral gardens, then shoot up to the surface with six shells clenched in his skinny little arms. One day, though, he came within an ace of getting his hide thoroughly tanned, as Dick had often promised him. He was giving Billy a breather, and that good-humoured aboriginal commenced to roll a cigarette. Little Paddy slipped overboard, and attracted Dick's attention by standing on his head in the water and flashing his tail.

"You'll show that face of yours once too often, young feller-me-lad," called Dick. "One of these days I'll be close enough to land you such a dinyhayser that no one will be able to tell your face from your tail again. Not that there's much difference anyhow."

Little Paddy's face popped up where his tail had been.

With a derisive grin he turned a couple of somersaults, sharply smacked his stern in Dick's direction, and vanished.

Dick grinned and went on with his job of tending Alor San and Ah Matt. My dinghy was working only fifty yards away. Presently, Dick glanced up. Little Paddy had not reappeared.

"Where Little Paddy?" called Dick, as Big Paddy broke surface.

"He no come up yet," called Billy. "He long time?" questioned Dick.

"Ou ail" agreed Billy unconcernedly, and went on smoking. Alor San and Ah Matt broke surface and threw their shells into Dick's dinghy. They clung to the gunwale, noisily refilling their lungs. Dick was watching the water by Billy's dinghy.

"Little Paddy go down," said Dick uneasily. "You see him? He no come up yet."

"No see," answered Alor and Ah Matt. They gazed unconcernedly towards Billy's dinghy.

"Paddy," called Dick, "Little Paddy dive, he no come up, look overboard longa him."

With a grunt Big Paddy lowered his head in the water, gazing all around to the bottom. Presently he bobbed up with a snort.

"No see 'im," he called.

"Well then, dive and find him straight away!" shouted Dick. "Quick! Something happen longa him!"

Big Paddy slid overside, took a deep breath and vanished.

Dick's alarm communicated itself to Alor San and Ah Matt. Filling their lungs they sank, turned over and swam swiftly down. Billy had smoked his cigarette, and now commenced to roll another. Dick waited a few more seconds, then shouted, "Never mind dinghy, Billy, me look after 'im. You dive, too, quick-feller-find Little Paddy-quick-feller, Billy."

"Ou ai," grunted Billy without moving. Then he looked up with a grin, rolling the cigarette between his fingers.

"Little Paddy he arright," he called. "He ony play about."

"What!" shouted Dick. Then glanced behind him.

And there, peeping above the dinghy side behind him was an impish little black face. Dick breathed deeply, very deeply, measuring the distance. Then he grabbed.

The imp vanished, the dinghy swayed violently, Dick overbalanced and splashed overboard.

11

HAPPY DAYS

AT the first pearly streak of dawn, Dick or I would be up on the Look-out. Such magnificent dawns, the sun a ball of molten gold rising up in its cloak of flame from behind the Great Barrier Reef. Carefully we'd scan the lightening sea in every direction. Only when certain there was no sail in sight" would we signal the *Nancy Bell.* Cross-eyed Joe would wave acknowledgment, then the shore party at the camp would stroll to the dinghy and row out to the cutter, and away she would chug to the fishing grounds. Whoever was on look-out duty would be in for a quiet, somewhat lonely day. I used not to mind, being of a somewhat lazy nature. But I knew the energetic Dick was lonely when his turn came, and Man Friday, of course, was always lonely when he was away from Dick.

On misty dawns the look-out man had to be very sure before signalling, for it is surprising how easily a little vessel can hide, or remain unnoticed in the mists. Only when certain that the seas were clear was the "All Clear" Signal given.

A couple of hours later, and the look-out man had again to be very careful. He must watch that no craft came sneaking out from behind any distant isle to take the *Nancy Bell* by surprise. When a vessel is "fishing" with all dinghies away and all hands busy she is at a disadvantage, liable to be surprised.

Such could not happen if the look-out man remained alert for from his height, and aided by the glasses, he must see any approaching vessel long before those aboard could see the *Nancy Bell.* But – there must be no dozing off to sleep.

Only a few miles off shore the *Nancy Bell,* the dinghies and the men at work were so close that I used to bring their faces up to me in the glass. I often amused myself by "telling" what they were saying and joking about, judging by their expressions in the glass. On some days I could even follow them through the glasses to the bottom of the sea. But this depended upon brilliance of sunlight, the angle of the rays, and the type of sea bottom on which the divers were working.

But their faces above water were always interesting.

The keen, animated face of Dick as he congratulated a diver breaking surface with arms fairly 'bulging with shell"; the shrewd, smiling brown face of Alor as he cracked a sly joke; the moving lips and saturnine face of Ah Matt who could express so much with so few words and so little change of expression. And in the other, dinghy were the broad, deeply-wrinkled, primitive face of Big Paddy, rugged as if hewn from the Rock of Ages-as indeed it was; easy-going Big Paddy, liable unexpectedly to fly into a fury, like all aboriginals; the shaggy face of Billy, with keen eyes set in even deeper more cavernous sockets, with his shrug and grunt and chuckle that meant a quiet joke at the expense of anyone. Aboriginals are by no means so dense as many of us believe them to be. I often used to keep an eye on Little Paddy. Tending his dinghy with a shouted joke to Dick now and then, or diving like a Trojan to bring up all the shell he possibly could while either his dad or Billy was spelling, and all for Dick's benefit, but sooner or later I'd catch him in a mischief. With a long, underwater dive, he would fasten a huge bunch of seaweed to the keel of Dick's dinghy. so that Dick would wonder why it reacted so sluggishly to his oars. One day I noticed him swimming under water to Dick's dinghy, then lost sight of him. He had poked his head up just under the bow, and was very gently pushing the bow round. Dick, gazing overside at the divers below, did not notice for quite a time. Then he put an oar overside to swing her round again. The divers broke surface, went down again, and again Dick found himself drifting round in the opposite direction. Irritably he thrust an oar over¬side, and pulled her round; I could guess that he wondered what queer tricks the tide was playing on him. When the dinghy drifted round the third time, though, he stepped to the bows. I saw his fist raised threateningly, then, yards away, a little black backside broke surface in a familiar gesture. I could faintly hear Dick's shout of wrath. But Man Friday's cleverest trick was to throw a live fish splashing into the dinghy when Dick was preoccupied with his divers.

For there are some species of fish which can be caught alive down below, if you are expert and know how to do it. These fish lazily rest just under a coral ledge, the side fin gently pulsing, sometimes visible to the experienced eye. The diver slips his fingers under the ledge and gently tickles the fish with his fingertips, slowly working up along from the tail, under the belly, to the head. Gently feeling at this with comforting fingertips he suddenly grips it, and the fish is a prisoner.

Dick, gazing down at Alor and Ah Matt diving below, would leap up with a start as a fish splashed into the dinghy behind him and flopped about his feet. Of Little Paddy there would be no sign – not until he was well out of reach.

Cross-eyed Joe was always busy on the *Nancy Bell,* either below or on deck. Occasionally he would be squatting in such a position that I would get his face in the glass. At such times, concentrated upon his job and believing himself to be unobserved, I would again get that glimpse of "two men", depending on which side of his face I could see best.

At times I used to think how very lucky we were, not only in finding the trochus, but in finding it so close to an island that was such an : admirable base. At this very moment there were scores of vessels cruising the Coral Sea prospecting for trochus, and here we had found a patch. right up against a sheltered island blessed with fresh water and wood.

Thus, once again, our quest strangely resembled prospecting for minerals. Many and many a man has walked over gold near his own camp door, and trudged away for weary miles seeking it. In the course of time numerous vessels seeking trochus surely must have sailed over the patch on which the *Nancy Bell* was now working.

The days and nights flew by. With sundown the *Nancy Bell* would come steaming back to anchorage and the look-out man thankfully climb down the Hill, eager for a yarn and to hear the news of the day. After the evening meal we'd hardly "hit" the blankets when we were sound asleep, to be awakened a moment later with a cry, "Shake a leg! Shake a leg, sun he rise!" Many a time I could not believe it.

Soon we had won and cleaned and bagged five tons of shell – a full cargo for the *Nancy Bell.*

That evening Cross-eyed Joe smiled at us across the fire-light.

"What you say, Dicky-Jacky? We do well?"

"Bonzer, skipper," answered Dick enthusiastically. "Five tons of shell in a few weeks. Worth £80 a ton when we left Cooktown. That means £400 – why, there's many a cutter will only make that in a whole season."

Joe nodded in evident pleasure.

"We got load full up for ship now," he grinned. "You want to go back – home to Cooktown now?" he added softly.

"Not on your life," replied Dick emphatically. "But you are the skipper, Joe. What do you want us to do?"

“We make island proper station until we clean up all the shell," replied Joe, smiling, and we could see that he was pleased. "Make proper big money that way. When we get all shell, then plenty time load up, sail for Cooktown. Some stay here, mind camp. We come back, load up again."

"Of course," agreed Dick. 'We were sure you'd work it that way. We're not anxious to hurry home just because We've made a few pounds quickly. Clean up the patch first, get every shell we can. There'll be plenty of time to sail for home, then."

"Good boy," said Alor San smiling.

"Proper-feller work that way," remarked Ah Matt with a grin. "Make proper good money. Buy plenty horse, Jacky."

"You bet," I replied. "Dick and I will get a real outfit out of this."

And so it was still a very happy ship. We could see that Cross-eyed Joe and the two Malays were relieved that Dick and I did not hanker to return to Cooktown. Why, had us puzzled a little. It would have been short-sighted to have done so for one thing. Then, again, we were under the orders of Cross-eyed Joe who, as skipper, was responsible for the ship and the success of the cruise. The obvious way to work was to use the island as a fishing station on which to stack the shell until we worked out the patch. Any day might see a lugger come spying upon us. Once they got wind we were on a patch they would gather round like hawks. Every day was valuable. Whereas, if we loaded up with five tons and sailed for Cooktown, it would mean some days before we unloaded and got back to work again. And – the secret would be out. I've could not possibly unload five tons of shell and sell it to the Chinamen after such a short cruise without sharp eyes, or quick wits and gossip putting two and two together. When we came to sail back to Lizard Island there would be boats following us, twenty-four hours behind, working in teams. Sooner or later they would spy our hide-out.

All hands knew this so very well that we wondered why the Filipino and Malays were so pleased that we were content to remain at sea.

"It's got something to do with a ship," mused Dick as we lay in our bunks smoking that night, ashore.

"Why on earth should it have anything to do with a ship?"
I asked, lazily.

"I don't know," replied Dick. "But it has something to do with a ship," he added determinedly, "the ship Alor San watches for from the Look-out of nights."

I flicked away the cigarette butt.

"Fiddlesticks!" I yawned. "Bullswooll" And, rolling over, fell asleep.

12

BILLY FIGHTS FOR HIS LIFE

WORK went on apace, ceaselessly, from dawn to sunset. The time soon came when we had bagged ten tons of shell, eight hundred pounds' worth, and all hands were in the seventh heaven of delight.

One evening after the camp-fire yarn I turned in, feeling dead to the world. It had been Dick's day on look-out duty, and on those days he helped pass time by baking a cartwheel damper. I only cooked on emergency now, and Dick definitely did not like my cooking. The others had been joking about it this very evening. When they stepped into the dinghy to row out to the cutter I was already asleep. Dick woke me.

"I examined Alor's hide-out today," he said. "I found, none of those tell-tale cigarette butts."

"Wha'?" I grunted, only half awake.

"Alor doesn't leave his cigarette butts lying about anymore," said Dick. "He's too cunning; he's taken a tumble."

"Wha'?" I growled. "Bullswooll" and was asleep.

But next morning Dick was insistent. He brought up the subject again.

"You've been dreaming." I yawned. "Cheese it."

"But," protested Dick, "you don't pick up real cigarette butts in dreams."

But even he ceased to puzzle about it.

In busy work, time flowed on, and the day came when we had bagged fifteen tons of shell. Dick and I felt so, wonderfully happy we hardly knew what to do with ourselves. For now beyond all doubt our share would be ample to buy us a jolly good outfit. Instead of just enough money to buy a couple of old horses, we now had earned sufficient to buy a complete team, with saddlery, and tools, and firearms, and twelve months' rations. We could start out from Cooktown thoroughly equipped and go bush in any direction we wanted, even to the wild west coast. No wonder Dick could hardly refrain from whistling the day long. As for me, all my little troubles had vanished like the mists that dissolved every dawn up above the Look-out. We were set, we could buy our team of horses. There was only one thing to keep us delightfully uncertain, and we discussed it every night by the camp-fire – what would be the price of trochus when we returned to Cooktown.

That was the burning question. For trochus shell fluctuates in price. By now it might have dropped to £60 a ton, to £50. But then, it might have risen to £90. We hardly dared think of what would be our share of this wealth if the price should rise higher than £80.

To ease the strain a bit we "bought the world" for Little Paddy, and made him as excited as ourselves. But he simply could not grasp the vast fortune that was to be his – a few pounds.

"Plenty money altogether too much!" he gasped. "Makes his eyes stick out like coco-nuts," laughed Dick.

"Why, he could buy all Cooktown with that money!"

"You like buy hotel?" chuckled Cross-eyed Joe. "Maybe you like buy Great Northern?"

But Little Paddy was speechless.

"Maybe you like buy horse," suggested Alor San, laughing. "Plenty-feller horse – you got money altogether too much now. You buy box altogether full up bacca? S'pose you buy plenty-feller does, plenty-feller dress belonga girl-friend belonga you. Maybe you like buy shop longa Chinatown. What you like buy 'im most feller?"

"Me buy 'im– " whispered Little Paddy, and paused for breath. "Me buy 'im– " he tried again, and out it came with a rush – "Me buy 'im bullick!"

"What for you buy 'im bullock?" asked Joe.

"Me eat 'im!" answered Little Paddy triumphantly.

We laughed. But Man Friday was going to be one of the happiest little men in the world. For we reckoned that his share would buy him his heart's desire. What a hero he would be when he treated his tribe to a full-grown roast bullock!

And then came near-tragedy.

It was a beautiful morning, and we were doing very well. I was staring down into the water at Billy on the sea floor with trochus clenched in his arms, turned upward to swim. I was thinking how bright his magnified eyes were, deep sunk in those shaggy sockets; his thick lips and primitive brow as distinct as if he were staring at me face to face. He was not half way to surface when the shadow came at him. Billy dropped the shells as he threw out his arms and with a Sideways twist writhed round the shark, thus avoiding being bitten in two as he kicked for the surface again – terror stamped urgently on his face.

The shark had got him-not badly, but it had got him, and now he was shooting up, with the shark coming again in a white Hash of belly as Billy writhed convulsively, and seemed to twist lengthwise round the shark's body, his thumbs frenziedly gouging for its eyes. Again the baffled thing sped away as Billy came spiralling up. Like phantoms to right and left the bronze bodies of the Malays and the deep chocolate of Big Paddy were speeding up. Dick, in his dinghy, was thrashing an oar on the water. Billy was very close to surface now with the shark speeding up under him again. And again that white flash of belly, and again that sideways writhe as Billy Hung his arms round the shark, his thumbs gouging its eyes, as Alor San and Ah Matt broke surface and leapt up into my dinghy. Again the shark sped away, and Big Paddy was beside Billy as he broke surface, his upstretched arms grabbed by Dick as he was pulled and pushed into the dinghy with Big Paddy splashing in beside him.

Billy's chocolate-black body was bathed in spreading scarlet, strips of flesh hanging from his thighs. The shark came on like a maddened thing, to be greeted by thrashing paddles and a vicious spear from Paddy.

Billy was lying in the dinghy panting, his eyes rolling up at the sky, his face ashen-grey. Alar San jumped in beside him and knelt down, rubbing practised fingers along his bloody body. Alar turned him over, lightly rubbing his hands amongst the torn flesh, then rolled him over again and grinned into his questing eyes.

"You arright!" he laughed. "Belly he arright! No bones he break! Big feller fright you catch 'im – tha's all!"

Billy's frightened eyes slowly sank back in their sockets.

He sighed deeply, his face relaxed, the Sickly greenish-yellow colour slowly drained away to the rich black again.

He grinned, showing wonderful teeth.

Big Paddy stood up and roared his triumphant relief.

"That plurry shark got him big-feller pain longa bingey," he assured his tribesman with expressive action. "Spear belonga me catch 'im proper-feller longa belly." And Billy derived obvious consolation from this revenge.

Fishing was finished for we could not tell how long now.

Speedily we towed back to the Nancy Bell and lifted Billy aboard. Cross-eyed Joe spread a blanket on the deck and we held Billy above it while Joe' straightened out the strips of flesh hanging from his back. Joe kept his hands to the strips while we carefully lowered Billy on to the blanket. Calmly Joe examined him. To Dick and me he seemed a terrible, bloody mess.

"He arright," declared Joe, and looked up with a smile.

"Little bit of meat chewed off, tha's all. We soon fix him."

We breathed in relief. Billy grunted with deep satisfaction; he was perfectly satisfied now. Joe gave him a smoke, and Billy puffed away in content. "Up anchor," ordered Joe quietly. "We steam for island – soon fix him."

Dick and I jumped for the winch while Alor slipped below to the engine. The sea was deathly quiet, not even a ripple. It had grown cool, too, and as we chugged back to the island we noticed a little black cloud coming up, away over the great reef.

"Feels like a bit of a blow," nodded Dick. "Yes. I wonder what we'll do now."

"Most likely load up with shell and run for Cooktown and hospital with Billy," replied Dick. "Stiff luck, though, if it comes on to blow just now."

Joe was busy below, he called me down, and there he was by his bunk laying out bandages, and bottles, and jars and things. They appeared to be of the simplest, though there was no telling what ointments the jars contained. The engine was chugging urgently.

"We bring Billy ashore soon, you make bunk for him, Jacky. Tell Little Paddy put plenty water on to boil." I nodded, watching Joe at his preparations. He was tearing a sheet into broad bandages. Carefully then, with a thoughtful squint at the point, he chose a needle, a large sewing needle. He tested the point with his finger. Then he chose a reel of strong thread, a small razor, a jar of black ointment, a jar of thick yellow ointment, a bottle of some sort of oil, a bottle of iodine, another of Condy's crystals, and several jars of unfamiliar Eastern medicines-one was a powder. Smoking a cigarette, Joe's lithe brown fingers sorted out these things he wanted, his squint-eye lending his scarred face a grim concentration.

Now he bent over his job, and I saw only one side of his face, and it flashed upon me that here again was that "other" Cross-eyed Joe, not, the scarred, squint-eyed half. This half-face was the face of an entirely different man, the man that but few people ever saw. As he reached for something he "vanished" – he was Cross-eyed Joe again.

The effect was so striking, it was so strange again to see two different men in one that the impression only slowly wore off. Even then it faintly lingered.

I pulled myself together.

Carefully he was packing his things into a clean little box, absorbed in the job. I wondered if that was how doctors in hospitals looked while sorting out their instruments before operating on a patient. I felt jolly glad Cross-eyed Joe was not going to operate on me, and then I thought that in a case of emergency a crippled man might do far worse than trust himself to this cool, confident Filipino, to the Filipino with that "other" face.

The engine chugged itself softly into silence; the hook splashed down, the chain rattled out. Joe was ready.

"Plenty hot water, Jacky," he instructed. "Boil all buckets."

I climbed up on deck, jumped into the dinghy and swiftly pulled ashore to light the fire. Little Paddy came running down from the Look-out as Big Paddy came in the other dinghy with Billy's few possessions – his beloved pipe, his knife, his blanket, and his fish-spears – and three dishes from aboard ship. Quickly he arranged a comfortable bunk, then Dick hurried to the dinghy.

"Tell Joe the buckets will soon be on the boil," I called.

"Right-oh," answered Dick. "Put on the billy, too. Billy will feel like a pannikin of tea."

So he would. But for a wonder I'd thought of that. They carried him ashore in his blanket and laid him down beside the bunk. Joe proceeded to spread out his needle and thread, and razor and jars; all in order.

"Just little hot water, Jacky," he said, nodding at the prospecting dish.

Quickly I brought it. Joe tipped in a few Condy's crystals. "Fingernails – you clean them," he smiled.

I stared. He handed me a pocket knife, nodding at my fingers. Sheepishly I cleaned the nails.

"Good," he nodded. "Now wash hands and arms. Plenty soap, then plenty hot water. You doctor too," he added. "You help me."

Thoroughly I washed hands and arms in the hot Condy water, Billy and the others looking on wonderingly. When Joe was satisfied, he nodded.

"Good. Clean them all dish, plenty hot water, scour with sand first time. Then wash with Condy."

And he proceeded to clean his own fingernails, thoroughly washing hands and arms in hot Condy's. Then in a tiny dish he put boiling water and Condy's, dropping into it the needle, razor, a bright little scissors, and thread. Dick gave Billy a hot pannikin of strong tea, with plenty of sugar. Billy drank it in thankful gulps, and his eyes asked for more. Since we had hauled him aboard the dinghy he had riot murmured, had never once whinged. He drank three pannikins of hot tea, then lay back with a satisfied grunt. Alor San lit him a cigarette.

With a dish of hot Condy's beside him, Joe now swiftly got to work on Billy, washing him with a sponge. From chest to toes he was blood, while ribbons of flesh hung from his thighs. He began to look much more human as the filth was washed away, and the rich chocolate-skin began to show out. But the crimson-pink of the raw flesh, and some white-looking threads like chewed sinews or something made me feel a bit sick.

13

THE BLACK LUGGER

IT was not until all Billy's front, from his chest to his toes, was thoroughly washed that Dick and I began to realize the reason for the skipper's surprising cleanliness. For, with clean Condy water he now began carefully to bathe the raw gashes and strips of flesh. As he squeezed open the gashes to swab them out we saw that all manner of dirt was adhering to them, even shreds of sea-weed. There was slimy stuff, too, and dirt, and fish-scales that had seeped into the wounds, or stuck to the raw flesh when Billy was lying in the dinghy, and there was fluff from the blanket. With absorbed brow and steady hand Joe straightened out each ribbon of flesh and washed it.

Every now and then Dick held a pannikin of nearly scalding tea to Billy's lips. Ugh! He needed it.

We watched everything in silence. Occasionally, I became aware of birds singing outside.

When Joe had thoroughly cleaned everything he washed his hands in fresh Condy water, then deftly held open a long, deep gash and poured a little strange oil into it. From the end of this gash a strip of flesh was hanging. He dipped a finger-tip in the yellow ointment, and lightly touched all along the under part of this strip of flesh. Then he dipped another finger in the black jar, and filmed this ointment on each side of the strip. Stretching open the wound from the base, he held the strip taut, and slowly worked it right back into the gash, all the way up to the very end, opening out the gash and working it with two fingertips, while the other hand drew up the strip and worked it into place. When he had finished, I just stared.

It seemed that along this awful gash Billy had been made whole again.

But Joe had not finished. Washing his hands in steaming Condy's, he oiled his finger-tips, and, as a man might touch the wings of a butterfly he began unwinding the crinkled flakes of skin and working them back over the scar. It was wonderful.

Joe did that to every gash made by those terrible teeth.

Then he folded a clean sheet in a certain way and laid it down over Billy's front, pressing gently. Then we rolled him over on his side, and Joe got to work on his back. When it was washed we carefully lifted him on to his bunk. Joe pulled at the sheet, and it spread out on the bunk. We lay Billy on his back then, and he was lying on a clean sheet.

It was a fascinating lesson in rough surgery, destined to stand Dick and me in good stead during future wanderings.

Joe then cleansed the back as he had the front. Here, it was Billy's buttocks that had suffered the most, and we attempted one or two rough jokes. Billy tried to laugh the loudest, but I guess he felt too sick. We became silent again.

The edge, here and there, on some of the flesh was chewed a deep purple, several other places were lumpy looking. Joe sliced these off cleanly with the razor blade. Billy shivered a bit. In places, Joe used the scissors on little knotted pellets of skin, and snipped jagged edges of flesh off here and there.

When Joe had finished he washed his hands, with the expression of a man satisfied with a good job.

"More better he eat now I think," he said. "Make him strong feller. We soon finish him then."

We gave Billy what he could eat and drink, and had a feed ourselves, yarning as usual beside him just to make it feel a bit matey like. But Cross-eyed Joe, I could see, was very pleased when Dick enthusiastically congratulated him on a wonderful job, and asked questions that proved what a keen interest he had taken in the operation.

Joe began washing his hands again, while glancing knowingly at Dick. "Billy boiled, Dicky?" he inquired. "Maybe Billy like 'nother cup of tea by-ern-by."

Dick grabbed the billy and hurried to the fire as Joe took out the reel of thread, then the needle. I wondered what was coming now.

Joe carefully threaded the needle, then, leaning over Billy, began to sew up the edges of the deeper gashes – just stitches here and there.

I had never dreamt how tough is the skin of the human being, what force is necessary to push a needle through that skin, then through the flesh, and draw out needle and thread through the outer edge. Billy had not made a murmur so far; but now he grunted once or twice as Joe drew through the thread, and tightened and knotted it.

Billy *did* need that tea.

When Joe finished, he covered the back with oil and ointment, placed broad bandages under Billy, then rolled him on his back and set to work again. And Billy's screwed-up face showed that it was more painful now. But he did not murmur.

"We finish now," said Joe at last. "You arright now Billy. Soon now you bin diving longa trochus again."

"Wah!" grinned Billy. But it was a sickly grin.

Joe covered the wounds with oil and ointment, then bandaged him fairly tightly. It looked a wonderful job. We sighed our relief when it was all over, gave Billy another pannikin of tea, and set about getting a meal for all hands.

We stepped out of camp into a strong wind. The sea was alive with white horses and the sky with swiftly moving clouds. We had not even heard the wind rise.

"It's coming on to blow," exclaimed Dick wonderingly.

"And we didn't even know it."

Joe squinted at sea and sky, nodded, then walked to the dinghy, followed by Alor San and Ah Matt. Big Paddy grunted encouragement to Billy, then followed after them. They would make all snug aboard in preparation for the coming blow.

'Well," said Dick. "If ever I meet with an accident out in the bush, I hope there's someone like Cross-eyed Joe handy to doctor me up."

"Same here. What a surprise the skipper is! When you come to think of it, he must have doctored up lots of men in his time."

"No doubt. He's seen many an accident – and many a brawl at sea."

"It doesn't look as if they're going to hurry Billy to hospital."

"No, it's not so serious now; there's no bones broken, and the shark didn't bite into his insides. Besides, the tossing about wouldn't do him any good anyway, judging by the blow that's coming. I suppose we'll take him in when the blow is over."

"Looks like the end of our fishing – for some time, anyway."

"Yes," sighed Dick. "Just when we were making a fortune. We've done wonderfully well though, like a dream come true. Anyway, this blow might have stopped us by the look of those inky clouds it's going to be nasty. It might disturb the trochus, too; they might move into deep water."

"By jove, yes," I answered. "Billy couldn't have been bitten at a better time."

"He timed it to a T," grinned Dick. "It would have been stiff luck if the shark had grabbed him two or three weeks ago."

That would have made a big difference to our fishing. We would have lost a lot of shell. All hands work from dawn to dark when on trochus, for sometimes they are "here today, gone tomorrow". They probably *would* go now, for, should this blow develop continuously and strongly, then the shallows would be stirred up; it would be rough down below, sand and sediment swirling about making it too unpleasant for the fish within the shell to enjoy a decent meal. If the blow was prolonged, the trochus might migrate to the calm of deeper water.

Just like humans, animals, birds, and even fish are affected by violent changes in the weather. To lesser degree, so are trees and plant life. It is rather strange to ponder on. We believe that man "runs" this world, but a cyclone; a drought; an earthquake, or a Hood can affect millions of us, upset our plans, even kill us.

As storm birds went shrieking by we spoke about it.

"Aw," protested Dick, "there's always been storms and bushfires and icebergs and things. Mankind's got ,along pretty well through all of them for thousands of years."

"No, he hasn't! He blows out his chest on a sunshiny day, then runs like a rabbit to his burrow when it rains."

"He'd be a silly goat to stay out in the wet," replied Dick.

"How about if it kept on raining and raining, and didn't stop?"

"But it does stop," protested Dick.

"Of course!" I said triumphantly. "If it didn't stop we'd all die."

"Bullswooll" snorted Dick. "It's too we'll regulated for that!" .

"What if something went wrong with the regulator!" I demanded.

"Nuts!" snapped Dick. "And you've got 'em today. What you think has gone wrong with Jacky, Man Friday?" he asked. "Maybe regulator longa him gone bung, eh?"

"No savvy that feller talk longa alligator," answered Little Paddy solemnly. "Maybe Jacky hungry-feller-boil 'im billy more better."

"Why it's not an hour since you ate a feed big enough for two grown men! You hungry-gutted little savage!"

Man Friday patted a well-rounded stomach. "Bingey belonga me no savvy that one 'gator talk," he grinned.

"You brainless little eating-machine," laughed Dick. "We weren't talking about alligators."

"There's no doubt about his regulator anyway," I said.

"It's always ready for action. Come to think about it, I suppose it's the first regulator man ever had, and still is."

"Cut it out!" said Dick, and sprang up. "For heaven's sake come and let's put the billy on. Perhaps it may quieten your regulators for the time being anyway."

Night came with a bowling sou-easter, while the surf on the reef developed into a pounding roar. The wind-swept shriek of some storm bird wailed dismally over. the camp. Dawn came with sunless, leaden skies.

Billy was ever so much better. His eyes rolled contentedly and he grinned up at us from a mighty mouth.

"You're all right," laughed Dick. "You look as if you could eat a horse. We'll put the billy on."

We stepped outside the bush-shed into a howling wind.

Sea and shoreline were a fury of spray and hissing foam. The wind whipped our voices away, and bent the scanty trees almost to the earth. We were pleased to be ashore, and glad of a safe anchorage for the *Nancy Bell.* Dick shouted, but I failed to catch the words. He pointed. In astonishment I gazed at a rakish black lugger, at anchor barely a hundred yards from the *Nancy Bell.* She must have come in with the storm in the night.

"Japs!" shouted Dick. "They've found our hide-out."

In a flash I thought how our luck still held. Had these Japs come sooner their presence would have forced us to abandon our fishing until they sailed away.

"They think they're jolly smart," shouted Dick. "But they've come a thud."

"If they come ashore they must see the stack of shell," I shouted back.

"Let them. They don't know where the fishing grounds are; the trochus bed may be a hundred miles away for all they know. Joe will take the trochus to Cooktown now, and that will mean three trips. If they hang around that long then we'll sail somewhere else, and lead them a wild-goose chase."

Soon after breakfast Joe and Alor San came ashore. Dick nodded towards the black lugger. Joe grinned sourly, Alor shrugged.

"They find us out, Dicky," said Joe in his quiet voice.

For a moment I imagined some question in his smiling eye.

"Yes," replied Dick. "But they found us too late – bad luck to them!"

"Dicky no like Jap man?'" grinned Alor San. "Jacky no like him, too?"

"We do not!" declared Dick emphatically.

Cross-eyed Joe smiled relievedly. "No matter," he murmured. "They watch us all a time now but they no find where we fish." And he stepped inside to look at Billy. But Billy was so well that Joe didn't even take the bandages off him to dress the wounds.

"No need," explained Joe. "Poison all killed – wounds clean – Billy soon arright." And Billy grinned cheerfully.

Within a week Billy was hobbling about camp, though only just. Many a white man, suffering those wounds, would have died from shock and loss of blood. But Nature gives her child of the forest as great recuperative powers as she does animals.

A week went by in howling winds and thunder on the reefs. The Japs did not land. We saw there were eight of them in the lugger, a smart, seaworthy vessel, three times larger than the *Nancy Bell.*

On the seventh day the wind dropped, and the island seemed now to shake from the waves thundering upon her ramparts.

"The blow is over," said Dick. "The seas will soon go down. We'll have to make a move then – or they will. I wonder what Joe will do."

14

TWO WATCHERS ON THE HILL

AT midnight Dick woke me. He winked meaningly, nodding seaward. Billy was snoring like a wild boar, Little Paddy lay coiled up in his blanket, dead to the world.

I rolled out of the blankets, slipped on pants and boots, and stepped outside. The night was pitch dark, the wind had dropped considerably; the thunder on the reef was dying down to a sullen, rumbling growl.

Only hazily could I make out the outline of the *Nancy Bell*. It was impossible to distinguish the black lugger on a night like this.

"What's doing?" I asked, yawning.

"Nothing," answered Dick hesitantly. "Couldn't sleep. I've got a hunch, that's all."

"What about?"

"Do you feel like a walk up to the Look-out?"

"What I This time of night! Black as the hobs of Hades –"

"We might see something."

"See what?"

Dick shuffled uncomfortably. "It's just an idea of mine," he mumbled.

"Surely you don't think Alor San still watches up there by night?"

"Why not? If he watched for one night, he'd watch another, until he saw what he wanted to see."

"He'd need the eyes of an owl to see on a night like this," I answered grumpily, "unless he can see ghosts. Why don't you leave him alone to see what he wants to see, anyway? What on earth you're chewing over in your think-box I'm blessed if I know. Come on, then." And we strode away to climb the Hill on the inland side. Thus we were climbing up "behind" the Hill. Any watcher up there would be sitting with his back to us, facing the sea. Not that I believed anyone was up there, but Dick was my mate and we always stuck together;

We climbed by feel of foot and hand, more than by sight, stepping warily when near the crown of the Hill. We peeped over into space, stretching out above the darkness. of the sea. Dick crawled over a break in the summit so as to avoid the skyline, though I hardly think there could have been a skyline in that all-enveloping blackness of sky and sea and land. I followed Dick, crawling along just below the top of the Hill.

I guessed he wanted to peep across at the little hollow just below the crest. It would be black as the pit in there. I stubbed my face against Dick's boots, swore in a disgusted whisper, then crawled up beside him. We were peering across and down, into blackness.

Suddenly, a star blazed in that pit, quivering into a glowing flame, held a moment, then slowly dimmed.

For a moment I stared amazed; only at Dick's triumphant. pinch did I realize that the star was a cigarette, glowing within cupped hands. Someone was down there smoking, watching.

For the first time I grew a bit excited, staring across through the blackness towards this invisible watcher. He did not know we were there, but we knew he was there, and we knew him. For again the cigarette end glowed, brightly illuminating the calm face of Alor San.

What on earth was he doing there? Why did he watch in secret here, night after night?

And then I hissed, and nudged Dick. Two hundred yards further down the ridge another cigarette glowed redly.
There were two men watching!

What on earth could it mean? Neither man knew the other was there. But we did, for we could see right along the sloping ridge, down over that blackness that turned the occasional glow of a cigarette into a star.

We lay there for two hours, whispering and wondering until I grew tired of it. At last Dick hissed, "I told you so!"

I opened sleepy eyes and there, far to the south-west, was a fairy glow, gliding through darkness – a ship, brilliantly lighted, travelling fast and steaming north. Soon she was opposite us though nearer the mainland, and miles away. But, from that height her lights were a fairy vision gliding through velvet blackness.

"The *Taiping*," whispered Dick excitedly. "I felt sure Alor San was waiting to see her or the *Changte* pass by. Only now there are two of them waiting. How I'd love to get a glimpse of the other's face, but he's too far away, and the angle isn't right."

"I wonder if he's Cross-eyed Joe," I whispered.

"Of course not. Alor is watching for Joe."

"What is he watching for?"

"The *Taiping*, of course."

"What for?"

"What do you think?" muttered Dick disgustedly. "I don't even know myself."

"Then what is the other man watching for?"

"The same thing, of course. You are jolly dense tonight."

"Who is he, then?"

"How the devil should I know?" whispered Dick crossly.

"He's one of the Japs from the black lugger, of course."

"Well then, why is he watching here?" I persisted.

"Ask my grandmother," muttered Dick.

We were silent then, watching that brilliant little comet glowing dimmer as it glided away into the north. And then we both thought –

"Did you hear it?" whispered Dick.

"Thought I heard an oar in a rowlock, away down below," I answered. "But wasn't sure."

"It was," whispered Dick. "I heard it, too. Come on, it's all over now for the time being, we'll go back to camp and put the billy on. They've gone aboard to report."

"How do you know?" I whispered.

Dick stood up. I could feel his disgust.

"Of all the stupid goats you've been tonight all over now for the time being, we'll go back to camp and put the billy on. They've gone aboard to report."

"How do you know?" I whispered. Dick stood up. I could feel his disgust.

"Of all the stupid goats you've been tonight – !" he growled aloud. "Come on."

Humbly I followed him, and fell head over heels when half-way down the Hill. What I said was nobody's business; all the Cross-eyed Joes, and Alor Sans, and Japs in the world could have heard for all I cared.

Billy, the convalescent, was harshly snoring, and Little Paddy wrapped in sound sleep when Dick brought the tea into the bush-shed. At the rattle of the pannikins, though, their faces popped out from blankets, eyes then mouths wide with anticipatory grins.

"Must have smelt it," said Dick sarcastically. "They wouldn't wake up so easily if a job was to be done."

We yarned until daylight, trying to put two and two together. Dick had something at the back of his mind but he wouldn't let on, and did not seem to be too sure of himself. Grumpily I gave it up, rolled a cigarette, and stretched out by the galley fire. Little Paddy brought his blanket and coiled up beside Dick, like a puppy at the feet of his master.

"Anyway, I know something you don't know," I puffed. 'What is it?"

"Both those men know the other was watching away up on the hill. They didn't know – but they know now."

"You're telling me," said Dick in a resigned voice.

"How did you know, then?" I demanded.

"Because they each must have heard the rowlocks of the other."

I threw the butt away in disgust, and snatched forty winks.

Dawn came in a blaze of fire and orange and gold up over the Great Reef. And we knew that good weather had come again. Dick stepped outside, then yelled.

I jumped up, staring towards the anchorage. Both the *Nancy Bell* and the black lugger had gone.

"Come onl" yelled Dick, and began to run towards the Hill. Quickly we climbed up to the Look-out, and stared north.

There they were, in plain view, bearing nor'-west as if for Howick Island, the *Nancy Bell* about ten miles ahead of the black lugger.

"She's dogging the *Nancy Bell,*" pointed Dick.

"This is strange, Dick," I protested. "Why did Cross-eyed Joe sail away without letting us know? And why did he sail north? Why didn't he load up with shell and take Billy aboard and sail south to Cooktown?"

"Because Billy is quite all right I suppose," answered Dick. "Joe has slipped away to the north to lead the Japs on a wild-goose chase, away from our trochus find, just as we'd planned to do."

"We know what he's doing, of course," I said. "But I'm blessed if I know why he didn't take the shell to Cooktown first, then lead them away on a chase. Anyway he won't shake them off today, for a Jap at the masthead with glasses could see the *Nancy Bell.*"

"That's so. And you can bet that old Cross-eye knows it. He probably won't try to shake them off tonight, either. He might anchor off the Howicks, then sail on in the morning and lead them a chase farther north. The farther he gets them away from here the better. He'll probably do a bit of fishing as if he's prospecting for shell and try to put them off the scent. Then he'll dodge them, some night, and double back."

"What if they double back, too?"

"They won't for a couple of days afterwards, at least; they'll scout all over the place, trying to pick up the *Nancy Bell* again. She'll dodge back here and that will give us plenty of time to load up. with shell. And the *Nancy Bell* can sail south for town while the black lugger is scouting the sea, looking for her."

"But the Nancy Bell must return here from Cooktown – she must make three trips to land the fifteen tons of shell."

"Yes. But she won't return after the third trip – if they're still here. They can hang around here for a week if they like, a fortnight," said Dick, laughing, "and still they won't see her. For she'll stay out of sight of a ship until we signal Joe the 'all clear' from the Look-out."

"I'd forgotten that. A great idea, this Look-out. Joe can be out of sight of any ship, yet we can 'talk' to him and he 'talk' us."

"You're learning," remarked Dick quietly.

"Thanks, that's nice to know. Oh well, the black lugger can chase the *Nancy Bell* all over the seas till she grows tired of it," I said lazily. "We'll diddle them all right. A cunning old bird is this Cross-eyed Joe."

"Yes," replied Dick soberly, "a cunning old bird."

The black lugger had gone...

15

THE FOOTPRINT!

WE were not worried by the turn of events; it was all in the game. The next three days went pleasantly by, 'made better still by the wide grin of Billy, hobbling about camp with the aid of a stick. Longingly, though, he watched Little Paddy manfully wading the shallows, fish-spear in hand. On such lovely days as these Billy longed to be doing the same.

"You'll soon be all right now, Billy," Dick said sympathetically. "Quick-feller time now you spear "im plenty fish."

"Ou ail" answered Billy, grinning. "Quick-feller time now legs belonga me grow strong feller."

Cooking was a regular job, now that the three of us were alone. I dodged it as long as I could.

"How about baking a damper, Jack?" suggested Dick in desperation. "I've a job on hand, strengthening the bough-shed since that blow."

So I built up the fire and the coals, mixed the wretched flour into dough, thumped it a bit here and there, and baked the damper. It was burnt a bit and seemed a trifle solid, which wasn't surprising. When tucker time came, I noticed that both Billy and Little Paddy had their eyes on my masterpiece, and lost no time in getting it inside them.

"Plurry proper good-feller damper Jacky," growled Billy enthusiastically. "Plurry damper stick longa guts belong mel" And he thrust his huge mouth into a hunk of soddy damper.

It was the first time a damper of mine had ever been praised, and I got a surprised thrill out of it.

"Good-feller damper too true!" crowed Little Paddy, chewing. "Strong-feller longa guts!"

Obviously both abos were enjoying my damper immensely. It gave them something to chew on. It would give them something to digest, too.

"Bah!" spat Dick in disgust. "It sticks to a man's ribs like glue – makes his belly feel as if he's swallowed a hunk of lead." And he threw his hunk away. Little Paddy grabbed it.

Dick took over the cooking after that, which suited me down to the ground.

In the mornings I'd climb up to the Look-out to watch for sign of the *Nancy Bell*, though we didn't expect to see her for a few days more at least, perhaps a week. Dick would busy himself with the few camp jobs, especially the cooking.

In the afternoons Dick went line-fishing, and I'd join him after the sunset meal. It was the big fellows, too large to spear, that we sought. And there were plenty of them, especially in the deep holes by night – lovely nights, with a myriad stars low down, just the whisper of a breeze, a murmur of surf, and the lapping of the tide. Every now and again the dark velvet water was whipped into a blaze of phosphorus where some great fish chased its prey.

The most exciting sport is to be had in hooking, fighting and then landing those big, savage fellows that rip and tear and fight to a finish. I've seen Dick struggle an hour at a time to land a fighting hundred-pounder, and he was all out at the finish.

We had plenty of bait-fish, and slices of fair-sized fish that would have been cheerfully bought for the table in any town.

Dick was the enthusiast. From the moment he threw out a line his eyes and hand never left it. I would throw mine out, hitch the end to a rock or stump, then loll back and smoke and wait for something to happen.

We seldom had long to wait. Generally it was Dick's line that slowly tautened or hissed out, according to the kind of fish biting. In the hole below the rocks on which we usually fished we had lost some big fellows since camping on the island. The strongest line would hiss out to its limit, then snap; or else it would be taken slowly and inexorably under, despite our desperate clinging to it. In this latter case we knew an old giant groper would be slowly swimming to his den in some subterranean cavern, and once there, he could never be shifted.

Dick used to get wild every time he lost a good line; he took it as a slight on his fishing prowess.

"Fancy a big, overgrown swab of a fish beating a man," he would snap, scowling at the broken line.

"You'll land him next time."

"Fat lot you care!"

He was right. I didn't care much. Anyway, life was nice and cosy, sprawling here by the water. Dick was enjoying great sport and we had plenty of lines, and plenty of wire, without which the snapping teeth of these beauties would shear through the thickest line in one vicious tug.

After midnight we'd call it a day and tramp back to camp for some shut-eye, Dick swearing he'd be back next night to hook the so-and-so that had taken his line – to the delight of Man Friday, who scorned to fish with a line!

"You fish," said Dick witheringly. 'Why, you don't know what fishing is! First of all you've got to see your fish. Then you throw a spear in the water, and the fish hasn't got a chance."

"Me catch 'im that one pish," answered Little Paddy boastfully. "He no run away longa line belonga me!"

"Here, young-feller-me-lad," snorted Dick, "are you throwing off at me?"

"No more," grinned Little Paddy. "Me no more laugh longa you! Pish he laugh, tha's all!" And he dodged Dick's foot.

On one particular night Dick was keenly vengeful, for he had lost two favourite lines the night before. Cunningly now he selected his line, and strengthened it with several more strands of wire. Baiting the hook tastefully he threw out the line, then settled down to catch his revenge. He caught something neither he, nor Little Paddy; nor I expected.

We landed some small fry for a start, some four or five pounders, then a couple of twenty-pounders. They weren't what we sought, but they promised bigger things. At length there came a queer bite on Dick's line. The line would quietly go out, then flop slowly back. Then again. Then a bit of a tug. Then it went out to a steady, though not strong pull, as if something was testing what was on the other end of it. Then it flopped again.

"What is it?" I murmured.

"Blessed if I know," whispered Dick, with eye and finger on the line. "It feels exactly as if something had taken a soft hold on the line and was gradually crawling about and down into some hole or other. I've never felt a bite like this before."

Then his eye gleamed, his arm stretched taut. But he was disappointed.

"Thought he was going to take it that time," he whispered. "'I wonder what it is."

And then the line was sharply tugged, and Dick tugged back and began pulling swiftly in. I saw by the line something was hooked.

"What is it?"

"I can't tell," answered Dick with puzzled face. "Feels like a wriggly bag of meat – heavy meat. I hardly believe it's a fish at all!"

The three of us were staring down inta the water as Dick hauled in the line, now making heavy work of it. Suddenly there was a howl from Little Paddy as a snake-thing, followed by another, lashed up and viciously smacked the water. Then came an upward surge of phosphorus as the writhing tentacles of a hideous shape broke water.

"Debil-debill" shrieked Little Paddy, and vanished.

"Octopus!" shouted Dick. "And a big one. Look out!"

We jumped back as the tentacles flailed out in all directions. Then the two longest gripped the rocks, and the thing surged towards us.

Dick held to the line. It was hooked all right; how, I don't know. Its loathsome black bag of a body was squeezed to the rocks at the waterline, twelve feet below us. As we peered over we saw a sort of beak gnashing about down there.

"Look at its eyes!" shouted Dick.

No need. Those enormous, liquid green eyes held us – glaring, awful things. Its floppy mass was slimy with living phosphorus in shimmering colours emphasizing the hideousness of the thing as its dripping tentacles writhed out and up, reaching for us. Dick tugged hard, and the thing whipped a tentacle round the line, then another, and fastened to a crack in the rocks.

"It's clinging to the line," cried Dick. "And gripping the rocks, too! I can't shift it."

It whipped another feeler round the line and began fiercely tugging and sawing, as if it were a reasoning thing, its eyes fairly swimming in liquid green. I suppose that hook in its soft body, and the pull of the line, urged it to do the one thing possible. Its other tentacles now spread out, fan-shaped, clinging to the rocks. Dick and I both tugged, but the line now felt as if it were tied to a tree-stump. Suddenly the line broke, and the tentacles whipped around the thing as it sank back in a whirl of phosphorus.

"Gone!" cried Dick. "Now who'd have thought of *that*?" and he stared at me.

"He sawed the line through," I said. "An octopus, a big fellow like that, was the last thing we expected! If any big fish ever gets on my line I'm not going to follow him into this hole, anyway."

"Me too!" whispered a shivery little voice behind us.

"So you've sneaked back, have you?" growled Dick. "A big, brave he-man warrior you are, I don't think. Anyway, I'll be a bit more careful myself," he added soberly. "No slipping into this hole. I thought sharks were the worst. But just fancy a thing like that snatching you and dragging you away down below."

"Of course you would think of something pleasant," I replied. "Come on, wind up the lines, I've had enough for tonight."

"Maybe more better put 'im billy on," eagerly suggested Little Paddy.

"You bet your life, Man Friday," agreed Dick. "We'll have a feed, too, while we're at it; that water looks too dark, and close, and clammy for me tonight." And for a wonder Dick seemed quite willing to knock off early.

At noon, next day, I strolled to the spring for water. The spring was away behind the camp, on the Hat towards the old ruined hut. Our feet had worn the first tracing of a pad between it and our camp by now. As I approached near the edge of the grassy plain quail Hew up with a startling whirr. Curious to test my eyes I veered off the pad, and strode out through the grass with the idle thought of finding a quail's nest. It was extraordinarily difficult. Again and again they beat me, though flying from right at my very feet. When about to cross one of the little gullies running from the Hill I glanced down, and almost tripped with surprise.

In the sand was a footprint!

It was one of those sandy little gullies we had prospected for tin, and there was a prospecting hole near by. Plain in the sand was the footprint of a strange man – a Jap!

Not the slightest doubt – a jap. There were the two imprints, like two big claws, with, further back, the imprint of the heel – a Japanese pearler, a *beche-de-mer* man. or a trochus sheller; it was all the same.

The Jap seamen wore these peculiar, though very comfortable shoes. Canvas, generally; they had one compartment for the big toe, another for the four other toes, with a cleft between the big toe and the four.

No one aboard the *Nancy Bell* owned such a shoe.

I knelt down, staring at the track. Even I could see it was fresh.

There was a Japanese with us on the island.

16

THE SPY

FORGE'ITING all about the water I hurried back to camp. Dick was baking a damper, while Billy cheerfully watched fish frying in the pan.

"There's a Jap on the island," I said excitedly.

Dick looked up with a puzzled squint, wiping the flour from his hands. 'What?"

"A Jap! A Jap is on the island with us!"

"A Jap?"

"Yes, a Jap."

'What are you gassing about?"

"Dash it all! Don't you savvy? There's a Jap here on the island with us! We're not alone! I've seen his tracks!"

Dick stood up, a startled look in his eyes. Billy frowned in a maze of wrinkles.

"Come on!" I said. They followed at my heels.

Dick stared down in consternation at the track.

"Phew!" he whistled. 'What does this mean? Billy, you look about quick-feller now."

Billy hobbled down into the gully and bent over the track, then stood erect, and stared fore and aft.

"Him bin come this way." He pointed at the grass-edged bank on which we were standing, and there was the faint impression where the grass had been pressed into the edge of the bank when the man had stepped down into the gully.

"He's been spying on us from behind the camp!" exclaimed Dick.

"Him bin go that way," and Billy pointed out over the flat. "Here, too," he grunted, pointing towards a few wisps of grass still bent over the bank edge. Then he lifted the grass and showed us where the shoe had pressed slightly into the soil where the wearer had stepped up on to the low bank.

"What time him bin walkabout?" demanded Dick.

"Longa breakfast time," replied Billy instantly.

"This very morning, a few hours ago," declared Dick.

"He was watching us before and while we were eating breakfast."

"Who on earth can he be? How did he get here? And what is his big idea?" I wondered.

"To spy on us for his mates aboard the black lugger, the 'clever devils. They guessed the *Nancy Bell* would run for it and try to fox them. So they left their man back here, landed him in the night. They'll dog the *Nancy Bell* all right, but if she gives them the slip they'll sail leisurely back and anchor behind one of those little islets during the night. They'll keep a look-out from there with the glasses. Their man back here will know when the *Nancy Bell* returns. He'll see her sail out to the fishing-grounds. Then, he will signal them from our own Look-out, and the game will be up."

"H'm, They've planned it well."

"Perfectly. Those aboard the black lugger don't yet know we've got fifteen tons of shell, and that Joe will sail for Cooktown with the first five tons when he returns. But their look-out man knows, because he has been listening to us talking. And he will watch everything that we do. When Joe returns from Cooktown after the last load he'll take the Nancy Bell to our fishing-grounds again. And this Jap will signal the black lugger."

"Hard luck! Just when we were making a little fortune. If the trochus is still there they'll quickly make a hole in it with eight men. And if they send for other luggers, they'll clean up the patch before our eyes."

"No they won't," said Dick angrily. "Not if we can help it. I'm not going to stand for a spy living on the very island with us. Billy, you look longa beach, pick 'im up track. No more walkabout big feller, only little way."

Billy grunted, then turned and hobbled back towards the beach.

"I wish Big Paddy was here," frowned Dick. 'We'd soon track him then. Come on, we'll look round the waterhole. There's sure to be tracks somewhere."

But there were no tracks.

We gazed out over the little plain, beginning to realize how difficult it might be to track down our unwelcome visitor. The plain was thickly covered with grass, like a greenish-brown mat on which no tracks would be visible to our eyes. The few small hills were tufted with grass and covered with rocks and it would be very difficult to pick up tracks there.

"He'll dodge the sandy beaches," said Dick thoughtfully. "Yes. And any soft ground at all where tracks would show."

"If he had not made that one slip where you found that

track this morning," mused Dick, "he could have remained hidden on the island until Joe returned and we wouldn't have suspected a thing."

"That's so. And Joe is away out there somewhere thinking he is fooling the black lugger."

"Yes. And he'll sail right back into the trap if we don't do something about it. I hate to think of that Jap spying on us like this," Dick finished uneasily.

"He must have a hide-out somewhere."

"Yes, but I suppose he's buried his tucker. It would be tinned stuff that he could easily bury here and there. He'd have very little else with him, perhaps a blanket, and that's about all. So he really wouldn't need a permanent hide-out. All he'd have to do would be to leave no tracks, lie quiet, and keep out of our sight."

"That would be difficult. After all, it is a small island; it's mostly all bare, grassy plain. And there's not much cover along the ridge."

"There's plenty," frowned Dick, "for a sneaker who has only to dodge us two and a crippled aboriginal."

"There's Man Friday, too." .

"Yes. He's only a kid, but he'll come in handy."

"That Jap must drink, anyway. If we could find out where he gets his water from we could lie in wait."

"Yes," agreed Dick. "He could hardly get his water from here without leaving tracks. He'd be seen by day, so he must come by night. That would mean he could not help leaving a track here and there, in mud or sand. No, there must be water elsewhere on the island. Let's go back to camp and have dinner, then climb to the Look-out. We can look down pretty well all over the island from there, and we may spot a likely hiding place."

But when we climbed the Look-out we realized it would not be so Simple. It had seemed so easy. This peak overlooked practically all the island. And as it was nearly all a level plain it had seemed impossible that a man down below could hide himself from a watcher on the hill for any length of time.

Dick was gazing along the ridge, of which our Look-out was the highest point. From here it looked like a gentle slope, gradually tapering along one side of the coast in a series of smaller and smaller hills that dwindled into hillocks where they merged into a further shore.

"He could be hidden among the rocks in any of those little hills, watching us even now," said Dick.

"Yes. But what advantage is that to him, when we hold the Look-out?"

"Not a great deal," agreed Dick, "now that we know he is here – except that he can partly watch our movements, or keep an eye on what the Look-out man is doing, or signalling. Before we knew he was on the island, the whole island was his. When we came down from the Look-out, he would climb up along the ridge to this spot. From here he could look down on our camp, and all over the sea." 'Well, he's beaten now."

"Not quite," replied Dick thoughtfully, "but we've got him in a fix. We'll prevent him from using the Look-out, which is most important to him. One of us must be on watch night and day. Billy will have to hobble up here somehow; he can camp here from sunrise to sunset, it would be just the sort of job he'd like, anyway. You and I will take night watches. Man Friday must be our tracker."

"Right-oh. 1 suppose it is important to stop him signalling the Jap lugger."

"Of course it is. That's his job, that's why they landed him on the island."

"Those small hills are not much good for a look-out, or for signalling, either."

"No. This is the only hill that commands all the sea, to all points of the compass. And from this height we can see many miles further than he could from any smaller hill. We've got a clear view, particularly to the north and nor'-west; whereas this hill blocks his view in those directions."

"You're right. By Jove! If the Jap lugger were even now hiding behind that rocky little islet away out there to the north he couldn't see the islet, let alone signal to it. Nor could he see a signal from a man there."

"That's right. While we hold this Look-out we've got him beaten."

'What will Joe do when he returns?"

"I think I know what he'll do," answered Dick slowly.

"What?"

"Kidnap himl"

"By Jove! That would be acting a bit strong."

"Serve him right," replied Dick stubbornly. "He's got no right here spying on us. The seas are free to all. Why don't he and his dashed countrymen go and find their own trochus shell?"

"I feel that way, too."

"Of course: We found that shell ourselves. It's ours. It's the chance of a lifetime. And I'll tell you why 1 believe Joe will kidnap him."

"Why?"

"Because. he knows everything." "What do you mean?'"

"He knows exactly how much trochus we've got. He knows it is a rich patch, and he knows exactly where it is."

"How on earth can he know all that?" I asked incredulously.

"Because he's heard us talking about it."

I stared at Dick, not understanding what he was driving at.

"I was thinking it out when we were climbing the Hill," explained Dick. "Now we know that ever since Joe and the black lugger sailed that night, that fellow has been spying on us, from here, when we were not up on the Look-out, and round the camp at night. His job was to learn all he could, and," said Dick impressively, "you can bet your bottom dollar that he's crawled right up to our camp and listened to us talking of nights."

"Heavens!" I said. "He knows everything, then."

"Of course. He's listened to us talking about the fishing, about the trochus, about how handy it is to the island, and in sheltered water except in a blow. He has heard us talking about keeping a look-out here, and rowing backwards and forwards from the *Nancy Bell* – heard us talking about the horses we're going to buy with our share of the money. He's heard us talking about Billy and the shark, and about Alor San and his queer night-watches up on the Hill, and about the cigarette glowing that betrayed the Jap up there. He's even heard us talking about what we think Cross-eyed Joe is doing while leading the black lugger a wild goose chase. He knows all that we know."

"I see," I said slowly. "And the only way to save our trochus is for Joe to kidnap the spy – and hold him till we clean up all the patch."

"Yes. Even if he dodges us we'll soon lay him by the heels when Joe returns with Paddy and Alor San and Ah Matt. Then Joe could load up with shell and sail. He could either hold the Jap down below, or dump him on some handy island. Better still, on the mainland."

"Might be all right to dump him southward," I said doubtfully. "But if Joe dumped him on the mainland north of here, the aboriginals would spear him."

"That would be his look-out!" declared Dick. "Joe would then sail south for Cooktown."

"Yes," answered Dick, "and the Japs could follow if they liked. They'd have received no signals from their man, they'd be so puzzled by then they wouldn't know what to do."

"By that time they'd probably believe they were on a false scent. They'd sail back here to pick up their man. And what then?"

"We wouldn't know anything about it," replied Dick.

17

ON THE TRACK OF THE SPY

"WELL, what are we going to do about it, anyway?"

"Cause that Jap all the trouble we possibly can. And the first way to annoy him is to find his hide-out. Which way you think 'im that 'feller lie down, Man Friday?" asked Dick.

"Longa water!" answered Man Friday promptly.

"Ah, ha!" we laughed. "That cheeky Jap no fool him Little Paddy, eh?"

"No fool 'im me!" boasted Little Paddy. "Me catch 'im Jap man easy-feller."

"Don't be too sure young-feller-me-lad," warned Dick.

"I've seen you look silly before today. I remember a big old spotted goanna that put it all across you. But we'll try you out."

Little Paddy's eyes were fairly rolling to be away on the chase. Now was his chance to show us what he was really made of.

"He's right about the water," mused Dick. "The Jap would naturally camp somewhere near water. Which way you bin think him 'nother feller waterhole?"

"Longa that way!" And Paddy pointed away out over space, towards the southern end of the island. To our eyes it looked merely the end of the grassy plain, the merging of coastline with sea.

"There's no reason we know of why water shouldn't be away across there, as well as at our own end of the island," mused Dick. "Very well, Man Friday, you go back longa camp, tell Billy come up longa here – you come, too."

"Ou ai," nodded Paddy, and scampered away.

"He'll be a real little bloodhound," laughed Dick. "He'll give 'Slinker' a bit of hurry-up I'll bet."

"That's not a bad name for the Jap," I said, grinning.

"Let's call him that."

"Right-oh. Now listen. Billy, from here, can see out practically all over the island; it's nearly all plain. If a man stood up, or walked anywhere across that flat country, he must be seen from here?"

"That's so."

"Right. Now, the best cover is along this ridge, right from here to where it runs down to that shoreline. Even so, Billy can see right away along and down the ridge from here, though he can't see in between the little hilltops, nor those furthest mounds where the ridge runs out to the sea.

"That's right."

"Well, Slinker is almost certainly hiding along this ridge somewhere. He must be, because it's the only place from which he can see out to sea, and signal."

"That's right."

'Well, the only other cover is those low hummocks away along the south-eastern shore, except for bits of the shore-line here and there."

"That's right."

"Well, that means that Billy can see out over three parts of the island. He will keep a sharp look-out from here, while we three comb the remainder of the island, piece by piece. Little Paddy will be like a dingo on the scent, and we'll flush the Jap from cover, sooner or later. If we don't see him then Billy will, and he'll signal us."

"Right."

"We can't do much this afternoon, for by the time Billy hobbles up here, and we walk out there to where Man Friday thinks the water is, it will be fairly late. But we might find out where he gets his water from, and that will be something gained."

"Yes. And what will we do if we really corner him?"

"I'm not sure yet," answered Dick doubtfully. "The best plan appears to be to drive him right away from the ridge – and keep him away. He won't be able to do his job then."

"What if we corner him, and he just won't go?"

"He's got to go. If he won't, then – surely the two of us can manage him. And Little Paddy would hop in and fight like a wild cat."

"What if he's armed?"

"If he carries a gun," said Dick decidedly, 'be's got us beaten. But he doesn't know we've got no guns. What fools we were not to bring our rifles along!"

"Cross-eyed Joe told us we wouldn't be landing on the mainland," I pointed out, "And that there was no game at all on this island."

"True," replied 'Dick. "Neither Joe nor we knew that this was going to happen."

"We'll look fools," I said, "if we corner him, and he simply pokes a gun at us."

"We'll feel fools," replied Dick irritably. "You'd be sure to think up something like that. But we must do something. If once he signals that black lugger, and gets aboard, then its good-bye to us getting any more trochus."

"That's a certainty. And wouldn't Cross-eyed Joe and Alor San and Ah Matt be mad?"

"We too," answered Dick sourly. "But we may bluff him."

"How?"

"Well, he's spying on us, to help his mates aboard the black lugger – beat us for the trochus we've found. And we know very well, and so does his crowd, that that sort of thing is not taken lying down in the lonely seas – not if the other crowd can help it. Then again, he's got no legal right, no permit to be on this island, so he knows that so far as a distant and shadowy law is concerned he's in the wrong also."

"My word, you're right. Makes us feel a bit bossy. He'll be frightened of us."

"Yes," said Dick. "But I've got something else up my sleeve-that slipped out!" he added quickly.

"What?" I asked. 'What do you know?"

"Aw," he answered sheepishly, "forget it-it's only a silly idea of mine."

"I'm not surprised at that. What is it?"

"But I'd made a slip," Dick snorted indignantly. "Come on, Dick, out with it," I wheedled.

"Oh, I don't know," he answered hesitantly. "It's just a half-formed sort of suspicion – I've had it for some time now."

"What is it?"

"I'm just not going to tell you," he laughed, "because I don't think it's right, and if I let it out it might lead us on a wild goose chase a lot sillier than Joe is leading the black lugger."

I stared at my mate. He never kept secrets from me.

I felt intensely curious.

"Come on, Dick," I coaxed. Uneasily he picked a blade of grass and chewed it hesitantly.

"Don't ask me, Jack," he answered slowly. "It only slipped out – I didn't mean it to. I'll tell you all about it when we get back to Cooktown-then we can laugh over it."

"Well then, just suppose this wild suspicion of yours turns out to be true, would it make our position any stronger?"

"By Jove it would," he answered emphatically. "And maybe a lot worse," he added lamely.

"But it can't be 'yes' and 'no'," I protested. 'What on earth is it?"

"Here's Man Friday!" exclaimed Dick, and jumped up.

"Here's where we get busy."

And Little Paddy's beaming face poked up over the summit. Billy was only half-way up.

"He's not too good on his pins yet," remarked Dick, frowning as watched Billy slowly climbing, "but he'll only have to make the trip once a day. Once he's up here he's only got to keep watch."

As we explained Billy's job to him he glanced out over the island, grunted, and nodded,

"Me savvy. You feller soon catch 'im that cheeky-feller Jap!" And he glanced round for the best spot to overlook the island.

"And now for the trail of Slinker," laughed Dick.

Little Paddy was already hurrying down the hill to the plain. The ruined hut was behind the camp, away to the left. Our objective was along the base of the ridge on the inland side to the right towards where the end of the ridge tapered down into plain, shore, then sea.

"Man Friday is travelling like a scalded cat," grunted Dick. "If we were in the open bush we'd be hard pressed to keep up with him."

"He is travelling some," I agreed. "But we can keep him in sight. No matter in what direction you travel on this island you must soon be brought up by the sea."

"Yes. And that's a good reason why Slinker can't hide from us for long."

"We'll see. Little Paddy seems to be all out to find that water."

"Yes. And I bet he will find it."

"You've got a lot of confidence in your Man Friday." "I've spent a lot of time in training him," replied Dick proudly.

I thought of blackboy Romeo and Bill Baird. We all knew that Baird had spent a lot of time in "training" Romeo. As we walked over the grass I wondered if Kennedy had "trained" his faithful blackboy, Jackey-Jackey. I don't think so.

Within a bare half-hour, the little black figure ahead stood in the grass and waved back to us.

"He's found water right enough," Dick said, smiling. "See those little birds flying into those few trees? Hear them squawking? Man Friday's eagle eyes must have seen those birds from away up on the Hill."

"Yes," I answered. "The grass is growing greener, there's water here all right. And look, there's a small beach just over there, where the plain slopes down to the sea."

Little Paddy was triumphantly pointing near his feet.

And there, in the mud, where a seepage of water flowed through the grass roots, were tracks-tracks of a cloven shoe.

"Got him!" exclaimed Dick laughingly. 'We know now where he gets his water."

The tracks were so few they told that even here; where probably we would never have come, the stranger still was careful not to leave many noticeable signs. Little Paddy pointed to a flattened grass tuft where the man had knelt to dip water.

"Him come this way," said the youngster, pointing. "Him go back same-feller way-plurry fool!"

We looked out over the grass but could see no track.

The grass was not high, but it was tufted and very thick. We were facing towards the extreme end of the ridge, where it ran into the coast in a dwindling series of low hummocks. We gazed carefully along the ridge where it gradually grew higher into little hills and at last rose to the big Hill, away back towards the camp. Away up on the Look-out Billy was sitting, like a black crow perched on a rock.

Little Paddy stood on a grass tuft and, drawing himself to his full height, faced half-right, back towards the "crow on the hill". Stretching up his arm with fingers shut and palm towards the "crow" he held it still a moment, then slowly swept it round and back to his leg.

The "crow" stood up, squatted down again. Little Paddy held both arms above his head, hooked his thumbs together, then drew his hands down to his head.

The "crow" stretched out an arm, held it a moment, and resumed his crouching position.

"How distinctly you could see that movement from this distance!" said Dick admiringly.

"What name talk you two-feller bin talk about?" he asked.

"Me bin tell 'im find 'im water!" answered Little Paddy.

"Me bin talk longa him we find 'im track."

"Good work!" said Dick admiringly, and Little Paddy's face shone with glee. "Which way we bin go now?"

"Longa track," pointed Paddy, and began walking towards the ridge end with careful swiftness, head cocked to one side, eyes concentrated on the ground.

"More better we stop little-feller while," ordered Dick presently. "I've never seen them tracking over thick grass like this before," he said to me. "We may as well learn a bit while we're at it. You teach 'im this one me," he said to Paddy.

Paddy knelt down and spread out his hands just over the grass every here and there, his upraised eyes and expressive face fairly "talking" to Dick. Then he stood up as if surveying a line of tracks. Then he cocked his head to one side, and squinted along the line. Then Dick stood in the same place.

"Plenty-feller track," Little Paddy said earnestly. "You look-see. Grass he no look alla same, him lie down longa ground.

For quite a time Dick stared along the line, holding his head this way and that.

At last he cried, "I've got it, Jack, it's the way you hold your head, to catch the sunlight slanting across the track. It's a track all right, though we'd never see it. I don't believe Little Paddy could have, either, only Slinker has always come and gone the same way, as we all do, when he's come for water. He's never dreamt anyone would see an imprint on grass as thick as this. It's almost like the faintest shadow, just here and there, as you move your eyes. His feet: have pressed the grass down just a little each time he came and went until now the grass doesn't spring up quite to its natural level. And so the grass-tops to either side overhang it just a little. If you get your eye just at the right level you can see, now and then, a sort of fleeting imprint of a shadow, where slanting rays of sunlight strike the grass-tops to one side of the track, giving the impression of a shadow in the tiny hollow below.

"Why, yes, that's it! I can see away along now! I'll bet he's come over that little reddish mound, away in front! I'll bet his camp is behind it, away up to the right somewhere between the beginning of the little hills and the shore."

Dick was boyishly pleased, for his ambition was to become as good a bushman as the most famous of our Cape York Peninsula prospectors, while Man Friday was in the seventh heaven of delight now that he had taught his hero something.

"Good boy, Little Paddy," said Dick. "Your blood's worth pickling. Now run Slinker to earth before sundown."

And Paddy bent to the job.

18

WE FIND THE SPY'S HIDE-OUT

THE red mound ahead was smooth and hard, and here Little Paddy lost the tracks. He walked straight over,' and we followed him down the other side, on to a rubbly beach. He pointed downward, and there on a small patch of sand clear of shingle was the faint imprint of a cloven toe.

"He's stepped down on to the beach here," pointed Dick. "He probably follows it along, walking beside this bank. You see, it's the edge of the plain, where it drops on to the shore line; it's somewhat like a river bank. He could walk along the shore keeping close to this bank and no one would see him from away back on the Look-out."

"Well, its along here that he comes and goes for his water."

"Yes. And he's walked back to his hide-out. I'll bet he's stepped up among those mounds just ahead, where the end of the ridge peters out on to the shore."

He had. Little Paddy lost his tracks on the shingle and coral rock of this beach, but we kept on, walking slowly, Paddy's eyes searching the shingle. The sea was a murmur at our left. Shadows were falling. To our right the mounds now hedging the shore were gradually rising higher, clothed with coarse grass and stunted bushes. Ahead these mounds rose more steeply as they merged inland into bushy hillocks, and that in turn grew into rocky hills that farther back loomed up into the big hill overlooking our camp. Little Paddy wheeled round with finger to lips, and eyes sticking out like pickled onions. He was pointing to the bank.

Here, on the reddish edge, was a faint mark a man had stepped up from the beach and vanished amongst the bushes.

Warningly, Paddy rolled his eyes towards the bushes.

Our man was there-somewhere in among either mounds or hills.

Little Paddy crouched up on to the bank, noiselessly as a cat stalking a bird, staring down, with outstretched hands. he silently parted the bushes and stepped on. Dick followed, standing there awhile until Paddy found another track. Then I stepped up the bank and – slipped.

Of course, I had to be the one to make a mess of things.

The noise seemed awful in the silence.

Dick was abusing me with his eyes. I wanted to swear, too. We listened – not a sound except the murmur of the surf. Dick stepped on, and this time I climbed the bank quietly. Then halted.

Little Paddy's black head was darkly visible amongst the bushes, staring all around. Either he had lost the tracks, or suspected the quarry had heard us; by instinct he was trying to locate his hiding place. Suddenly he held his head aside, sniffed a moment, then crept forward like a black snake wriggling amongst the bushes, writhing up towards the crown of the mound. He bent down, and vanished. Then his black head bobbed up facing us. I could see the whites of his eyes as he beckoned excitedly. We hurried to him.

Just below the top of the mound the earth was hollowed out naturally, just like those tiny caves so popular as a camp with the wallaroos in the hilly mainland. This cosy retreat was screened on the seaward side by bushes.

Paddy put his hand to the ground, his eyes speaking to Dick.

"Warm," exclaimed Dick. "Feel it, Jack! He was lying here even while we were tracking him."

I felt the earth, it was indeed warm, as if a man had been lying there on a blanket. Lots of cigarette butts were scattered round, and Paddy picked up a butt triumphantly. It was still smouldering. Paddy had smelt that smoke when he was looking for .the hide-out.

"The slinking pest has been lying here enjoying himself," said Dick indignantly. "Living like a king while he spied on us."

"He can't be far away," I suggested.

"No!" exclaimed Dick. "He must have sneaked away when he heard you slip down the bank."

Paddy leapt up the mound crest and his arm went straight up. Billy, away on the distant Look-out, was signalling.

"Billy see him!" cried Little Paddy. "He go that-a-way, then that-a-way!" And he panted ahead and around.

The Jap had run down the mound, then round the one in front. The next one was still higher, and among bushes there he had vanished. Billy signalled no more. Down where we were the long shadows had fallen, and the cool air warned of evening approaching. But away ahead of us, and high up, the crown of the big Hill stood up boldly, with the rays of the setting sun a searchlight upon it. Crowning it like a black pillar stood the immovable Billy. Little Paddy was gazing round everywhere, listening intently. But there was no sign, no sound.

'We've lost him," said Dick disappointedly. "Slinker has given us the slip. But we've found his water supply and his camp," he added grimly.

"I wonder where he keeps his tucker," I said.

"Of coursel" exclaimed Dick, and wheeled around. "Let's go back to his hide-out and find it. We'll soon bring him to heel if we can find his tucker."

But we could not find his provisions. Except for cigarette butts, the hide-out was bare. The hard earth had not been dug up; nor could we find anything among the bushes.

"There's nothing here," said Dick disappointedly. "He's a cunning bird."

"Yes. But he won't dare use this hide-out again."

"That's right." Dick grinned. "And it won't be easy to find another. He knows we'll be on his scent again quick and lively."

"He's out in a cold, hard world, a hunted man trying to find a new camp amongst the bushes. Won't you feel sorry for him when we're back in our nice, warm camp?"

"I hope he shivers his teeth out," replied Dick savagely, "He daren't light a fire, either. But I do wish we could find his stores; he'd be a hungry outcast then."

"Probably his provisions are all tinned stuff."

"Of course – or most of it. Tinned stuff would keep, and he could hide it easily and throw the empty tins into the sea. We've seen no sign of a fire, but he might light a small fire now and then to cook his rice, and cover the ashes with sand."

"It's a cosy hide-out," I said.

"Yes," replied Dick, "a home away from home. He's been hiding here like a bandicoot nesting in the bushes. See how the crown of the mound shelters it from wind and rain from east, north, and south, while the bushes shelter it from the west. And just look!" He lay down, then rose on his elbow. "Right between these bushes I can peer out and see all over the anchorage. But a man aboard a ship, even with glasses, could not possibly see me."

"And by standing up," I pointed out, "we can see Billy plainly silhouetted."

"By jove, yes!" exclaimed Dick. "And the Look-out and flagstaff! So Slinker could see a ship come or go from the anchorage, and see every signal that we made from the Look-out. And when we left the Look-out he could climb up there and do his own signalling. If you hadn't seen that track we wouldn't have known a thing about it."

"That's so. But there's one thing he couldn't see from here, and one thing he couldn't do,"

"What's that?"

"He couldn't see a ship any distance out to sea. And he could not signal a ship."

"I forgot," replied Dick relievedly. "Of course he couldn't.

We hold the Look-out, though not the smaller hills below it. But the Look-out is the strategic post. And now that we know he's here we'll jolly well see that we hold that Look-out by day and night."

"That's so. But we'd better be making for camp, it will be dark before we get there."

"Come along then. We'll go back along the shoreline beside the ridge, that's the way old Slinker has gone. We'll give him as much trouble as we possibly can."

"With pleasure. Lead on!"

"Not on your life!" Dick replied. "It's Man Friday who must take the lead, every time we are hunting Slinker."

The delighted grin from Little Paddy was reward for the compliment. But Dick's light-hearted praise to the little blackboy was going to bring us greater reward than that.

We had barely walked a hundred yards when Little Paddy halted, staring down at a small, clear patch of gravelly sand, ringed round by shingle. There was no sign of track or mark on the clear patch. We gazed curiously as Paddy pointed to it, then turned to us with a grin – such a grin, it reminded me of Big Paddy's grin from ear to ear when he was very, very pleased. I had never imagined that Little Paddy would some day grow a grin like that. He knelt down and began scraping. He dug a little hole, then pulled up a tin of potted crab in fiendish triumph. I couldn't help thinking of Little Jack Horner who put in his thumb and pulled out a plum.

"Found it!" yelled Dick. "Found Slinker's tucker supply!" We really had. We knelt beside Paddy and scraped away the sand, unearthing tin after tin of fish, and crab, and pastes, and Japanese potted foods. Laughingly we spread them on the shingle.

"That's all," said Dick disappointedly. "Maybe Slinker was too cunning to hide all his eggs in the one basket. But this is a good supply, the loss of this will make him scratch for his tucker."

"He'll be pretty mad if he's up among the rocks, watching us raid his larder."

Dick stood up and gazed at the little hills ahead of us, stretching back towards the Look-out. He laughed and waved ironically.

"Very kind of you, Slinker," he shouted. "We'll enjoy this potted crab."

But neither the shadowed hills nor the coarse grey rocks gave reply.

"He's not speaking," laughed Dick. "Come on, whip off our shirts and make a bag of them. The three of us can easily carry the tins, then. If we don't get back to camp soon Billy will think the debil-debil has gobbled us up. What say you, Man Friday?"

Little Paddy glanced uneasily around at evening closing in. He was certain that "debil-debils" come with the night. 'Well, then," smiled Dick. "What do you say to a bright fire and the billy boiling and a good feed?"

Again that all-embracing grin spread over the impish face of Little Paddy.

Pearling Luggers, Cooktown Harbour, N. Queensland.

19

WHERE IS THE *NANCY BELL*?

THAT evening we enjoyed a merry feast – at Slinker's expense!

"He's a thoughtful host," chuckled Dick. "Supplied us with variety."

Dick was curious to taste the queer mixtures in the gay tins adorned by Haring covers of octopus and shrimp and crab. Though familiar with the contents of most, .among these tins some tricked him.

"I've never seen one like this before," he pondered, and examined it by the firelight.

"Potted dragon," I ventured, "judging by the label."

"Maybe." He smiled doubtfully. "Yes, I wouldn't be surprised if it was lizard or something." He opened the tin. "Phew!" With protesting hand to screwed-up face he thrust the tin at Paddy. "Throw tin in sea, quick-feller," he spluttered, "before it stinks the place out!"

The happy expectancy on Little Paddy's face chanced to alarmed entreaty.

"No more!" he implored. "No more trow 'im away! Him good-feller tucker!"

"You chuck him longa sea!" yelled Dick. "Quick-feller tool Here! Take it and skit!"

I was holding my breath, Dick his nose, as Little Paddy reluctantly reached for the tin.

"Good tucker!" exploded Dick. "Why, it hums like a cess-pit! It's a wonder it didn't blow the camp to smithereens."

Little Paddy edged backwards, clutching the precious tin. It would break his heart to throw it away.

"Phew!" yelled Dick. "Aren't you gone yet? Throw that tin into deep water before I lay my belt round you."

Little Paddy had a brain-wave. Thrusting dirty fingers into the tin he drew out a fistful of the greasy black mess and shoved it into his maw, chewing with delight.

"Good-feller tucker!" he gurgled earnestly. "Plenty good-feller too much! Taste him longa you-feller," and held out the tin invitingly.

"Spit it out!" yelled Dick. "It's poison, you fool! That-feller tucker killem you!"

"No more," gurgled Paddy, shaking his head earnestly.

"Plenty-feller good-feller tucker this one!"

"Get to the devil out of this!" yelled Dick, jumping up, while Little Paddy vanished. "Phew! I've smelt dead dogs, and 'cats, and horses and cattle, but never in my life have I ever smelt anything like that!"

Neither had I, thank goodness.

"It must be food of some sort, though," I suggested.

"Little Paddy had evidently tasted it before."

"Yes. When I opened the tin I thought it was fish paste or some other muck gone putrid. But Asiatics must eat it like that, so it won't harm Man Friday. He's not going to come back into this camp, though, if he smells-he can jolly well camp outside with the debil-debils."

We were enjoying tinned crab an hour later when a little black head peered into camp and spread into the friendly, ingratiating grin of Man Friday.

"Come longa me," ordered Dick suspiciously, and Paddy obeyed. "Wouff!" spluttered Dick. "Clear out of this and go and jump in the sea." And Paddy vanished.

"He hums, too!" said Dick. "No wonder, after eating that awful stuff. He can jolly well air himself outside until we go up to the Look-out to relieve Billy. Then Billy and he can have their feed. The hum should be out of the camp when we come down in the morning."

"I hope so. That stuff did pong."

So poor Man Friday had to squat all by himself in the outer fringe of firelight, watching Dick and me gorge.

I sneaked a glance at him. His eyes in the camp fire glow looked large as a cow's, mournful, and brimful of longing.

"This potted shrimp is tasty with soy sauce!" I winked at Dick.

' 'Yes, makes belly belonga me warm-feller."

"Sure does. The Chinese know how to make sauce."

"They do," said Dick, gobbling, "and the Japs know how to tin fish. I'm sure Little Paddy would enjoy this tinned crab."

"I'm certain he would. So would Billy – he must be feeling out of things away up there in the dark on his lonesome."

"By jove, yes, I was forgetting him. Here, Paddy," he called, "make 'im up fire big-feller, scare away debil-debil longa Billy."

As Little Paddy fairly jumped to the job Dick remarked, "A blazing fire down here will cheer Billy a bit. I'll bet he's growing a kink in his neck, staring down from that Look-out, imagining every whisper in the breeze is a spirit of the night come to grab him."

When we climbed up to the Look-out there was no doubt that Billy was glad to see us. Dick kept him a while until Billy explained just when and how and where he had seen Slinker. Billy could tell us it was only for a moment, when the Jap had run for cover and vanished round the further mound.

"All right," said DIck, "maybe we catch him tomorrow morning time. Now you go down longa camp, have a good feed longa Little Paddy. But only Jap-feller tucker!" he added warningly. "Eat 'im plenty-feller that one! No more eat 'im our feller-tucker!"

Billy's grin was all mouth as dreamily he patted his stomach.

"Me eat plenty!" he grunted. "Me proper hungry-feller."

"All right, buzz off!" And Billy "buzzed". There one moment, he was gone the next.

"A few more hungry spells like this," Dick laughed, "and those legs of his will get better 'plenty-feller quick'."

"I bet those two blackboys will make a hole in that tucker!"

"There won't be much of it left in a couple of days," laughed Dick as he settled his blankets for the night. "I suppose Slinker is down by that hole we dug, swearing fit to bust."

"Can you blame him, finding his larder bare?"

"Old Mother Hubbard," chanted Dick, "she went to the cupboard "

I did first watch with the listening night. A sky of blue speckled with myriad diamonds floated low down. The faintest whisper of a breeze breathed through pleasant coolness. The quiet sea was a velvety sheet, merging into the night. Away below, the fire illuminated all the familiar things round the camp. Billy and Little Paddy squatted there, gorging their hardest to eat "plenty-feller Jap tucker". I gazed far out into starlit space to north and nor'-west. No star of a signal light twinkled out there. Slowly I turned my gaze westward towards the mainland, then further round into the southern night. No sign there; we hardly expected any from that direction, nor from the east, for out there lay the Great Barrier Reef. Still I gazed out east-ward, then down over the crown of the Hill. The little plain seemed a ghostly carpet, dreaming under the night sky. The black walls of the ruined hut were splashed by starlight, abandoned and forlorn. I mused a moment on poor Mrs Watson. What terrifyingly lonely nights the young mother had suffered there, her tower of strength the faithfulness of the two Chinamen! How awful the shock when the first was killed, the other wounded! What desperation the stars must then have looked down on in the beseiged hut, what agonizing suspense! Softly my mind whispered that it was not star-splashes down there, but the tears of stars dried by the night on the hut walls. Abruptly I turned away and gazed along the ridge, south, kneeling down to silhouette the crowns of the little hills. For I must watch down there, too, for sign of Slinker trying to sneak up to watch for signals, or to signal. I felt just a little bit sympathetic towards Slinker. His was a very lonely job, and he must feel very sorry for himself now that he was found out, with enemies seeking him, tucker gone, his friends gone too; and now no home. Thus the night watches dreamed by.

The new day, from the Look-out, was nearly always beautiful. Dawn seemed to be born right beside us, out of night, popping up from the Great Reef, a wave of gold shining up through the coming day's bridal veil of mists. Then up shot fire from the furnaces of the sun, and a moment later up he popped himself, a swimming disc of molten gold magically dissolving the mists. We gazed away out, then, into a ghostly world of drifting mists swiftly harried by those far flung rays. As yet we could not see the peaceful sea, except by the Great Reef, where the King of Day was burning the waters a rosy red. And now we saw gulls gliding there, paying homage to their life-giver, the sun. Dawn brightened, there came breakings in the mists far and wide – just like tearings in a world-wide veil. And now to the nor'-west we stared into these breaks, but no ship came sailing into the open spaces of the sea. The mists were rolling as if trying hard to join together again. But they were forced to grow thinner, and rise higher, with ragged edges dissolving in wraithy vapour. We glanced down at the island at our feet. But there was no island, no little plain, no camp. There was a mass of smoky-white mist over all. Even as we watched it began moving up, the island a white mist, ghostily creeping up to engulf us. Away down there it had swallowed the base of the Hill; we saw granite rocks vanishing as it crept silently up, pressing up close against the cliff-face. As if anxious to swallow us in, great fleeces broke away and came rolling swiftly up the hillside. And now we could have leapt out, straight into the soft white cloud. In a moment Dick was a ghost beside me as the clammy nothing engulfed us. A moment more, and it slid above our heads, rising fast as it broke away into gliding sheets of mists. Then we were gazing out over a sparkling sea, with not a sail in sight.

"It's time we sighted the Nancy Bell," said Dick. "Cross-eyed Joe could not have shaken off the black lugger as easily as we thought he would."

"I thought he'd have turned up by now," I replied. "They must still be playing hide-and-seek out there. But there's been very little wind since they sailed away."

"Of course," replied Dick cheerfully. "I hadn't thought of that. Now what do you think of those lazy niggers?" He pointed down to the camp. "Not up yet, and the sun a mile high."

"The sun travels a bit faster than we do," I suggested. "I know, but I'm hungry as a hawk and the lazy beggars haven't even got the billy on. I suppose they're as full as butchers' pups from their feed last night."

"You can be sure they ate till they couldn't manage a mouthful more. I wonder what Slinker will do for his breakfast?"

"I'm not worrying about him," replied Dick cheerfully.

"I'm going below to put the billy on and shake those lazy beggars up. We've got a full day ahead of us, we must keep Slinker on the run."

And Dick started off down to the camp, while I turned again to the sea for any sign of the *Nancy Bell.*

I saw the Jap behind the sand hummock.

20

THE HUNT

BY the thorough manner in which Dick organized the search for the unwelcome Jap, I knew he must have thought it out during his watch the night before.

"Even if we can't catch him," he told us, "we must find every possy in which he could hide. There can't be many, for the island is so small and nearly all open plain. If we know his hiding places, then, when the skipper returns, we'll be able to run him to earth quick and lively. We won't have much time to spare if the Jap lugger follows the *Nancy Bell* back here. So keep your eyes skinned up on the Look-out, Billy. And listen, Man Friday feller-me-lad! If you go to sleep while looking for tracks I'll tan your hide!"

Little Paddy's grin implied he didn't take the threat too seriously.

"You might liven him up with the belt," I laughed, "but you couldn't tan that hide any blacker than it is."

"I'll warm it, anyway," Dick threatened.

Dick climbed up to the Look-out with Billy, their figures purposely distinct on the skyline to attract the Jap's attention.' We felt sure he would be lurking away down the ridge, somewhere towards the Hide-out. For there was his only cover and high ground that faced the vital anchorage. Only on the seaward side of the ridge could he see whether a vessel sailed in. Only from there would he be in a position to communicate with the black lugger.

Dick was to walk down the spur of the Hill, then up to the crown of the smaller hill adjoining it, and so on right down the ridge to the mounds and the farther shore. He would thus walk over every hill, and see fairly plainly to right and left.

Parallel with him, Little Paddy was to walk along the shoreline, while I would follow along the base of the ridge on the inland side. Thus if Slinker tried to dodge Dick by crawling round a hill and getting behind him I should see him if he came out on the plain side; while if he crept out towards the shore, then Little Paddy would see him.

Billy, from away back up on the Look-out, would overlook all. And the glasses would help him.

"The Jap will keep his eye on me," explained Dick, "as I'm walking over and down those little hills. But he won't spot you two coming along away below. So keep your eyes peeled."

And thus we started out. My job was the easiest. I had only to walk slowly along the foot of the ridge, keeping a sharp look-out, and being carefully examining each little hill as he walked to it.

Midday came in brilliant sunlight. My bingey was demanding whether my throat was cut when I stopped dead in my tracks. Just in front, a little higher up, a man was creeping round a small hill. Pressed against the hillside, his outstretched arms were parting the bushes as he crouched, his head craned Sideways, gazing upward.

Dick was just climbing to the top of that little hill. He would stare round, then walk slowly down it to the mound in front. As he did so, this stranger would sidle round the hill behind Dick. I could only see the side of his face, for he was concentrating on where Dick must be. He was a sturdy Jap, with bow legs plain from his shorts, and a red headband round his forehead. He carried his muscular arms outstretched from his singlet. A sheath-knife was at his belt.

He crouched on, cautiously Sidling round the hill, gazing up, listening, taking clever advantage of a bump in the hill behind Dick to shield him from the Look-out.

I was wondering if I could sneak close enough to pounce and yell and try to hold on long enough for Dick to come. But I didn't like the idea of that knife.

He stepped forward and glanced straight down at me, the taut expression freezing on his face: He had a little black moustache and startled black eyes. He bounded round and ran like a hare. I yelled, and heard Dick's answering yell, heard him running. We sighted the fugitive rounding a hillock, leaping bushes like a wallaby. He vanished as a yell came from Little Paddy, then a long drawn-out cry from the skyline told that Billy had spotted him also. We got a glimpse of him as he dodged ahead down among the low mounds. Little Paddy's eyes were fairly leaping' from his head as he ran, jumping high now and then to try to keep the quarry in view. But we lost him.

"Hold hard!" shouted Dick. "Stay in your possies! Watch out where he goes. He may try to double back."

But we could not see him. Nor could Billy, away back on the Look-out, advise us.

"Keep a sharp look-out in case he breaks out on the plain, Jack," called Dick. "It's useless him sneaking out on Paddy's side, because the sea's there. And if he goes any further ahead the shore is there, too. He must be hiding among those low mounds right in front of me."

'What are you going to do when you spot him?"

"Yell, then the three of us rush him."

"Right-oh. But watch out he doesn't use that sheath-knife."

"If he draws it, then we'll stand off, and Paddy will dong him with a stick."

"I hadn't thought of that. Right-oh."

"Paddy," yelled Dick, "you go in look-about. Sposem you no find him quick-feller then look about longa track. Quick-feller now."

And Paddy jumped in among the mounds like a terrier scenting a rat.

But he could not find him, and lost time picking up a track in the shape of a broken bush. We were on the trail again, but it proved slow work. The long mounds about nine feet high, with channels running between, were of hard earth covered with tufted grass and bushes. Slowly Little Paddy worked his way along, seeking any sign of a fugitive in a hurry, while Dick and I kept to our observation posts.

And then Little Paddy jumped down into a channel between two mounds, where a broken bush showed where the Jap had slid down. I lost sight of Little Paddy then, but guessed what the Jap had done. Seeing he could not double back, he had apparently crouched down in the channels between the mounds, and crawled out on the seashore several hundred yards ahead. The shoreline there was the bank only about five or six feet above the beach we had walked along yesterday. By keeping close to the bank he would be able to run along the beach that walled in the plain. Dick was up on a hillock, but I doubted if it was high enough for him to see over the edge of the bank. I rolled a cigarette and waited, with an eye on the plain.

A shout from Paddy settled the matter. We ran down to the shoreline, and there was Paddy pointing at the Jap's tracks, plain to see where he had crouched close to the bank.

"Dash him!" grinned Dick. "So he's given us the slip again, just when I thought we had him cornered."

"He can't be so very far away."

"You can bet he's' gone for all he's worth," replied Dick.

"Going like a scalded cat. It took Paddy some time to track him here, but we've driven him away from the only decent cover on the island."

"He can sneak back at night."

"Yes, but he knows now we can hunt him away from the ridge any time we like."

"He won't feel too pleased about that."

"He won't," answered Dick cheerfully, 'but I will."

"Well, there's only one way for him to go now. He must keep walking along the shoreline. This is where we tracked him from the water yesterday. If he keeps close to the bank it will shield him from Billy, but if he once comes up on the plain, then Billy must see him."

"Yes, but if he keeps to the shoreline he could go on walking east, then all the way round the island."

"Yes, though every step would take him farther away from where he could do his job."

"Well, what do we do now?"

Dick looked at Little Paddy, then answered, "I think Man Friday wants to get on those tracks straight away."

But Man Friday gazed reproachfully at Dick.

"What say him you Little Paddy?" Dick queried, grinning.

"Belly helonga me proper hungry-feller!" sighed Paddy.

"I thought so," laughed Dick. "All right. You fill him billy longa Jap man waterhole – he not far. We eatem tucker." And Paddy departed in delight.

I was pleased, too. We were ravenous. Soon we had a fire crackling merrily.

A few minutes later I happened to glance away back at the Look-out. A coil. of smoke was lazily floating up.

So Billy was "hungry-feller" too.

I grinned. Inquisitive little birds, cheekily twittering, came from nowhere to share our damper crumbs.

Torres Strait Islanders preparing beche-de-mer, 1908.

21

SLINKER PLAYS US A TRICK

FEELING new men after the meal Dick made Little Paddy a cigarette, which lifted him into the seventh heaven of delight. He and I stretched out, puffing up at the lovely sky.

"Snap out of it," ordered Dick. "Here's where we get busy again."

"Aw," I growled, "give us a break!"

"Not on your life. You lazy shysters would snooze here all day if I'd let you. Come along."

"What are we to do now, then?" I growled.

"Set out on those tracks right away. I'm going to give Slinker no peace. Come on!"

Unwillingly we obeyed the taskmaster.

We followed the tracks easily, plain on the sand below the bank which in a couple of miles had risen higher, enabling the Jap to walk at ease-to Dick's disgust!

"I'd like to have seen him grow a hump like a camel," he growled.

"We've got him on the move now, but he'll double back in the night," I grumbled.

"Yes, but we'll drive him away again in the morning. Each morning it will be easier and quicker, because we'll soon know every bush and rock and gully along that ridge."

"If we keep him moving all day, and compel him to fish for his tucker by night he won't be feeling very happy."

"No," answered Dick. "It will give him other things to think about than spying on us. I was wondering," he added thoughtfully, "if one of us couldn't patrol the anchorage shore by night, just to disturb him in his fishing. It would make him nervy."

"Yes," I answered, "it would. And I don't feel like stopping a thump on the head from a stick in the dark."

"I suppose not," said Dick disappointedly. "Still, it shouldn't be difficult to interrupt his tucker supply. If we both did a bit of prowling along the anchorage beach--"

"I know who'd do the prowling," I declared. "And it wouldn't be me."

"After all," he persisted, "it's only an occasional possy here and there along the anchorage-front he could fish from. We could find them by day, then it would be a simple matter to visit them at night."

"And end up as feed for the fishes," I replied. "Forget it."

Little Paddy grimaced, and pointed, The tracks had come straight across the beach and vanished at the water.

It was high tide, the beach very narrow just here and the bank high. It was impossible for Billy, away back on the Look-out to see along the waterline here.

"A kid's trick," said Dick contemptuously. "As if we would fall for thatl"

"Still, it's not so bad," I replied. "I don't suppose he knows anything about the bush."

"Don't be too sure. Remember his cunning hide-out back on the ridge, and how careful he was not to leave tracks nor a trace of smoke or ashes of a fire. Besides which he succeeded in spying on us for days, and would be doing so still if you hadn't accidentally seen that one track."

We walked on silently for a while. On thinking back I realized the Jap must know quite a bit about bushcraft. He wouldn't have been trusted to do the job that was his, otherwise. For the first time I began to wonder about the men aboard that black lugger. Surely they couldn't be a match for the cunning of Cross-eyed Joe!

The Jap's trick here was plain to us. He had entered the water to lose his tracks. But we knew we must pick them up again wherever he recrossed the beach, for he could only go on and on all round the island, or re-cross the beach again, climb the bank, and step out on to the plain. There were but few trees, and little natural cover. We knew he could not have doubled back along the shore, for we must have seen him. So we strolled along unconcernedly, Man Friday with a contemptuous joke to Dick.

"Jap man he all a same fool," he laughed. "Piccanin' track him feller."

"You keep a jolly good look-out, young-feller-me-lad," snorted Dick. "Sposem you lose 'im they-feller tracks me tan him hide belonga you!"

Presently we came to what from the Look-out had always appeared to be a "corner" of the island, where the opposite coastline appeared to run back parallel to the ridge. I noticed Little Paddy keeping a more intent look-out at the beach edge. At this "corner" there were a few mounds, only about ten feet high, and a couple of hundred yards long, ending at the shore-edge.

"I'd expected to see signs of him by now," mused Dick. "I thought he'd cross the beach, climb up into those mounds and see if he couldn't work back across the plain, or drop back down on to the beach behind us and hurry back for home.

This was what I had been expecting also. But there was no sign of a track, try Man Friday ever so keenly to find one. We walked round the "corner" and soon came to a rocky place with deep water.

"He *must* have crossed the beach here," frowned Dick. "Otherwise he would have had to swim. And he wouldn't have chanced the sharks."

But there were no tracks. Little Paddy was obviously puzzled, hunting round like a fox terrier that has lost the scent.

"You've made a mess of it," said Dick disgustedly. "Come and see if Billy has seen him." And he climbed the bank to the mounds

We stared out over the plain to the ridge opposite. Back along it to the big Hill, where Billy was perched up on the Look-out, apparently no bigger than Little Paddy.

"You talk longa Billy," suggested Dick, nodding.

"Billy no more see 'im," answered Paddy miserably.

"How you know?" demanded Dick. "Billy no more see us-feller yet."

"Sposem Billy see him-feller Jap man," explained Paddy, "he talk longa smoke."

"Of course he would," said Dick sheepishly. "But Little Paddy wouldn't have seen it."

We stared over the plain, then back along the beach. But there was no sign of the Jap.

"He's dodged us somehow," grumbled Dick. "I'm certain he's made back towards the ridge. But how did he do it?"

I sat down and rolled a cigarette, camouflaging a grin.

"I didn't think a Japanese seaman on a strange island could outwit an Australian bushman and a famous Australian tracker," I ventured.

"You're telling me!" replied Dick sarcastically. 'Well then, how did he do it?"

"I leave that to the bushman," 1 grinned.

Dick was wild that we had been outwitted so easily. If I should be mean enough to repeat this story to Dick's friends in Cooktown, his reputation would suffer. And he was proud of his reputation as a tracker. He was staring back along the shoreline. It was so very plain – the long line of bank that was the edge of the plain, the strip of beach-sand like a narrow road running beside it, and the quiet water hemming it in.

"I have it!" exclaimed Dick. 'What fools we are! Blind as bats!"

"Do you see him?"

"Of course I don't! He must be nearly back to his old hide-out by now."

"What do you see, then?"

"Stand up here, you lazy loon, and see for yourself."

I stood beside Dick and he pointed away back along the beach.

"See it?"

"See what?"

"The tree. Do you see a black stick there, leading from the water's edge across the beach, nearly to the bank of the plain?"

I could see it.

"Well," explained Dick, "that's the trunk of a dead tree blown down by the wind; it lies right across the beach. From the water, he's walked over it to the edge of the plain, climbed up, wriggled a few yards further into the grass, then lain there till we silly goats strolled by. 'Then he's slipped back to the beach and quietly walked back, while we carried on with our nice long walk right to here."

"H'm," I said doubtfully. "I didn't even see a tree."

"Neither did I. We were talking too much, felt so sure of ourselves that we stepped over it without noticing."

Little Paddy's downcast expression told us that all was now plain to him.

"All the same," I protested, "there are no trees here large enough to stretch right across the beach, even though it is narrow with the tide in."

"That's what puzzles me," said Dick. "If it lay right across the beach from the bank to the water we simply must have noticed it. But that's what he's done, all the same. Come along, I'm going to see how he did it."

It was a fair walk back to the tree. Once there, however, it was easy to see why we hadn't noticed it. It was a long dead sapling, without branches, part embedded in the sand. Dick and I had simply stepped over it while talking. It did not reach to the bank by a good ten feet, while there was another ten feet of clear sand between it and the water.

"What you say?" asked Dick.

"Ou ai! Him go along that a way." Paddy nodded at the sapling, and bending down pointed to a few grains of sand here and there, pressed to the dry wood.

"But which-feller way he come from water longa stick?" asked Dick.

Paddy walked beside the sapling to the bank: At the bottom of the bank lay two tufts of seaweed, cast there apparently by storm or tide. Paddy picked up the seaweed, and walked back across the beach, and into the water. At the water's edge he turned and, stretching out, laid a clump of the seaweed on the sand before him. Reaching out his foot he carefully put it on the seaweed and, balancing on one leg, placed the other seaweed before him and stretched his foot to this. Lifting up his other foot, he reached behind, grasped the seaweed, and threw it carefully before him.

Reaching out his foot he carefully put it on the seaweed and, balancing on one leg, placed the other seaweed before him and stretched his foot to this. Lifting up his other foot, he reached behind, grasped the seaweed, and threw it carefully before him. Thus he proceeded, step by step, on a. thick pad of seaweed right to the log. Then, with the seaweed in each hand he walked along the log to its other end, and from here, across seaweed again to the bank. Reaching up, he grasped the grass tufts, leapt up, and disappeared over the grassy bank.

"Well," said Dick grudgingly, "it was a clever trick. But what fools we were not to have seen through it!"

Little Paddy's black face, with an ingratiating grin, appeared over the bank.

"You can wipe that grin from your face," called Dick.

"You, an aboriginal training to be a warrior, and you let a little Jap man beat you! Why, you couldn't track pussy , if she had a tin tied to her tail!"

Dick turned his back on Man Friday's woebegone expression and winked at me.

"Come on, Jack. I bet you we'll find Slinker's return tracks just a few yards down the beach. He would only have waited till we'd passed on a little way. Then he'd jump down and take his time back to his hide-out-if he's found a new one."

And so it proved.

As we strolled back to camp across the plain in the sunset, I remarked, "You're a bit hard on Little Paddy."

"We've got to be, Jack, to keep him up to the mark. This jolly old Slinker is no fool. And we'll have to impress it on Billy, too, to keep a double sharp look-out for sign of the *Nancy Bell*. I don't know what is happening to Cross-eyed Joe and the cutter, but our job is to look after the camp with all that trochus while our ship is away, and get in touch with Joe before Slinker gets in touch with the black lugger. Remember, we don't know what these Japs are up to."

22

WE KEEP THE JAP MOVING

NEXT morning there was still no sign of the *Nancy Bell*. Under a light breeze three luggers heading south, away towards the mainland, held only a passing interest for us.

"Joe should have arrived back by this time," said Dick soberly. "If he does not turn up within another week we'll be in the same boat as old Slinker – forced to fish for our tucker."

"He'll turn up all right," I yawned. "The devil looks after his own. I wonder what price trochus is fetching in Cooktown now."

"It may have gone up in price," replied Dick hopefully. 'We never know. Confound that shark! Everything was going so well until the shark attacked Billy."

"Billy will soon be all right, and we haven't done so badly."

"A hundred times better than we dreamt," agreed Dick.

"But I wish we had that trochus in Cooktown, all the same. Oh well, I'll go below to camp and shake up those two lazy abos. I bet they'd rather pick up their fish-spears and stroll away fishing than chase Slinker."

"You're going to worry him again today, then?"

"I feel easier in my mind if we know what he's doing, Jack. Or rather, prevent him from doing anything."

And Dick climbed down the Hill to the camp while I gazed away over the sea to the nor-west, lazily wondering what was delaying the *Nancy Bell*. It must be something important or Cross-eyed Joe would have been back by now. Knowing the local reputation for cunning possessed by that shrewd old sea-dog, I could hardly believe that the Japanese lugger had managed to keep on his tail all this time.

It was a good hour later before Dick came climbing up the Hill with Billy, and settled him in his job.

"Little Paddy is keeping the billy hot for you, Jack," said Dick. "He's eaten enough breakfast for two men, but you can be sure he's counting on you to invite him to another feed."

"I won't be able to resist giving him another crust," I smiled. 'What's doing afterwards?"

"Pretty well the same as yesterday. Slinker will be away down the ridge there, gazing up here with a hungry look in his eye. When you're ready I'll start from here, same as yesterday. I've a feeling we'll have an easy day. Slinker will know it's little use playing hide-and-seek now we know the ridge so well. When he sees we're coming the same way he'll sneak down on to that same beach, and walk quietly up along it where he had to hurry yesterday. He'll just lead us for a nice, long walk. That will do us. So long as he's away from the ridge he can't do any harm should either of the boats appear, whereas Billy can signal us."

"You seem to have it all thought out."

"Mother reckoned I had it in me," replied Dick with a grin.

"Gee whiz!" I exclaimed admiringly. "After that one I retire down to your little boy Friday for breakfast."

And I did.

It worked out as Dick had thought. As we advanced along the ridge the Jap retired towards the shoreline, taking his time. Billy saw him several times and Signalled us. When eventually we reached the shore there were his tracks, sure enough; he was walking close to the bank, as yesterday. We took our time, with a jump up the bank now and then to see if the distant Billy signalled us. Little Paddy, now that he had not to be on the *qui vive* before his hero, cast longing eyes at the water's edge, wishing he had dared to bring his fish-spear. Every now and then a ripple out there told of a fat fish snouting for his dinner, close in shore. When we came to the fallen tree that had enabled the Jap to bamboozle us the day before, we stood looking at the tracks.

"Him stop, too!" stated Little Paddy, pointing. "Him look about."

And the Jap's tracks, deeply imprinted, showed where he had stood while he examined and read our tracks of the afternoon before. Then he had stepped on over the log and made his leisurely way along the beach.

"That will show him," said Dick in satisfied tones, "that he's not as smart as he thought he was. We know all about his little trick."

"He won't 'try it again."

"No, he won't." Dick stared, now frowning at the tracks.

"I'm not so sure," he added thoughtfully, "that we are so smart after all."

"Why, what's wrong now?"

"Nothing much, only that we've still got a lot to learn."

"In what way?"

"Well, if we'd used our heads yesterday we could have got Little Paddy to blot out our tracks where we came along this log and climbed back, just as the Jap did. He would then have come along this morning and thought we hadn't seen through his little lark. He would have put the same joke across us again. We would have carried on, and given him time to feel safe to jump down the bank and start back on his homeward way. Then the three of us could, have hopped up the bank, gone out on the plain a little bit, then run along parallel with the bank. Little Paddy could have peeped over the edge and seen just where he was. Then the three of us could have jumped straight down on top of him."

"That's so," I said. "We've missed a good chance to surprise him."

"What thick-headed fools we are!" said Dick regretfully.

"I would have loved to have seen his face-the three of us jumping on him from out of the sky."

"He would have looked silly," I laughed, "sprawling there in the sand with us on top of him."

"He could have known all the ju-jitsu in the world," said Dick, "and it wouldn't have helped him. The shock would have been too sudden. What a pity we didn't think of it before!"

"Too late now," I said as we walked on. "You must think of these things beforehand."

"Then why the blazes didn't you think of it?" demanded Dick. "You're a bloke from the city where they've got all the brains."

"I'm in the bushman's country," I replied. "I'm only a learner." I lit a cigarette.

"H'm," replied Dick. "You've had all the luck, anyway. I'm becoming really curious to meet old Slinker face to face."

"Look out he doesn't shove a knife between your ribs," I warned. "He doesn't seem as anxious to meet us."

"He catch 'im crab!" exclaimed Little Paddy.

And there were the tracks where they'd suddenly run to the water's edge, chasing the sharp-cut little tracks of a large crab scuttling to the safety of the water. There was a graze on the sand where a foot had kicked it back to the shore.

"He's got to hunt for his tucker," said Dick grimly. 'We'll keep him on the move, anyway. Come along."

We did keep him on the move, but he tried us out, with a few tricks all the same. At the corner of the island he played hide and seek with us among the low mounds before we could drive him back to the shoreline again. And a little farther along, where inequalities in the ground gave him shelter from the watcher on our distant Hill he crawled out amongst the grass on the plain and kept crawling on, and it took Little Paddy an irritating hour to track him down. Dick was a hard taskmaster, and kept his Man Friday with his nose to the job. I took things easily. So long as we kept the Jap away from the ridge it did not seem that he could do any harm. We kept a look-out towards Billy, but he neither signalled us sign of the *Nancy Bell,* nor the black lugger, nor the Jap.

It was late afternoon when Dick called a halt. We had driven the Jap nearly three parts round the island. He would have all that way to trudge home, mostly in the dark, whereas we were now almost directly opposite the big Hill.

"We've only got to stroll across the plain to camp and put the billy on," said Dick complacently, "but he's got to walk round the island to a hide-out he'll be scared to camp in. And he's only got a crab for his dinner – and I hope it's a skinny one."

"He'll be feeling pretty mad with us," I said, "for forcing him to trudge all that way back when he could have got in a few hours' sleep. And now he must watch for his friends all night on an empty stomach."

"Yes," agreed Dick. "And he can't even do that job properly because we hold the Look-out day and night now. Any distant signals, or any vessel that comes to anchorage, we must know of long before he does. And, after he's been awake all night on an empty bingey, we'll chase him away again in the morning."

"Me think 'im mad-feller Jap that feller!" said Little Paddy, grinning.

"You'd better keep a sharp look-but, young-feller-me-lad," warned Dick. 'Watch out all a time. Sposem that feller Jap catch 'im Little Paddy, him knock Paddy longa head, eat 'im!" And Man Friday's hushed face showed he believed Dick's warning not to be all a joke. He had heard tales round his tribesmen's camp-fires that assured him such things had really happened.

It was sundown when we reached camp with ravenous appetites. Billy, away up on the Hill, staring down at the bright camp fire, must have felt the same.

"I wonder how old Slinker feels?" Dick laughed. "I wonder if he can see our fire away out there in the cold, hungry night." And he enjoyed a mouthful of damper and tinned meat, and washed it down with half a pannikin of tea.

Next morning at dawn, Dick and I were staring out over the sea as usual, away to the nor-west. The drifting mists were there, but suddenly, as if at some vast breath, they vanished, and there was left a clear, sparkling sea.

"Not. a sign," said Dick at last, "nor a signal from anywhere."

"The *Nancy Bell* should have returned before now."

"Yes," agreed Dick, 'but I'm beginning to think."

"Surely not," I murmured.

"Someone's got to," grunted Dick. "The black lugger may be lying behind that little island away out there. If the *Nancy Bell* came in, then the

Jap skipper would expect Slinker to signal him by night. But old Cross-eye may be wise to the move, and he, like as not, could be hiding behind one of those other islets."

"That might be the explanation."

"I think it is. But why Joe doesn't make a break for it in the night beats me. If there's no breeze, he's got petrol. If he knew Slinker was here waiting to signal his arrival I could understand his not coming. But he can't know that the [aps left a spy on the island."

"It's beginning to seem a bit of a mystery to me."

"Me, too," replied Dick, soberly. And he gazed out to sea.

We made a late start that morning, to Dick's disgust. "Just because of you two lazy combos," he growled to Billy and Man Friday. "Too tired to wake up and put the billy on. And now Slinker has Had time to catch enough fish for a dozen men's breakfasts."

However, we started off as usual, fully expecting that Slinker would dodge down. the ridge before us, and out on to the distant beach. We saw no sign of him, and when we stepped down on to the beach there was no sign there, either.

"He must have come out higher up," said Dick with puzzled face. "You pick 'im up track, quick-feller."

Little Paddy hurried along the beach by the bank, while we followed leisurely. But there was no expected track, only the tracks of yesterday and the day before.

"He's come at some monkey trick or other," declared Dick. "Carry on."

But in half an hour's walk there was no sign of a track. "We've missed him," declared Dick in disgust. "He's back in the ridge somewhere, probably taking it easy in his hide-out, and laughing at us. We'll have to root him out of that ridge." And we started back, Little Paddy very woebegone.

"Call yourself a tracker," snapped Dick. "Why, you couldn't track pussy!"

From the beach we combed the mounds carefully, then the hillocks, and then the little hills right to the base of the big Hill. Not a sign. We tried all over again; we must have searched round every rock and bush, let alone every gully and mound – or so it seemed. But not a sign did we see, and it was well after midday when Dick exclaimed, "I know what he's done! He's crossed the plain before dawn and made for the corner, while it was still too dark for us to see him from the Look-out. Then he's. dropped down on to the eastern beach and fished in peace all the time we've been fooling about looking for him. Come on."

But though we hurried at once to the corner and stepped down on the beach, there was no sign there but our tracks of the day before.

Dick was very disturbed. "We've lost him," he declared. "And while we can't keep in touch with him it means he might be in a position to signal his friends. When we don't know where he is, we don't know what he's up to."

"He can't be far away," I insisted. But I was just as deeply puzzled. Little Paddy was in despair; he had failed his hero.

"Of course he can't be far away," snorted Dick, "but that makes it worse. We don't know whether he is at the opposite end of the island or whether he is in a signalling possy, right under Billy's nose."

It was late afternoon when we were forced to give up.

As we turned towards the camp Man Friday yelled and pointed. A smoke signal was arising from the Look-out.

"Jap man he be that a way!" Little Paddy pointed excitedly towards the eastern corner of the island. "Billy see him longa beach!"

We turned and gazed that way, it was the nor-eastern corner, while the Hill and our camp were the nor-west, We had scoured the island for three parts of the way round it, and here he was all the time, directly opposite our camp.

"He's had a clear day's fishing all to himself," said Dick disgustedly. "He must have cut across the centre of the plain in the night; no wonder we couldn't find his tracks. But now we' know his new hide-out we'll easily root him out in the morning. Come on." And he turned back towards camp.

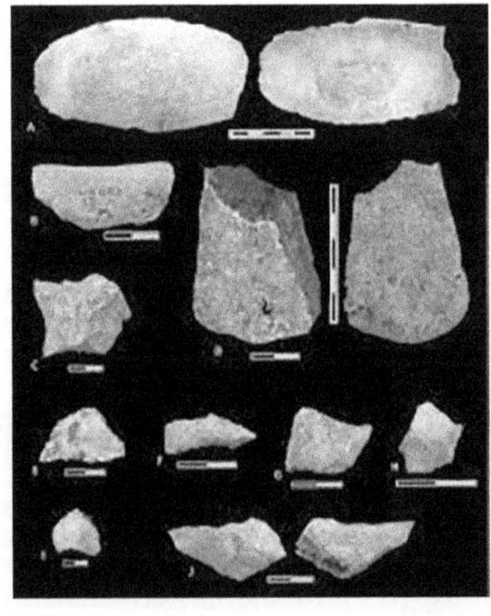

Aboriginal impliments, Lizard Island.

23

OUTWITTED

TIRED and hungry, but cheerful again, we reached camp, where Little Paddy fairly ran to put the billy on. We ate ravenously till Dick snapped, "Leave a share of that damper for Billy, you savage little guts! Billy plenty hungry-feller too!"

Little Paddy, with longing eyes, gazed at the remains of the damper. He had already gorged enough for a man and a half.

"I'll have to cook some johnnies for breakfast," growled Dick, "then bake a damper for night-time. I'll come down the Hill an hour before dawn and get the cooking done so we can get an early start."

"Slinker won't be enjoying a feed like this."

"He will not. What fish he's caught he'll cook on the coals and that's all he'll have. With no camp and a chilly night for compapy. And he'll have nothing to eat tomorrow night, for we won't give him the chance," Dick added with a grin.

"He tricked us again today."

"He did," admitted Dick grudgingly. "He's using his head, and a knowledge of bushcraft I never knew a Jap possessed. It doesn't say much for us, four of us against one on a small island with very little cover, and yet he's dodged us all the time."

"Hardly as bad as that. We have found him out, driven him from his post, commandeered his tucker, and kept him constantly on the move."

"That's so," agreed Dick more cheerfully. "So long as we prevent him from doing his job, that's all that matters to us. But I'm worrying over something else."

'What?"

"Our tucker supply. If Cross-eyed Joe doesn't turn up soon we'll have to start fishing in earnest to keep ourselves going. That means we won't be able to chase the Jap."

"That's not so good."

"It isn't. Of course, Joe should be here, he must arrive any time now. But come on, Billy must be starving – if the bad spirits haven't scared him stiff."

Up on the Look-out we found Billy starving indeed, and inclined to be sulky. We were very late. However, he brightened up when Dick mentioned the "billycan longa tea, plenty-feller tucker" waiting below for him.

Billy explained that, through the glasses a little before sundown, he had seen the Jap appear leisurely here and there, just beyond the few trees fringing the beach, away across on the nor-east corner. The Jap was walking about quite unconcernedly, as if looking for crabs.

"Well soon hunt him out of there now we know where he is," declared Dick.

"We've only got to walk straight across the plain."

Billy had seen three sail, distantly to the west, sailing north. But no sign of the *Nancy Bell* or the black lugger. With a grunt he vanished down the hillside.

"His legs are nearly better," said Dick. "A white man would have died of the shock."

I rolled up in the blanket, smoking up at the stars.

Dick woke me at midnight. "Come and have a look at this," he said urgently.

We stepped to the crown of the hill, gazing east. And there, in the nor-east corner, shone a bright little fire.

"He's there, all right," nodded Dick, "just where Billy saw him."

"He's there sure enough, blow him!" I yawned. 'Why did you wake me up?"

"To show you, of course, you sleepy coot. It's your watch, anyway."

When Billy relieved me at dawn I walked down to camp, hastened by a healthy appetite. Little Paddy greeted me with the amiable grin that told he had enjoyed breakfast. Dick, with the drawn expression of the conscientious cook, was squatting down with outstretched hand over the camp-oven lid, testing the heat. The lid showed just above the round hole in the ground in which sat the oven, and a glance at the blackened coals and ashes covering it told me the damper must be about done. So Dick had got to work early. After a hurried wash I got busy with breakfast, and knowing the touchy little ways of a cook, even if he is your own mate, I showed enough interest to grunt, "How's the damper doing?"

"Should be just about done," mumbled Dick, with serious face.

He slipped the fencing-wire hook under the ring of the lid then, careful not to disturb the ashes, lifted the lid up and off.

A glorious vista! A dome of golden-brown damper crust coyly peeping from the oven. Dick rapped it testingly with his knuckles.

"Sounds good," I suggested.

"Just about done," murmured Dick.

Not satisfied, he picked a long, clean straw of grass and carefully pushed it down through the top of the damper, as carefully withdrew it, and examined it anxiously.

It was perfectly clean, not a sign of the moisture that would have betrayed the damper was not quite cooked.

"Done to a turn!" he grunted and, slipping the hooked handle into the rings on the side of the oven, he lifted it clear of its pit, placed it tenderly on the ground, tilted it, lifted the damper and stood it on its side in the oven to cool. He smacked it top and bottom – a bonzer damper, a dinkum "cartwheel".

"We won't go hungry tonight," said the satisfied cook.

I praised the damper; it pays to praise the cook. Always remember that, whether you're at home, at sea, or in the bush.

Before I'd finished breakfast Dick was itching to be on the move. He carried the damper into the camp, wrapped it carefully in a clean cloth and laid it on his bunk.

"Ready?" he asked.

"Right-oh," I replied, and we walked away.

"It will be easy today," grinned Dick, as he strode out. "We'll give Slinker an early surprise. And," he added to the grinning Paddy, "if you don't get on his tracks quick-feller I'll tan your hide until you look like a white boy."

But Little Paddy only grinned with dog-like devotion at his beloved hero.

It was easy this morning. We headed straight out east across the little plain, across the wee swamp, past the old hut, then straight on towards the opposite coast from the camp.

"You know," frowned Dick, "this Slinker is a shrewd old bird. We thought we'd combed every yard of the island, but didn't give a thought to that other little corner out there right behind the camp."

"That's because we're used to chasing him along the ridge, then up along the southern shore."

"Oh well, we've got him on toast now," declared Dick. He laughed. "And we know now there's not one little spot on all this island where he could hide and we wouldn't know where to look for him." And we strolled on, with quails whirring up from our feet, and the screech of gulls coming over from the sea.

We stepped on to a wide beach fringed by a few trees.

The tide was out, and sea-birds were fishing along a strip of coral-sand and mud. A quiet sea stretched away out to the Great Barrier Reef. We glanced along the beach, but caught no glimpse of a lonely brown figure. There were plenty of signs of him, though-tracks everywhere.

"Just think of it," said Dick disgustedly, "he enjoying himself here all yesterday while we were hunting everywhere but in the right place for him."

Little Paddy soon spotted where he had been fishing; there were the remains of his fire, with several fish-heads and crabs claws all charred from the cooking.

"He won't enjoy a feed like this tonight," declared Dick.

"You find him track now quick-feller, Man Friday."

But Little Paddy could find no fresh track, hunt he ever so eagerly, and with growing anxiety. There was *no* fresh track.

"There *must* be tracks," exclaimed Dick angrily. "He can't be far away."

But Paddy could find no tracks.

"He's up to his old tricks again," declared Dick. "Cut him track alonga water!" he ordered Little Paddy. "Try longa beach back towards camp first time. Quick-feller now!"

And Little Paddy hurried to the water's edge and we followed it along to where the island's northern shore led westerly, back towards camp. For Slinker, to deceive us, might have walked in the water in this direction. We must cut his tracks where he merged from the water.

But we did not, although we retraced our steps along this portion of the coastline, half-way back to camp.

"He wouldn't have come back any further," said Dick at last, "for Billy would have seen him. It was stupid of us to come back so far. He's diddled us again!" he added savagely.

I tried to look wise; Man Friday looked the picture of misery. For the life of me I couldn't imagine what the Jap had done to hoodwink us so completely.

"I know!" exclaimed Dick at last. "What fools we are! To let Billy see him, and to light that fire last night was only to fool us – and it did. He guessed we'd come looking for him here today. I bet last night, after he cooked his fish, he piled the wood on that fire, then walked back across the plain to his old possy on the ridge. That's where he is now, laughing at us while keeping a look-out for the *Nancy Bell* and the black cutter."

"Of course," I laughed, "that's what he's done – what goats we are."

"Pleased to hear you admit it," growled Dick, then seemed to hesitate. "Let us think first," he said slowly. "No, not the ridge first. He's such a slippery customer he might think that's just what we'd do. No, we'll walk along the coast to the south-eastern corner. He may be fishing there. If we don't find him there then we'll know he must be back at his old hide-out on the ridge somewhere."

We did so, carefully watching for tracks, stepping back to the plain every now and then to see if Billy had seen our man. He hadn't. It was a long, slow walk. But there were no tracks round the south-eastern corner. We tried all in among the little mounds there, but found no sign of him.

"Oh, well," said Dick disgustedly, "boil the billy. We'll have a feed, though we haven't earned it."

Little Paddy ate in silence, trying to say sympathetic things to Dick with his eyes. But Dick was too annoyed at the way the Jap had outwitted us to take notice. For my part, I'd come to the conclusion that this Jap was a particularly experienced man, and must have done this type of work often before. Why, I wondered, and in what countries? But there was no answer to that.

It was well after midday when Dick hurried us back along the southern shore, on over the old log, and away back to the mounds at the extreme end of the ridge.

"Now look about quick-feller," he snapped at Little Paddy as we climbed up into the mounds. "Find 'im track!"

We spread out and carefully searched the mounds, then on into the beginning of the hills. No sign. The sun was going down when we climbed up among the little hills. No sign. Sunset came.

"Beaten again!" groaned Dick. "Completely outwitted by a Jap!" And he kicked a bush in futile anger.

In silence we trudged round the base of the big Hill and back to camp. It was dark.

As Little Paddy went quietly to light the fire, Dick stood by the bush-shed a moment, staring out at the anchorage. The quiet water looked soft and lovely. Stars were bursting out overhead.

"I don't like it at all, Jack," said Dick quietly. "Cross-eyed Joe so long overdue, no sign of the black lugger, and this Jap so completely baffling us."

"I suppose it's all got some simple explanation," I ventured.

"Maybe – but I don't believe it. Anyway, there's nothing simple in the way that starving Jap has beaten us today. If there is, explain it."

But I could only shake my head. "Beats me," I muttered as the fire blazed up.

"I hate to admit that," growled Dick. "You and I and Billy and Little Paddy on this small island and yet one lonely Jap can trick us. And we kidded ourselves we were going to be bushmen. Light the lamp!" he called savagely. And Little Paddy hurried inside the camp to light the hurricane lamp.

I was gazing at the billy and the bright flames crackling under it, not knowing what to say, when the strange silence made us both turn towards camp.

Then Dick stepped forward. I followed. We stepped into camp. Little Paddy stood there, his hand still on the lighted lamp, his eyes sticking out like pickled onions.

Thrown untidily on the camp floor were three freshly emptied meat-tins. An emptied jam-tin. Some rinds from the last of our precious bacon. Some golden brown damper crusts.

With a catch at the breath I glanced towards the damper.

It was goner.

I didn't dare look at Dick.

View to the West over Mangrove Bay on Lizard Island.

24

LITTLE PADDY VANISHES

"HE'S pinched the damper," howled Dick. "He's wolfed our tucker! He's camped in my bunk! He's-he's-look – smoked our tobacco! Look at the butts! And here's a butt still smoking! Tracks!" he yelled at Paddy, who dived out of the tent as if the devil were at his heels.

We followed with the hurricane lamp. Little Paddy was instinctively on the tracks made only a few moments ago. Fresh and clear back to the beach along the anchorage front, leading round to the ridge.

"He waited there till we arrived home," sputtered Dick, "lying in my bunk smoking our tobacco, with his belly full of our good tucker. And now he's gone and taken the damper – and we don't know what else besides!"

That wonderful damper that Dick had cooked! This was worse than insult, this was tragedy. We walked on a little further. Dick was boiling.

"It's no use," growled Dick. "He's gone for the night."

And we turned silently back to camp.

Dick waved a hand. Automatically Little Paddy hurried to get the dish and flour-bag. Automatically Dick washed his hands, prepared flour in the dish, and began to make johnny-cakes, while Man Friday prepared the coals.

A glance at Dick's tragic face and I had to turn away as if miserably seeking consolation from the night. I dared not glance at the picture of abject misery that was Little Paddy, or I would have burst out laughing.

But it was no laughing matter, as Dick explained when, an hour later, we had relieved the very uneasy Billy.

"Another knock like this one, Jack, and we'll be in afix. He's got away with a fair amount of our tucker, and as you know we've none to spare. We'll have to start regular fishing very soon, which means we must leave him to his own devices. And that means he will then be handy when the *Nancy Bell* or the black lugger turns up to the anchorage."

"That's true," 1 remarked.

"'I'll tell you something more!" declared Dick. 'We're now a man short."

"How do you make that out?"

"He's added another possy to his list of hide-outs," resumed Dick savagely. "Our camp, that's all! We can never tell now when he'll make another raid. He's turned the tables completely, the cunning devil."

I was silent awhile, gazing out over the starlit sea so deceptively peaceful – the air so sweet, just the breath of a whispering breeze.

"How did he work his stunt today that we fell into the trap so easily, I wonder?"

"Simple," replied Dick disgustedly, "seeing the simpletons he has to deal with. He thought it out first. Then yesterday afternoon, late, he showed himself to Billy. To make doubly sure, he lit his cooking fire so we could see it from here at night. Then he walked straight across the plain and hid right behind our camp-the very last place on earth we would have expected him. When we walked out this morning, he walked in!"

"And made a jolly good day of it." .

"That's right, rub it in," snapped Dick. "After I'd cooked that damper, too."

"It was a bonzer damper. I'd like to have my teeth in a hunk of it now."

"Which you won't," snapped Dick in a more satisfied voice. "But just you imagine Slinker with his teeth in it at this very moment."

The picture did not appeal.

"Well, what's the programme now?"

"I'm going to give him a jolly good shake-up tomorrow; he won't venture near the camp for a few days at least, he's not a fool. And," Dick went on impressively, "we won't give him our timetable as to when we're starting out. He's watching from away down the ridge, staring up along here at Billy on the Hill just after breakfast. And silly me, walking away from Billy down the ridge towards him – and he knows Little Paddy is coming along the shore side, and you along the inland side."

"We certainly have shown him a thing or two," I mused. "He's shown us a thing or two," replied Dick disgustedly.

"Tomorrow he's going to wake up. Tomorrow Billy will be standing up here staring down the ridge as usual, but-by that time you and I and Little Paddy will be half-way along it!"

"Ah!" I chuckled. 'We'll be on top of him before he realizes we've started."

"That's it," replied Dick. "He'll be forced to break cover in a hurry. And, in the surprise, we might get back most of that tucker."

"That's a brain wave! Yes, we might get that tucker back – unless he buries it tonight."

"A very difficult job," replied Dick, "to bury it in the darkness so as to leave no trace for eyes like Little Paddy's."

"That's so."

"Better turn in," suggested Dick. "It's my watch, and we have to be on the move well before dawn."

We were. I was becoming a bit tired of the Jap; he and that wretched black lugger had completely upset our happy cruise. It was cold, with a heavy dew, and pitch dark as I felt my way cautiously along the base of the ridge. Every dim shape of a bush, every dull boulder seemed to be a crouching man – and could have been, too, for all I was to know. But I had to admire Little Paddy, he was away over the other side of the ridge walking along opposite me. He had accepted his job without a murmur, started out into the dark like a young Briton. Yet I knew he must be scared. For the aboriginals, especially the children, are afraid of travelling by night.

Dick, though, would have by far the worst walk. And, if there were any risk in this business, then he must face that risk alone. For the Jap would most likely now be up on one of the little hills, as near as he dared go to the big Hill, watching out over what he could command of the sea for sign of the black lugger, or of whatever it was he was watching for, And Dick would be up there, walking down, and up, and over the crown of those little hills. If he came face to face with that silent watcher – but the Jap must hear him coming first, no matter how quietly Dick tried to walk. I did not like to think of what might happen.

We knew just how far we had each to go to the last little hill; and, if dawn had not come then, to wait, and keep eyes and ears open. Yawning, I prowled on.

The ridge side suddenly was there – a moment before it had been darkness. I glanced out over the plain. There, too, night was mysteriously dissolving away, exposing a ghostly plain. Quickly came the steel-grey of dawn, and I breathed thankfully. The east grew pink, bringing grass on the plain, while the ridge side, reflecting dawn, grew rapidly into tiny hills with rocks and trees. A bird twittered sleepily, another answered grumpily. The Great Barrier Reef burst into fire and our tiny spot of world was beautiful. High up, the ridge crest now seemed to ripple into a thin line of grass afire- the reflection of that titanic fire blazing up out of the great Reef near by.

I was almost opposite our meeting place. Then the plain grew hazy, a cold breath crept over me. The plain had misted over, the base of the ridge grew hazy. I crept cautiously on through a wraith-like veil.

We had not allowed for the lifting of the mists. Suddenly, they slipped up overhead, and all was daylight. 1 glanced up and stood stock still.

There, with his back to me, crouched on top of the tiny hill now bathed in rosy gold from the rising sun, was the Jap, staring out over the anchorage.

I glanced back, and there was Dick, just appearing on the crown of the next hill. He and the Jap saw one another at the same instant.

The Jap leapt up, staring. They stood a moment, silhouetted like bronze statues in the dawn. Then the Jap vanished as Dick yelled and ran towards him. I ran, and Little Paddy would be running, too. Up the little hill, jumping the boulders, pushing through the bushes. Panting, we met at the top.

"Quick!" yelled Dick. "He went that way! After him!" Like greyhounds hot on the scent of a 'roo we leapt high to catch sight of him above the bushes as he vanished down the gully.

Little Paddy was right at his tail, for the sound of his running and the broken bushes were clear signs to Paddy's eyes and ears. Then he vanished. We learnt afterwards that he had simply lain behind a bush and let us run by. Then he had sneaked away.

But he had led us on to his old hide-out, and the sight of empty meat-tins halted Dick.

"Look about!" he called to Little Paddy. "Find him tucker belonga him. We've flushed him, anyway," he laughed. "Our camp is safe for today. He can only clear out along the shoreline, on his old tracks. We'll follow him directly. If we can only find that tucker he raided from us we'll put him right back where he started from."

But we could not find his plant, though Little Paddy searched until it seemed his eyes must roll from his head.

Obviously the Jap could not have buried it without detection in the hard earth of the mounds or rocks of the hills, nor was it hidden among the ridges. And if it were buried somewhere in the sand or rubble of the shoreline Man Friday would certainly have detected some sign. My idea was that the Jap had hidden the tinned stuff under a rock, below low-tide level, where he could leave no trace.

I suggested this idea to Dick. He grunted. But when it was obvious that we might search the coastline for days, he gave it up.

"I've got another idea," he said. "Tonight you keep a look-out alone. After dark I'll sneak down here and hide near his hide-out. He must have hidden the tucker near here somewhere. I'll watch him if I can, and see where he digs or fishes it up from,"

"And what now?"

"We'll make sure he's gone back along the shoreline. If he has, we'll keep him moving all day, anyway."

We did. And by mid-afternoon we were playing hide-and-seek among the small mounds in the south-east corner. He circled round and round them, with Little Paddy like a fox terrier on his tracks. I wondered why he did not stand and challenge us, then remembered it must be because he had been left behind to do a particular job for the black lugger. He doubled away along the shoreline, but Little Paddy soon picked. up his tracks and we quickly followed to where he had jumped up the bank and confused his tracks in the grass.

"He's slowed us down again," said Dick. "He may be hiding near by, or he may have doubled back behind us and be running back along the beach."

"We've given him plenty of hurry up for today," I suggested. "How about knocking off? It's getting late."

"Yes," agreed Dick, "and we didn't get much sleep last night. How about if you cut across to the camp and knock up some johnnies? Little Paddy and I will Hush him from cover just once more, then we'll knock off."

"Right-oh," I agreed, and set off across the plain. I was tired of chasing this wretchedly elusive Jap.

Back at camp just at sundown I made up the fire and set about preparations for cooking johnnies on the coals. A wretch of a job – cooking. When finally I flipped the johnnies off the coals, charcoal was plentifully embedded in them. However, Dick and I both had good teeth, while Billy and Little Paddy could chew bone. The billy was boiled and tea all ready well after dark. But Dick and Little Paddy had not turned up. Surprised, I lit a cigarette, and stared out into the deepening night.

Half an hour passed before I heard Dick's approaching footsteps. As he strode into the firelight he glanced swiftly round.

"Where's Little Paddy?" he asked.

"I dunno. Isn't he with you?"

"No."

"Well, he's not here. I haven't seen him since I left you."

"That Jap has got him!" said Dick tragically.

25

THE MIDNIGHT VIGIL

WE stared at one another. Dick's face looked drawn in the firelight.

"Nonsense!" I murmured.

"It's not," replied Dick. "It's fact."

He sat down, and began to roll a cigarette.

"After you left us for camp I didn't see him again," he said soberly. "I took no notice for a while, because I knew he would appear when he picked up the tracks. So I continued searching on my own. When it grew late I looked round for him, then cooeed. No answer. I thought then he might have popped up from somewhere earlier, noticed you walking across the plain, and thought we'd both knocked off. So he must have followed on. But I couldn't understand his knocking off without me, so I kept searching and shouting. At last I decided he *must* have followed you."

Dick stared at the fire. His little blackboy friend was dear to his heart.

"He may have fallen down a gully," I suggested.

"Knocked himself out."

"Impossible," replied Dick abruptly. "That could only happen on the ridge. Where we were a baby could fall over and not hurt itself."

For the life of me I could make no other suggestion. "But why should the Jap grab him?" I asked.

"What would *you* do," demanded Dick, "if you were hounded day after day by a little aboiginal with a scent keen as a bloodhound?"

I remained silent. I knew I would have clouted the little wretch if I'd got the chance.

"If he hurts him--" exclaimed Dick furiously. "Oh, why didn't we bring a gun!"

"He wouldn't dare hurt him," 1 protested. "He'd be too scared of the police."

"The police!" snorted Dick. "Don't be silly. How much water is between us and the nearest police! And when the black lugger comes then lugger and Japs will vanish."

The Jap could do what he liked with Little Paddy. He could throttle him and throw him into the sea for the tide to take away for sharks' feed. Little Paddy could vanish without a trace. And not a soul would ever be able to prove anything.

Tragedy stalked our happy cruise.

"I'm going to get Billy down from the Look-out," exclaimed Dick. 'We'll search the island all night!"

As he jumped up I suggested, "Better have a feed first. We'll need it."

He sat down again. "Yes," he answered morosely. "I suppose so. If he's going to harm Man Friday he's done it by now."

Dick ate unheedingly, staring at the fire. Suddenly he smiled across at me.

"What fools we are!" he cried gladly. "The ruined hut! The one place on all the island we've never thought of searching. He'll hide Little Paddy in the ruined hut if he hasn't killed him."

"By Jove!" I said hopefully. "That sounds likely."

"Yes," replied Dick eagerly. "He'll manhandle Paddy across the plain then tie him up in the hut – and it's in the hut floor that his remaining tucker might be buried. Then he'll walk across the grass and climb the ridge, for he must keep that look-out for his lugger. When he returns to the hut before daylight, you'll be waiting in the hut for him."

"What!" I exclaimed.

"Yes," said Dick, nodding. "You'll be waiting for him. You'll have Little Paddy with you so you'll be all right."

Privately I did not feel so "all right", but Dick, as usual, was working everything out to his own satisfaction.

"He may not return to the hut," he resumed. "By Caesar, I don't believe he will, the cunning hound! But if he doesn't then you'll be able to liberate Little Paddy. The Jap may stay somewhere along the ridge and keep his look-out, he'll let us see him. He'll think he's got Little Paddy safe and sound. He knows that Billy is still a cripple and that, whether or no, one of us must keep a look-out up on the Hill. That will leave only two of us to chase him about without the blackboy to track him. And the cunning devil knows it really means only one of us, for now we're forced to keep a sharp eye on our camp. He can stay on the ridge and do what he likes – all except signalling from the Look-out. If he's thought it out that way," added Dick hopefully, "then he'll see there's no need to hurt Little Paddy."

"I believe you've solved the problem," I agreed. "That plan should be plain as daylight to the Jap – Little Paddy trussed up like a fowl in the old hut, and the Jap's tucker buried there. It's a hide-out he thinks we'll never guess. I believe you're right, Dick. Don't worry about Little Paddy, he'll be quite all right."

Dick stood up with almost his usual cheerful grin. "Pick a good waddy," he warned, "a heavy one. Then sneak down to the hut. If he's there then hit him a clout over the head. And when you hit him, think of Little Paddy. If he's not there when you arrive then wait inside for him. You'll surprise him-with a thump on the head."

Dick was rooting amongst the firewood. He picked out a hefty waddy, felt its weight and swung it round. I saw he imagined he was bringing it down on the head of a certain Jap.

"What will you do?" I asked. "Mind camp?"

"Mind camp my eye!" he exclaimed. "Do you think I could sit here doing nothing while Man Friday is away out there somewhere! I'll climb the Hill to Billy and he can come down here and get his tucker and mind camp. We won't be able to keep watch tonight. At the same time the Jap will never think we've abandoned the Look-out for the time being. I'll just carry on down the ridge and try to find him there, just in case he's not at the hut."

"He'll come there all right," I replied confidently. But I did not feel too sure, for the Jap had been one move ahead of us too often.

"Ready?" asked Dick.

"Right," I replied, and grasped the waddy.

"Mind!" warned Dick. "This Slinker is a slippery customer. When you hit him, don't miss, or you'll feel his knife between your ribs."

"I won't miss," I promised.

"Right. Then we're on our way. And Jack –"

"Yes."

"Don't forget Man Friday."

"I won't forget. I'll do my best."

Dick nodded and turned towards the Hill while I walked out into the night, towards the plain.'

It was a cool dark night, though the sky was brilliant with stars. As the grass began rustling underfoot I trod more cautiously, staring through the night at the ghostly grasses of the plain and the dim outline of gnarled pandanus palms. A vague loneliness chilled everything. I wished I was back by the cheerful camp-fire. Night voices now whispered I was setting out after an elusively dangerous man, a shadow by day, let alone by night.

An experienced, full grown man, strong and wiry, sure to be familiar with ju-jitsu, and armed with at least a knife as well. A hunted man, all alone. A hungry man, entrusted with some important job. And we four had been harrying him day and night. Sleepless, hungry days and nights some of them. He must be feeling pretty savagely towards us by now. Desperate, too. He had proved that by grabbing Little Paddy.

I shivered, feeling by no means sure what he might have done to Man Friday. I knew the Japs thought an aboriginal life was nothing-probably he had strangled the boy and thrown him into the sea. And now here was I, all alone, setting out to get him. I could imagine his fiendish delight if he "got" me instead, his enemies delivering themselves into his hands, one by one. And there was no help either here on the island, or far away. A violent whirring underfoot made me jump with a smothered cry.

I stood trembling, with thumping heart. It was only a wretched quail. I must have stood on the dashed thing in the grass.

Softly but heatedly I cursed the Jap. He had grown into a dangerous enemy by now, very different to "old Slinker".

The ruined hut loomed up squat and dark. I knelt down so as to silhouette it as much as possible. The walls stood out much plainer now, so I peered along its front where the open doorway was. Among the shadows was no moving shadow. A deathly silence layover all.

I crept forward, listening, drawing nearer and nearer to the hut, darkly plain now. The sea seemed to be murmuring a warning close by. I crawled along, lifting hands and knees well above the grass, lowering them slowly, softly. I halted in the black shadows of the hut.

Not a sound – yes! – a mournful sigh – silence.

Cursing that shivery sigh from the long, drooping pandanus leaves at every ghostly breath of a breeze, I listened again. But no other sound issued from the night, nor from within the hut. I crawled to the open doorway, and listened. Not one faintest whisper.

Within that silence I *must* have heard his stifled breath.

They had not come.

With intense relief I crawled into the hut, peered round, then looked up. Enclosed thus within dark, roofless walls, the sky was a blaze of stars. Plain were the stones in the walls, the earthen floor smelling of mildew and dust.

I took up a position near the broken doorway, where I judged I could glide behind a man should he enter the hut – strove to imagine the position of the Jap as he would push Little Paddy in before him.

Then, with hand on waddy, I waited, encompassed in silence.

One faint sound – a pump? My heart.

Time passed, and it was borne in upon me that I did not wait alone. For all this little world was listening, listening, listening. I knew there was only me and the ruined walls and God's stars above, the plain around and the faintly sighing pandanus palms, the ridge and my distant comrades, and, somewhere, the Jap and Little Paddy, with the murmurous sea embracing us.

I shivered and glanced round. The dim walls, splashed with starlight, held some tiny movement, like the grass outside vaguely rippling under some tremulous breath of air.

Time dreamed on, and imperceptibly there seemed to be two silences-the outer silence of the night, arrested by the still, the breathing silence within these walls. Perhaps because I was all keyed up for soft footsteps outside my own' breathing may have made me feel that the silence within these walls was really *breathing*! There *was* life here – a tremulous flickering of life in the walls. I glanced up and sighed with relief; it was only a drifting cloud, like a wraith of mist, floating below' the stars. Its silent passing dimmed the star-beams and played ghostly shadow-tricks on the walls.

So far above – oceans of worlds above, yet those effects touched the walls down here. Just as those buried furrows under the grassy plain betrayed an old garden. All vanishes – all is with us.

Midnight brought thoughts merging into breathless form –the woman crouching behind the barred door, her rifle through the loophole, a star-beam on her cold, desperate face; the wounded Chinaman crouching beside the baby, whimpering in its corner, smiling through pain as his lips moved in noiseless whispers to quieten the child; the hut listening for stealthy footsteps. I was staring, listening, listening until it hurt – that lingering, mournful sigh!

With a shudder I pulled myself together. This would never do. There was only the open doorway, the shadowy walls, the stars above, the night outside – the moaning of the pandanus leaves.

Presently, my misty thoughts began to re-form-the presence of the woman, the horror, the baby, the thirst, the stifled gasps of the wounded Chinaman. This very floor was stained with blood. The woman, with heart in her throat as she listened to "outside", and knelt over the Chinaman and cut and pulled and cut the tough flesh, dragging the barbed spearheads from his body. He had not whimpered, had smiled up at "Missy".

This very silence had forced her make her choice – to fight it out, though even if she won she must perish of thirst, or run the gauntlet and put to sea in an iron tank.

A terrible choice; I felt it imbedded in these sun-baked walls, oozing up from this floor, breathing in this silence.

Again I pulled myself together and determinedly thought of other things, of Dick and Cross-eyed Joe, and the *Nancy Bell,* and the black lugger. Another silent hour dragged by. Strange that I had not thought of Mrs Watson and the baby and the Chinaman when I left Dick to keep my vigil in the hut! The spirit-presence of these humans was with me just as those long-dead furrows remained, though buried deep under the smothering grass. This hut that had absorbed such bitter tragedy, this hut in which silence was alive – my heart beat like a sledge-hammer – what was that? Yes, again! A footstep – outside!

I listened, clutching the club. Yes, again –a footstep– faint swish of grass – a soft, barefoot step.

Someone –the Jap– he was coming from outside. I crouched, gripping the waddy. Starlight in the doorway was blotted out by a big black shadow, then – "Crack!" With a surprised grunt a body hurtled into the hut and fell with thump and whouff!

On trembling legs I crouched and stared at the doorway, while the black body on the floor grunted and groaned. Another shadow had leapt back into the night.

I stood there trembling. That groaning body on the floor – it was far too big for Little Paddy.

With shaky hand I struck a match. It was Big Paddy.

26

THE MYSTERY DEEPENS

I GASPED, and shook burnt fingers, then lit another match. It was Big Paddy all right, six feet of groaning aboriginal clad in a soiled lava-lava. He was grunting on his knees, hand to head, his corrugated visage screwed into dismay as he glared round. He recognized me as the match burnt out.

"Jacky!" he growled. "Some-feller man been hit 'im me longa head. What name?" he demanded.

But I did not know why Slinker had hit him on the head.

"What name?" he demanded again. "That-feller man hit 'im me two-feller time!"

"Two times?" I questioned.

"Ou ai. Longa beach he hit 'im me, too! What name that feller?"

"That-feller man Jap man," I replied.

"No more!" growled Big Paddy unbelievingly. "Jap man he long-feller away, longa black lugger."

"One-feller Jap man he stay behind. He hide longa island," I explained.

Big Paddy frowned, it was too much for him, as indeed it was now for me.

"Where Cross-eyed Joe?" I asked. "Where cutter?"

"Him no more here?" inquired Big Paddy.

"No more. No come back."

He frowned painfully, his shaggy eyes and squat nose and lips all screwed up.

"Why he no come back?" he growled.

"We no can tell," I replied.

Paddy obviously expected the *Nancy Bell* to be here.

He tried hard to think, which apparently hurt him. "Maybe he long way away," he suggested at last. "Maybe he pright longa black lugger."

"H'm," I murmured

"Where Dicky?" he demanded abruptly. "Where Little Paddy? Where Billy?"

Where Little Paddy? Alas, I did not know. I longed for Dick to appear.

"Dick look all about longa Jap man," I answered evasively. "He want us wait here, keep look-out longa daylight."

Because I needed time to think, and because the matches would not last, I went outside the hut and, keeping a sharp look-out, scraped round for tinder and put a match to it. Only when the flames were throwing cheerful light into the darkness did I draw a breath of relief. The Jap would not return now he knew two of us were here. It seemed Dick had guessed correctly; the Jap was coming to the hut all right, but what about Little Paddy? What had he done with him? Had he been coming to the hut when he ran across Big Paddy? Had he hit Little Paddy on the head before he tried to do the same to Big Paddy? What was the meaning of everything?

A hundred thoughts chased themselves through my mind as I built up the fire, wondering what to do. I could not tell this surly primitive that his little son had vanished. Dick must do it.

Big Paddy came striding out into the firelight, glaring like an animal. Thank goodness he had recovered from that crack, but blood was welling down one cheek. With his rugged black face and shaggy eyes and teeth bared in an animal-like snarl he looked pretty ghastly. I suppose he had a headache.

We wheeled round as a flame shot up quickly, distantly illuminating the camp and the black form of Billy carrying armfuls of dry grass to feed the flame.

Billy was signalling Dick that something had happened.

It would be just what Dick would think of, that if anything happened then Billy was to light a signal fire. And Billy had seen our fire.

"Dick come back soon," I reassured Big Paddy. He grunted, lapsing into surly silence. The telephathic instincts of the aboriginal warned him I was holding something back, something concerning him.

I rolled a cigarette, pleased indeed at Billy's signal fire.

Even if Dick were on the other side of the ridge he must see the reflection, and would answer.

Dawn was breaking, and we were on the point of returning to camp when we saw Dick striding rapidly over the grass. In the dawning light I could see the amazement on his face as he came towards us. He strode up, cast one swift glance round, then looked inquiringly at me. I shook my head, and saw his glum disappointment. His eyes then were all for Big Paddy, Big Paddy's for his.

"What name?" demanded Dick.

Big Paddy answered in a torrent of aboriginal, Dick broke in now and again and thus Big Paddy told his story; He was silent a moment then quietly asked a question. I knew he was saying, "Where is Little Paddy?"

Dick's unhappy expression gave the answer.

Big Paddy's face hardened; he glowered at the ground.

"What's it all about?" I asked at last.

Dick turned to me in relief.

"When Cross-eyed Joe sailed from here he doubled in among the Howick group, and anchored one night to give the black lugger the slip. Before dawn he put Big Paddy ashore telling him to fish until he returned, promising him he'd be back that sundown. Paddy climbed the peak after Joe had sailed, and saw the black lugger anchored behind Coquette Island. Coquette is about four miles across the channel, only a flat mangrove island, and from the peak on Number One Howick you can see over and round it. The *Nancy Bell* was heading north. The black lugger followed two hours later. Joe never returned for Big Paddy. But several days later the black lugger did, sent a boat ashore and told Paddy that Cross-eyed Joe had asked them to pick him up, that all hands were returning to Lizard Island. Paddy was only too glad of company and did not suspect a trap until they were sailing north. They treated Paddy well, then by degrees tried to get out of him all he knew about what Cross-eyed Joe was doing. Paddy acted dumb, didn't savvy anything. For a week they played hide-and-seek, the black lugger and the *Nancy Bell*. It dawned on Big Paddy that the Jap skipper and crew were 'plenty mad' against Cross-eyed Joe and Alor San and Ah Matt for something. He believed the Japs would cut their throats if they could catch them. Finally they lost all trace of the *Nancy Bell*. They sailed straight back then, and hid behind one of those little islets away out there. They've been there these last few days, with a man with a glass perched up on the islet day and night, keeping watch towards the Look-out. No doubt he's been awaiting a signal from Slinker. Big Paddy waited his chance and quietly slipped away in a dinghy with the tide by night. It's been perfect weather for a dinghy, but he had a long pull to get here. The tide turned against him near shore, and as he couldn't make the anchorage he was carried down past the camp to just opposite the old hut. He beached, stepped out and was about to drag the dinghy above high water mark when something hit him on the head. He fell, but jumped up again and ran. His head was 'singing' and he couldn't run fast. He ran straight towards the old hut, but he doesn't know why. Then he was cracked on the head again and woke up with you striking a match 'on his face'."

"H'm." I grinned. "So that's the story. Poor Paddy's face would strike a match all right! If you hit it with a lump of iron it would throw out sparks."

"I'll bet he saw more than sparks last night," replied Dick grimly. "He's got two nasty cuts on his head."

"They'll only give him a headache, that head is as solid as a mast."

"I know," replied Dick. "I'm glad it wasn't *your* head." So was I.

"I don't know what to do," mused Dick. "This Jap holds the trump card."

"We'll soon lay him by the heels now that Big Paddy is here."

"We daren't try," replied Dick miserably, "for he's got Little Paddy – or I hope he has."

This brought us back to earth. Judging by the Jap's attack on Big Paddy, Little Paddy probably was food for the fishes by now.

"The Japs will be mad at Big Paddy getting away with the dinghy," I suggested.

"The dinghy!" exclaimed Dick. "What fools we are talking here and doing nothing! Quick! Big Paddy! Where you leave him that-feller dinghy? Pick 'im up Jap track there longa dinghy, maybe Little Paddy track, too."

Like a shot Big Paddy was on his feet and we hurried down to the beach fronting the hut.

But the dinghy was gone. And there were no tracks – it was a spring tide, the water coming right up to the grass fringing the shoreline, obliterating all tracks.

"Not a sign," said Dick disappointedly. "We don't know whether the dinghy drifted away, whether. the Jap took it, or if the Jap had Little Paddy with him. We know nothing – except that Little Paddy has gone."

The Jap had struck him when he came ashore.

27

MAN FRIDAY AND THE JAP VANISH

BACK at camp, we sat down to a quiet breakfast. When Big Paddy and Billy met they had carried on an animated conversation, then lapsed into a sullen silence. After breakfast Big Paddy picked up a fish-spear, frowning at the four iron prongs. Grimly, with strong black fingers he began straightening out the dents in each prong. Then he poked them into the coals, staring down as the iron slowly took on a dull red glow. He would make those prongs strong and straight, and sharp.

If Big Paddy came within spear-throw of the Jap there would be bloodshed. Billy, too, commenced to straighten out the prongs of his spear. Just as Dick and I had not brought a gun, neither had the two aboriginals brought either hunting- or war-spears. We never dreamt we would need gun or spear on this cruise. The fish-spear has a very short range compared to the hunting-spear. But at fairly close quarters, if the four long iron prongs penetrate a soft portion of a man's body they make a nasty and very probably poisonous wound.

We left the two men at their job and climbed to the Look-out. The sea was a lake glistening under sunlight, not one ripple, not one sign of a drifting dinghy.

"He's probably pushed it out past low-tide level, then sunk it," said Dick to my unuttered question. "They'll easily raise it when the black lugger returns. I do wish we could find Little Paddy," he Sighed.

"What are you going to do?"

"We'll comb the island, that's all we *can* do. Big Paddy will never let up until he finds Man Friday – and the Jap, And then there'll be trouble."

"Big Paddy will spear him."

"Yes. I don't think I can stop him now, either he or Billy."

"What if the Jap has a gun?"

"Then so much the worse – for us."

"Cross-eyed Joe must have been hard pressed when he left Big Paddy on Howick Island and did not return for him."

"Yes," answered Dick absent-mindedly.

"These wretched Japs seem determined to find our fishing grounds," I remarked.

"Yes." His reply sounded half-hearted.

"I suppose both the *Nancy Bell* and the black lugger are away out there in hiding, waiting for one or the other to make the island."

"Yes," agreed Dick, "and both may know the other is waiting. But there's no signal yet from Cross-eyed Joe. I can see the islet through the glasses today almost as if I were standing on it."

"How long are they going to play at this hide-and-seek?"

"Goodness knows. What worries me now is Little Paddy."

And Dick stood up. "Come along and we'll start searching. Billy must come up here and keep a look-out as usual. You and I and Big Paddy will comb out every hide-out in the island. And I wouldn't like to be in that Jap's shoes when we lay him by the heels."

"Neither would I," I thought, remembering the look on Big Paddy's face when he was straightening out those spear prongs.

With Billy keeping a sharp look-out from the Hill, we searched that island as never before, Big Paddy with fish-spear in hand grimly seeking for tracks. We searched all along the ridge and anchorage shoreline first, combing out the Jap's favourite haunts. But not a trace of him did we find. Our worries increased, for we had been certain that if he had Little Paddy with him he could not have avoided leaving tracks. Little Paddy would leave a hundred signs for us to follow. But there was not one fresh track-not one single broken bush, nor overturned stone, nor dragging foot in beach or mud or shingle, not a shred of cloth Man Friday would have torn from his trousers – nothing. Not only had we hoped for tracks, but for signs for us to read a "sign talk" of innocently placed sticks pointing the way, a carelessly broken bush hanging at a certain angle, two or three pebbles that when "read" would have a distinct meaning, two or three 'stubs of the big toe in sand or mud or soft earth. For aboriginals can leave signs on the earth as directions for others to follow, and although we believed Little Paddy knew nothing of Big Paddy's arrival still he would have thought that we would quickly get Billy on to his tracks. We had confidently believed he would have left plenty of signs, no matter what precautions that Jap might take. But there was not one.

Leaving the better cover of the ridge we began anxiously to comb the southern shoreline. Still not a sign.

Not pausing to eat, we searched throughout the day, right to sundown. Not only Little Paddy but the Jap himself had vanished. And without a trace.

In unhappy silence we trudged across the plain in the dark. I now really believed Man Friday had gone for ever. His quaint little face, his impish grin, his skinny figure, his adoring eyes, all for Dick, seemed again and again to rise before us out of the plain. Several times I turned round, half expecting to see him following behind us as he so often had followed Dick. I could guess what Dick was feeling, for Man Friday had followed in his footsteps since a piccaninny. As for Big Paddy – well, Big Paddy had not even grunted for hours past.

We sat down to a silent meal. Then I climbed the Hill to relieve Billy, leaving Dick and Big Paddy alone.

That peaceful, starry night was far and away the loneliest and most miserable I had spent on the island. Here on top of the Hill there was just the breath of a whispering breeze. The breezes must have played here as long as the stars had shone. They seemed almost living things, these wraiths of breezes, kissing the grasses on the hill top, playing with the star-beams that gleamed on rock and shrub. Tonight this breeze caressed my cheek, softly lingered in my ear, then sighed away. Unnoticed, presently it came again, a persistent flicker of some breath from the skies.

If the stars had seen things for ever, so had the breezes.

And they had touched things and heard things. They must have seen, must have touched the first strange, animal-like man to climb these shores. Perhaps he boated over on a log from the mainland – a very, very venturesome mariner. Captain Cook had been venturesome in these very waters, but how many thousands of years after that first ape-like mariner had stepped upon these shores! He must have climbed this Hill and in awe gazed out over this vast, lonely sea. And the breeze must have kissed and comforted him, as it was whispering to me now. It had heard his guttural sounds of surprise. I wondered if he had come with a mate, or if he came alone. He may have stayed here, lived and died within his island kingdom. The breeze never dies; it vanishes, but comes again. If only the breeze had a memory and could talk, what could it whisper-sounds of many men who had sat just where I was sitting, strange men throughout the ages. Yet today anyone could think this uninhabited isle one of the loneliest in the sea.

It was alive with memories. Old-time aboriginals had gazed from this Look-out. Perhaps even some wandering voyager of fair-skinned, mysterious people that crop up in ghost-like legend every now and then among coloured people of the South Pacific-people who built cities that vanished under the sea; or those others who made the stone urns and pots occasionally dug up from deep down under New Guinea soils; or the supermen of the Torres Strait Islanders, those mysterious legend-gods like Abob and Kos, and others who vanished after building the miles of fish-trap mazes that surround the shores of Eroob, three hundred or so miles to the north. Perhaps early Portuguese and Spanish craft crept along these waters; certainly then an officer would come ashore here and gaze from this very Look-out to seek a way of escape from the terrifying reefs, just as Captain James Cook did long afterwards. The breeze must have whispered to him as his troubled eyes at last found, in the differently tinted waters, the channel that was to lead the Endeavour to safety. MacGillivray of H.M.S. Rattlesnake had also gazed from here. I wondered what other famous men – the breeze tried hard to tell me, but I could not understand. Mrs Watson had also gazed from here. Here she had sat with her baby, and waved and watched her husband's little vessel slowly vanish into the north. Here she had sat gazing nor'-west, longing for his return.

I pulled myself together, stared down the blackness of the ridge for some sign of the Jap, then turned and gazed nor-west for a pinpoint of light that would mark a signal from Cross-eyed Joe.

What *could* be keeping the *Nancy Bell*?

The remnants of Mrs Watson's home on Lizard Island.

26

THE BIG SURPRISE

THROUGHOUT that lonely night Dick did not come to relieve me. I guessed he and Big Paddy and Billy had trudged away in some forlorn hope of laying the Jap by the heels. Though he appeared to have utterly vanished from the island, Dick would not be able to remain inactive.

Dawn broke coldly to the complaining twittering of little birds as they shook the dewdrops from moist feathers. From out there somewhere came the harsh cry of a sea-gull. The mists rolled up, unwillingly absorbed into the blue of space. And all around lay the sea.

One glance to the nor-west, then I turned and searched the island through the glasses. No sign of the Jap – or of Little Paddy.

With heavy heart I turned round and glanced down at the camp. It was quiet – no breakfast fire.

I glanced out across plain and shoreline towards the hut, feeling that Dick might have laid a forlorn ambush there. Billy stepped out of the hut, and almost at the same time Dick rose from some bushes about three hundred yards further east. Then Big Paddy appeared up out of the grass, away behind the hut. The Jap had not walked into the ambush.

Dick waved an arm and all three commenced walking back towards the camp. Carefully, then, I trained my glasses to the nor-west and north. But on the open sea there was no sign of the *Nancy Bell.* Nor was there any sign of a signal on the few little islets.

When breakfast was ready down below Dick stood out and waved to me. He must be feeling pretty desperate to call the look-out man down from the Hill.

When I reached him he glanced at me. I shook my head.

His worried face was matched by Big Paddy's and Billy's which bore brooding frowns.

"Better have breakfast," suggested Dick.

We had just finished a silent meal when we sat up as if at a rifle shot.

Across the quiet water had come the distant sound of rowlocks. We listened – it came again. We jumped up and hurried out from the camp.

Along the anchorage shoreline was coming a dinghy, a Jap leisurely at the oars, a little black monkey crouched in the stern.

"Slinker!" cried Dick. "And he's bringing Man Friday home!"

As we stepped down towards the water I noticed Big Paddy and Billy each dragging a spear across the beach with their toes. Dick didn't notice, his face all smiles as he gazed at the oncoming dinghy.

It came to just out of spear-throw. The Jap rested on his oars and turned towards us. It was Slinker all right, with his unblinking eyes, little black moustache and expressionless face. Man Friday, crouching in the stern, seemed all eyes. We stared at them, they stared at us.

"Well!" called Dick at last. "Come ashore."

"By an' by, maybe," answered the Jap. 'We make agreement first time."

"What agreement?" questioned Dick.

"Mind own business," came back the answer. "Me mind business, too. You no interfere, me no interfere. You give me back food you steal belong me. I give you little nigger boy. Mind own business."

"You land that nigger," called out Dick angrily, "and be smart about it, or I'll have the police on you quick and lively."

"No more!" shrugged the [ap.

The simple reply expressed everything. In that lonely place, and under these circumstances, to try and frighten the Jap with mention of far distant police was ridiculous.

And the Jap knew it.

Dick glared at him awhile, It was a queer situation. Then he tried again.

"You stole that little nigger boy," he called. "Then you tried to murder his father. You hit him on the head."

"Nigger boy chase me," answered the Jap calmly. "You all chase me – you no right. Me right stay here till my captain pick me up. You steal my food. That nigger man steal dinghy belong my captain. What police say that way?"

"They'll say you deserve five years' jail," called back Dick. "And I'll see that you get it!"

"Police talk fool talk," replied the Jap coldly.

Dick sat down and commenced rolling a cigarette, playing for time.

'We'll see about that!" he answered threateningly, and casually struck a match.

With the tide, the dinghy was imperceptibly drawing closer. Out of the corner of my eye I saw Big Paddy's big toe stealthily gripping his spear haft. At any second now he would whip it up to his hand and leap out into the water, within spear-throw, before the startled Jap could pull away. Even as I breathed apprehensively, the Jap quietly bent to the oars, and the dinghy was shooting further out. It came to rest again.

"A shrewd old bird is Slinker," said Dick disgustedly. "Perhaps it's just as well, Dick," I replied. "After all, he doesn't appear to have hurt Little

Paddy – and we don't want tragedy now."

"But he's got us fried to a frazzle," frowned Dick. "He's beaten us all along the. line. He's got us beaten now."

"Yes, I know. But, after all, we can get Little Paddy back, so no harm really has been done. But a dead or dying Jap on bur hands would take a lot of explaining away."

Without turning his head, Dick said softly, "Call out Little Paddy, tell 'im jump overboard quick-feller."

Instantly Big Paddy called out in aboriginal, but there was no movement from Little Paddy; he just stayed crouched there, only his head and big eyes visible. Pathetic eyes they were. Then he called back in aboriginal.

"Little Paddy tell 'im me Jap man tie him foot belonga him longa dinghy," growled Big Paddy.

"Ah," puffed Dick. "Old Slinker is a wise old bird."

I lit a cigarette and squatted down; it was more comfortable than standing. The morning was warming up nicely.

"Ask him Little Paddy which way Jap hide him yesterday," said Dick. "Ask him whether Jap good-feller man or bad-feller belonga him."

Big Paddy bawled out. A shrill torrent answered.

It appeared that yesterday they had dodged us simply by remaining in the dinghy behind a little rocky islet just off shore, No. wonder we had found no trace of Jap or boy. The Jap had dumped him in the dinghy the night before then rowed around to the rock. He'd not given him a thing to eat. The last bite he had was his lunch with us two days ago. I had detected something of the sort from the wail in Little Paddy's voice. He added that now he was "plenty-feller hungry-feller".

"I suppose so." Dick grinned. "Tell him," he said to Big Paddy, "that we're nearly out of tucker, haven't got enough for ourselves, that he'll eat too much if he comes ashore. In fact, that I think he'd better stay with the Jap."

Big Paddy's questioning glare spread into that huge, familiar old grin that we'd missed so much. With gusto he roared Dick's message. There came one agonized wail in reply. I bent my head so as not to see that imploring little black face trying so hard to crane up out of the dinghy.

But the Jap thought we had dallied enough.

"What you say?" he called. "You agree?"

"We say you can go to blazes," Dick shouted back. "Arright," answered the Jap calmly. "Then nigger boy come, too!"

And he bent to the oars and with strong, steady strokes began pulling out to sea. A pitiful wail burst from Man Friday.

"Him say," grumbled Big Paddy, "[ap' man leave 'im this-feller islan', go find lugger belonga him. Him say goodbye belonga Dicky."

We stood up, staring at the dinghy forging out to sea propelled by long, steady strokes. Dick's face was a study. At last he shouted and waved his arm to the Jap to return. The Jap hesitated, then, as if unwilling, turned round and began pulling slowly back. When within earshot he rested on his oars and called, "What you want?"

"You land little nigger boy."

"No more." The Jap shook his head. "Maybe you agree, yes!" he added.

"You land that boy," called Dick in one last attempt, "or it will be the worse for you and all aboard your ship."

The Jap pulled the dinghy round, and bent to the oars. "No come back this time," he called, and began to pull away.

"Where you go?" shouted Dick.

"Find lugger," came back the answer. "Maybe find him, maybe not. Only enough tucker, no more for nigger boy. No good me stay here any more, you no let me." And he pulled strongly at the oars.

We could not do a thing, except "agree", or let Little Paddy go, which I knew Dick would never do. We had no dinghy; the Jap was master of the situation. He almost certainly would know where to pick up the black lugger, if the weather held good. He could throw Little Paddy overboard and not a soul could ever prove it. Besides which, he could disappear with ease.

"All right," shouted Dick, and waved his arm. "I agree."

Slowly the Jap pulled around, came back towards shore. "You agree?" he called once. Dick nodded and answered, "Yes."

Without hesitation the Jap came straight for the shore.

Dick turned to Big Paddy and Billy.

"You two-feller stand back," he ordered. "Leave him spear! No more touch him Jap man now! Savvy?"

Sullenly the two aboriginals stepped back. I knew that once Dick had given his word he would keep it. I felt tremendously relieved, and grinned at the big eyes of Little Paddy, now so close in shore. The lad was holding his breath lest at the last moment something might go wrong.

The Jap pulled in his oars, as the dinghy grounded on the beach. The Jap stood up, and walking to the stern bent down and cut a lashing which bound Little Paddy's ankles to the dinghy bottom. To make security certain the Jap had taken down the boy's trousers and lashed them round his ankles as hobbles. Bashfully Little Paddy pulled them up, then stood up as if straightening a creak in his joints.

"Come along," said Dick, and Little Paddy stepped stiffly ashore. His eyes and his grin were all for Dick.

"A nice mess you've made of it," growled Dick. "You've gone and let us be bluffed by a Jap." But there was a smile in his voice.

Then he turned to the Jap, Terms were quickly confirmed. We were to return to him just as many tins of foodstuffs as we had taken of his. We were not to interfere with him on the island. He was to stick to the ridge below the big Hill, but must not come up to the Look-out by night or day.

"All right," said Dick nodding. "You stay with him, Jack, while I get the tucker. It will just about skin us out of tinned stuff. Keep an eye out that Big Paddy and Billy don't try any funny business; one of them might try to slip back while I'm getting the tucker. Come longa camp!" he sternly ordered the three aboriginals. Sulkily, they walked ahead of him.

I turned to Slinker. I suppose I wore a half-grin, I was so relieved at the way things had turned out. Slinker grinned back. I offered him the "makings". He accepted with a nod of thanks, and calmly rolled a cigarette. I was curious about this nuggety little brown man who, all alone, had led us such a lively dance. We smoked, with an occasional glance at one another, until Dick came from the camp laden with a bag of foodstuffs. He dumped the bag in the dinghy.

"Count it," he said shortly. "The same number of tins as we took from you."

"They all right," answered the Jap. Throwing away his butt he nodded to us, pushed the dinghy out, stepped in and calmly commenced rowing back along the shoreline towards his old hide-out.

"He's a cool customer, is Slinker," said Dick. And there was no malice in his voice.

"Aren't you glad we got Little Paddy back?" I asked. "You bet I am! I could almost forgive old Slinker for besting us now that he hasn't harmed the kid. Come and we'll hear his adventures."

29

MAN FRIDAY TELLS HIS TALE OF WOE

MAN FRIDAY was stowing damper and the last of our tinned beef into him at an amazing rate. As we walked up to the camp-fire we could only see the bottom of a blackened billycan, for Little Paddy had the rim of it up to his mouth. Big Paddy and Billy grinned expectantly. We stood there listening to the gulps, and presently the billy came down and the gasping mouth and big eyes of Little Paddy were gazing up at us. Those eyes took on a starey look at Dick's grim expression.

"You dirty little black tyke!" admonished Dick. "How often have I warned you I'd tan your hide next time I caught you drinking out of the billycan!" And Dick whipped his hand to his belt.

Little Paddy flinched. I'd seen him occasionally gaze with imploring trepidation at Dick when he uttered that oft-repeated threat, but I'd never seen him flinch before.

"All right this one time," growled Dick, and dropped his hand. "But next time I catch you drinking longa that billy I'll skin you alive. All right. You eat 'im brekfus now, then we talk."

Red-legged sea-birds were running along the water's edge, chasing their breakfast. A crab was clawing a bunch of seaweed on the beach. We sat down and rolled a cigarette, our minds at peace. It would have been awful to have lost Man Friday.

He finished the last of the damper, the last of the tea, and anything else he could lay his clutching little paws on. With bingey extended alarmingly he sighed with half-closed eyes, fidgeting to make himself comfortable.

"Stand upl" ordered Dick abruptly.

Man Friday grunted, and stood, regarding Dick from doubtful eyes.

"Turn round," ordered Dick. The startled little aboriginal hesitated. "Turn round!" snapped Dick.

Man Friday obeyed. We gazed at the little black back, wondering what was in Dick's mind. The boy's trousers were rags now, obviously they'd seen exceptionally hard service lately.

"Drop 'im pants belonga you," ordered Dick.

Little Paddy's entreating eyes appeared over his shoulder. "Undo your belt! Drop your strides!" roared Dick, and snatched at his belt.

With one last, appealing look Little Paddy reluctantly unbuckled his belt and let his pants drop. We gazed a moment, then I held back sympathetic laughter. Dick chuckled. Big Paddy and Billy threw back their heads and roared. We all laughed.

Little Paddy bent to his outrageous pants, pulled them up, then sullenly buckled his belt. I felt sure if we could have seen his face it would have been near howling.

His sit-me-down was streaked in weals, and they were weals. The Jap had thrashed him "proper feller". What Dick at times had threatened to do, Slinker had done with a vengeance. It was easy to understand. This imp had kept that Jap on the hop like a terrier scenting a rat, from daylight to dark, day after day, kept him constantly on the move, ferreted him out from hide-out after hide-out. No wonder, when at last he got the chance, he tanned his tormentor's hide with his belt.

Bashfully Little Paddy turned round and began to grin.

We all laughed the louder. It was good. Big Paddy and Billy had turned from rage to laughter in a moment, as often is the way of the aboriginal. I knew how pleased Dick would be, for he had given his word of peace to the Jap. Little Paddy squatted down, tenderly.

"Plenty-feller sore-feller I" He grinned at Dick. "Jap man belt 'im me plenty hard-feller, make 'im tail belonga me sore-feller."

"When him beltem you?" asked Dick curiously.

Little Paddy then explained that when Dick saw him last he was hot on the Jap's tracks. He had jumped down into a little gully and crept up through the grass in which he felt certain the Jap was hiding. Suddenly he was pulled violently to the ground with a hand at his throat. A knee was thrust into his stomach, and the wind gushed out of him in a stilled groan. The Jap's eyes were glaring into his, the Jap's teeth bared so furiously that Little Paddy was terrified his throat was going to be torn out. He was held thus a long time. Again and again he heard Dick calling, and each time the Jap grinned and hissed and squeezed a little harder. Then came dark, and Dick did not call any more. The Jap unbuckled Little Paddy's belt, turned him over, then knotted the belt round his ankles. Then he undid his own belt and pulled down Paddy's pants. He sat on Little Paddy's head and belted him, and belted, and belted. At each howl he sat Little Paddy's mouth down hard into the earth. And when Little Paddy couldn't howl any more the Jap grunted, and belted him until he did howl again. At last the Jap got tired. He paused awhile, and let Paddy breathe and try to cough the earth out of his mouth.

Little Paddy told his harrowing story with gusto and expressive actions, growing ludicrously funny as he noted his appreciative audience, his rolling eyes talking as vividly as his mouth. It was easy to visualize all that had happened. To the roars of laughter the little blackboy was soon laughing himself, now telling his story in fearful glee.

Later, so Little Paddy explained, the Jap undid the belt round Paddy's ankles, stood him up, but made him hold his pants up. He then got a ju-jitsu grip on the skinny little arm, and quietly they started tramping across the plain. Presently, Paddy saw they were walking towards the old hut, the pressure on his arm urging him to pass it on the right. When they were nearly behind the camp the Jap halted, glared down at Paddy, then made gestures towards our camp. Suddenly he whipped out his knife and with a fearful grimace slowly drew it across his throat with a horrid, gurgling noise. Then he held the knife at Paddy's throat, and snarled, and spat in his face, inviting him to yell. For one awful moment Little Paddy imagined his throat cut from ear to ear.

"Him proper prighten me," explained Little Paddy pathetically. "Me tink 'im neck longa me, cut all – a same belly belonga kangaroo."

"And you didn't sing out, either!" chuckled Dick.

"No morel" exclaimed Man Friday in horrified tones.

"S'pose me sing out me all-a same dead man!"

They passed close by the hut. They stood, listening for a long while. But there was not a sound. I knew that, for I had been very silent in the hut. Then they carried on cautiously towards the beach. When near there the Jap tripped Little Paddy, tore a strip from his pants, thrust a thick chip between his jaws and gagged him effectively. Then he jerked Paddy's legs up along his back and fastened his wrists to his ankles. Even Little Paddy, with his snake-like body and inborn bush craft, was trussed so efficiently that he could not move an inch. Just as the job was finished the Jap was startled by the noise of a rowlock. They listened. It came again.

Someone was rowing to the shore fronting the hut. The Jap quickly cut a waddy from a clump of bushes, then vanished towards the beach. No doubt, when he had. tied Little Paddy up like that his intention was first to reconnoitre the old hut, alone and unencumbered. "A cunning old bird is Slinker," as Dick so often remarked. I had expected him, if he came at all, to come with Man Friday. Thus they must have made some noise. But if he had come that night he would have first come alone – noiseless as a shadow.

Big Paddy could add but little to the story. Ruefully he rubbed his head.

"That Jap man proper strong-feller," he grunted reminiscently.

"Just as well your head is wood," grinned Dick. And Big Paddy threw back his head and laughed as at a priceless compliment.

"Proper-feller good-feller head," he chuckled. "No Jap man can break 'im this one!" And Billy roared in admiration.

It flashed upon me that it might not have been a laughing matter had I not been in the hut. As Big Paddy lay there dazed for the moment, the Jap might have cut his throat. He must have been a desperate man by then, his plans awry, and a new reinforcement arriving for us. He must instantly have realized that with Big Paddy to aid us, we had him at our mercy. Again, he knew the dinghy was from his own black lugger. He must have wondered what had happened to her. She might have struck a reef; she must have met trouble of some sort, otherwise how could our man possibly have got possession of this dinghy? He must have been certain that we never expected Big Paddy to land in the black lugger's dinghy. He would know that we did not expect Big Paddy. If he cut the aboriginal's throat and threw him into the sea, not a soul could ever know. It surely must have crossed his mind to do the same with Little Paddy. He then would have the dinghy, and could escape from the island if time proved that misfortune had fallen upon his mates aboard the black lugger. Otherwise, he had no retreat. That Jap's mind must have been in a whirl, trying to puzzle events out. In all probability my being in the hut saved the lives of both Big Paddy and Man Friday. Dick was thinking the same, for we discussed it later.

But not now because the aboriginals were in a good humour. To let Big Paddy know we thought the Jap might have killed him would have plunged him and Billy into a sulky, revengeful mood.

Little Paddy told us that when at last the Jap returned to him he was "proper sulky-feller". We could guess at the Jap's anger and alarm. He picked up Little Paddy and carried him across thick grass, parallel to the shore, until he came to a rocky bar jutting out into the water. He walked along this to lose his tracks, then turned and splashed back along the water's edge. Then he threw the terrified boy into the dinghy, got in, and rowed away. Any trace that he may have left was washed away by the big tide.

Little Paddy was first in terror lest his throat should be cut, then he felt sure he was to be drowned – or both. He was being rowed away out to sea; he was never to see his beloved "Dicky" again. So he howled up at the stars, and howled and howled.

Whether the Jap developed the idea of holding Little Paddy as a hostage when he rowed round the island in the chilly dawn, we could not tell. But he must, by then, have been thinking plenty.

Anyway, it was a shrewd idea to hide all day in the dinghy behind the big rock. By vanishing without trace and giving us that heart-breaking search we were convinced we had lost Little Paddy.

So that when the Jap rowed to our despairing camp next day with Man Friday we were in a very fit mood to accept his "terms".

"A wise old bird is Slinker," murmured Dick.

Beche-de-merlugger, at Townsville 1924.
State Library of Queensland.

30

THE BLACK LUGGER AGAIN

IT was near midday when we had talked it all over, so we boiled the billy again, all hands in good humour.

"You're a nice crowd!" exclaimed Dick. "You've forgotten all about keeping a look-out."

"So we have," I agreed in apparent surprise. "Why, a fleet could have sailed into anchorage and we'd have known nothing about it!"

"Fat lot you'd care, whether or no," growled Dick. "But it doesn't matter much this morning. Old Cross-eyed Joe has kept us waiting so long it would serve him right if we kept him waiting awhile. Anyway, we know now Slinker understands English perfectly, so he must know all about our trochus shell, and just where the bed lies."

"You were right when you guessed he'd listened in to us talking night after night before we found him out."

"Of course he did. He knows all our business from A to Z."

"Joe and Alor San and Ah Matt will be pretty mad when they do return."

"Yes," answered Dick. "But we can't help it. Who'd have thought the black lugger would have put a man ashore to hide and spy on us? We've done all we could. And now we'll have to do a bit of fishing to fill our tummies." And he chuckled like his old enthusiastic self again.

"I'll keep Look-out for this afternoon," I volunteered.

"You fellows are better at the fishing game than I am."

"Good-oh," agreed Dick, smiling. And the aboriginals grinned, itching for their fish-spears. All hands were pleased that the ceaseless game of hide-and-seek was finished. While keeping a look-out for the *Nancy Bell*, we'd fish the time away until she arrived.

"We'll have to spear and catch plenty," warned Dick, "or go hungry. All we've got to live on now is damper and what fish we catch."

This did not seem to alarm Big Paddy or Billy.

'We spear 'im plenty pish," laughed Little Paddy boastfully.

"You'll go hungry if you don't," promised Dick

When we started on our various jobs, Dick ordered Big Paddy and Billy along the shoreline back towards the old hut, away from the Jap's direction. Dick and Man Friday set out in that direction, along the anchorage shore; Little Paddy flourishing his fish-spear, Dick carrying his fishing lines. Meantime, I climbed the big Hill. The granite boulders were warm under the sun.

When at the summit, I saw the Jap on top of the next hill, squatting like a Buddha, gazing out to sea. I wondered how he was going to manage, for he could not see northward because of our big Hill, and only a little way towards the nor'-west. But he was in a far better position now than when we were chasing him. Oh well, it didn't matter much, the cat was out of the bag, and he knew all about the trochus. Away down below, Dick and Little Paddy were walking along the shoreline parallel with the base of the ridge. Little Paddy ran, then his arm shot up, paused a second, then the spear quivered out into the water. I saw the splash from the prongs, and, a second later, the white belly of a fish as the spear-haft tipped over.

Dick had got his bait quickly. He settled himself down on our favourite fishing possy, baited and threw out his lines. Man Friday kept walking along the shoreline, spear in eager hand.

Suddenly a stick shot out and splashed into the water.

The Jap leapt up and ran down his hill towards the water's edge.

So he had set lines! He was watching for the black lugger and watching his lines at the same time. I could see the line now, hissing out. It reached its full length, then began half-circling in a wide arc. It was a strong line, and a big fish was hooked to it.

The Jap reached the line and began playing the fish. He knew his game. It took him twenty minutes to land the fish – a kingfish, a beauty; it must have been all of forty pounds.

Then Dick got a bite, and landed a twenty-pounder.

Neither we nor the Jap would go hungry tonight, anyway.

It was a quiet, bright, dreamy afternoon. Lazily I thought how funny it was. Only a few hours ago and the elements of tragedy were fast gathering upon this little island. We might have killed that Jap; Big Paddy and Billy certainly would have, had they got the chance. He might have killed one or more of us. And here we were now in this quiet afternoon, enjoyably watching one another catch fish.

I turned my glasses nor'-west, but there was not a sail upon the sea. A gull flew low overhead, gazing down from bright, amber eyes. Birds have their "bump" of curiosity just as humans have. And they choose their mates, too, and they quarrel among themselves just as we do.

The next few days went cheerily by, with always one man on look-out duty while the others were kept busy fishing. And we needed fish. Dick and I enjoyed healthy appetites, but the food that Big Paddy and Billy and Little Paddy could put away was awe-inspiring. And this raised a howl from Dick one sunset.

"Here, Jack! Come and have a look at this!"

I hurried into the tent, and there was Dick standing with horrified face and half a bag of flour in his hands.

"Half a bag, Jack! Half a bag left among this pack of wolves! I thought we had another full bag. We haven't – we've eaten that, too!"

"We eat a fair bit," I murmured.

"A fair bit!" he growled. "We're cannibals." And he strode out to the shed and "roared" on the three aboriginals.

"All a time eateml" he admonished. "Eatem! Sleepem! Eatem! From now on you can sleep less and fish more, and eat fish until you look like fish. And when we run out of fish we'll eat you!" And he glared at Little Paddy. "You'll be the first one! We feller altogether hungry-fella belonga meat! We eat your Little Paddy gazed up with big eyes grinning from an unbelieving face.

"He's skinny as a rake," I protested. "There's barely a pound of meat on his bones; he'd hardly be worth boiling up for soup."

"Skinny as a rake, yes," growled Dick, "but eats as much as a horse. If that wall-eyed tyke of a Cross-eyed Joe doesn't turn up very soon, Jack, we'll all be skinny as rakes."

And I had to admit the position was serious. We could live on fish and crabs and shellfish for months if need be, but fish without damper would soon become monotonous.

That night was beautiful, as nearly all the sou-east nights are. Dark with a velvety darkness, brilliant with the tiaras of the heavens. At times, the blacker the night the brighter the stars, and the more multitudinous. A steady breeze tonight, a heavy murmur growing into a rumble as the tide slipped out and the livening sea heaved down on exposing reefs. We gave Man Friday the first watch.

"Not that he's any use," growled Pick. "If a ship sailed into the anchorage he wouldn't see it."

"Eyes belonga me good-feller," boasted Little Paddy, grinning.

"If they were as good as your bingey there'd be something in it," retorted Dick. He was still pondering over that half-empty bag of flour. I hadn't worried about the tucker position at all. Dick was in charge of the camp and, lazily, I left everything to him. In the worry over Little Paddy's disappearance he had forgotten to watch the tucker position so closely. The dawn watch was Dick's. I was sound asleep when urgently he woke me.

"Wake up, Jack. Quick!"

I rolled up on an elbow, yawning. Dick pointed down at the anchorage. I stood up, and gazed down. The black lugger lay at anchor.

world seemed just wonderful again. And how welcome was the first sign of man -the winding sluice race of a scrub-edge tin-scratcher. A few miles farther on and I was at the Rossville pub, waking lazy Bill Cleary from his snug bed. Assan could come if he liked now. A native saddled a horse while I gulped a hasty breakfast. Then I set out along the thirty-mile tin-mine's road to Cooktown, arriving there in the afternoon, delighted at the sight of Dick Welch in the old man's yard, greasing packsaddles. Quickly I explained the hurry. Dick laughed in boyish delight, eager for details. He thought the affair a great adventure.

"Why worry?" he smiled. "All the better if someone's killed, it's more exciting. Wish I'd been there. It's not your fault, anyway, you didn't kill anyone. The police can't do anything to you."

Dick's smiling philosophy was jolly comforting, if not altogether convincing.

"I've got the horses paddocked at the Four Mile," he consoled. "The tucker is already in the pack bags in the shed. We can get away if you're still thinking of old Assan!"

"He'll follow me to Cooktown for a certainty, immediately he comes to his senses. But he won't travel any farther north – he doesn't know the country. Get the horses right away, Dick; it would be stiff luck to stop a bullet at the last moment. Has there been any sign of the Filipino?"

"No. He hasn't come into the bay, and you can bet your life he won't."

"Well, get the horses in while I go up to the Signal Station and see if they've sighted the cutter. I'd just like to feel sure that the little coloured girl is safe, and I'd like to camp a few miles out of town to-night, too."

Up on Grassy Hill overlooking the town was the trim white Signal Station, with the caretaker in charge at his ceaseless job of watching for vessels coming from north and south.

From the closed-in glass veranda, with a deep feeling of thankfulness, I watched a tiny cutter beating past towards Cape Bedford, heading towards the distant north. The cutter had taken as long to do her thirty miles by sea as I had to do fifty overland.

"That's that Filipino *bêche-de-mer* fisher," nodded the caretaker as he handed over the telescope, "I wonder what he's doing running north with a woman on board and not calling in? He's beating against a head wind too."

I gazed at Mee-lele through the telescope, bringing her right close to me. She was sitting on the tiny cabin roof, gazing back towards Cooktown. The Filipino was at the tiller; five native seamen lazed up forrard. The wind whipped around in a freshening from the sou'-east; I could see the cutter responding as I gazed. Almost it seemed that the craft had just dawdled along to hasten now in farewell.

31

PIRACY

"HOW did she do it?" exclaimed Dick. "She's come in like a ghost ship. I didn't even hear the anchor-chain rattle down."

"Neither did I. She couldn't have come in during my watch, or I would have heard."

"They lowered the anchor foot by foot so we wouldn't hear," declared Dick. "And I didn't notice Slinker show a light, nor see any signal out to sea."

"Neither did I."

We stood there, gazing down. In the new dawn two men came up from the foc's'le, stretched and yawned, plunged overboard for the early morning dip. Leaping back on deck they went to the galley. They'd cook breakfast while the others snoozed below.

"Slinker!" exclaimed Dick.

"Where?" I asked. "I don't see him."

"He's aboard. See, there's his dinghy tied astern. The two other dinghies are lashed to the deck."

"Ah! He's down below with the skipper and his mates telling them all about us. They'll be out on the trochus grounds before midday. When the *Nancy Bell* does return, the first thing Cross-eyed Joe will see will be the Japs cleaning up our trochus patch."

"Yes," Dick agreed thoughtfully. He was frowning down at the black lugger.

"It means the finish," I protested. "They'll fish up all the trochus that's left."

"Yes," he murmured. He swept the glasses carefully north, then nor-west. "Not a sign of the *Nancy Bell,*" he said at last.

Man Friday was staring down at the black lugger, and there was no smile in his eyes.

"Plenty Jap man aboard," pointed Dick grimly. "Eight feller. Sposem they catch Little Paddy they cut 'im throat this-a time sure."

"Jap man no more catch 'im me," muttered Little Paddy uneasily.

"I wouldn't like to be in your hide if they do," warned Dick. "All a time you keep 'im sharp-feller watch out longa Jap man. Come along, Jack," he added to me. "You too, Paddy. Somehow I'll feel easier down in camp. We'll send Billy up here to keep a look-out.

The lazy beggars are still snoozing," he added. "They'd sleep their heads off if their bellies would let them."

We walked down the Hill with a glance now and then at the black lugger. Smoke was lazily coiling up from the galley where two Japs were squatting, busy with cooking pots. We strolled from the base of the Hill to the camp, Little Paddy at our heels. We entered the bough-shed and halted, Dick with a startled exclamation.

"Hullo! What's this? Where are they?"

Their blankets were on the ground, but there was no sign of Big Paddy or Billy. Dick entered the tent, then called out to me. As I stepped forward a shuffle behind made me wheel round. Four Japs stood there. One snatched at Little Paddy as he wriggled like an eel between them. He was gone in a flash with a Jap at his heels. In hazy bewilderment I thought, "That Jap won't catch Little Paddy."

Dick stepped from the tent.

"Big Paddy and Billy are tied up like trussed pigs in the tent," he told me. "What do you mean by this?" he demanded, turning on the Japs.

We stared at them; they stared back. Their captain was clad in singlet and shorts, a squat, powerfully built man with flattish face and black, expressionless eyes. His thin lips were a straight line as he stared at Dick. He was in no hurry to speak. Through the silence we heard the splash of a dinghy thrown overside from the black lugger. Then the sound of two pairs of rowlocks. The two Japs aboard were rowing ashore, each in a dinghy. It had been a perfectly laid trap.

"Where your ship?" asked the Jap skipper quietly.

"You know better than we do," answered Dick, "and it's no business of yours, anyway. What do you mean by burgling our camp and tying up our two men?"

"Where our goods?" demanded the skipper. "What goods?" asked the surprised Dick.

"Our goods that your captain steal! Where you hide them?"

"I don't know what you're talking about," replied Dick contemptuously. "You're crazy – or drunk."

The Jap shrugged, staring at Dick. The other Japs had not moved. In some queer way it flashed across my mind that Dick's surprise and contemptuous answer sounded just a shade unconvincing. Foolish thought! Like Dick, I had not the faintest idea of what the Jap was talking about. Just then the Jap who had chased Little Paddy returned, breathing heavily.

The skipper did not even look at him, merely shrugged.

Silently, two other Japs appeared. One was Slinker. It was quite a relief to see the familiar brown face, the black moustache of Slinker.

"So you've come along, too," sneered Dick. "But you'll find no more provisions here."

"Plenty aboard," replied Slinker. impassively.

The Jap skipper with an angry gesture silenced Slinker. "You no tell where your ship is?" he demanded of Dick. "You no tell where you hide our stolen goods?"

"We've got none of your goods," answered Dick hotly.

"And we don't know where our ship is. Now you get to the devil out of this, and quick and lively, too!" And he turned to the tent.

In a flash the skipper stood before him. They stared into one another's eyes. Dick's face grew very angry, but the only change in the Jap was his narrowed eyes.

"We mean business," he hissed. "Suppose you no give us back our goods, we take your trochus shell in return."

"What!" exclaimed Dick. No doubt he was amazed now.

"You'll take what?"

"We take your shell!"

"You take my aunty!" sneered Dick uneasily. "You've got another thing coming!"

"Your captain steal our goods," insisted the Jap impassively. "We take your trochus shell to pay back."

"You jolly well will do nothing of the kind," replied Dick energetically. 'What you'll do will be to land yourself in jail. Now clear out of this!" He pushed determinedly to the tent.

In an instant the skipper and Slinker tackled him. Dick struggled wildly, but was tripped up clawing and shouting, "You rotten pirates! You'll pay for this!"

I sprang towards him but three Japs tumbled me over and we all were struggling on the floor, But they handled us swiftly, neither my arms nor legs seemed to belong to me, they were numbed and helpless as the Japs trussed me up. Dick's gasping struggles were of no avail. As I glared towards him a four-pronged spear dived within an inch of Slinker's throat and buried itself in the floor. Slinker sprang back and his face had changed its expression all right. The skipper snatched a revolver. from inside his singlet as Dick shouted.

"Good boy, Little Paddy! Run quick-feller, run, run!" The skipper thrust the revolver at Slinker with a sharp command. Slinker snatched the weapon and doubled out into the open, murder in his eyes.

They tied us each to a tree just outside the shed. Slinker stood in a commanding position where he could look all around the camp, keeping a sharp look-out for Little Paddy. I hoped with all my heart the little blackboy would not attempt to use a spear again. They would shoot him.

To an abrupt command, the Japs went straight to our stack of bagged shell. Each man bent down, pulled a bag on to his back, and loped to the water's edge. Each tipped his bag into a dinghy, then hurried back for another bag. Slinker kept his look-out, the skipper superintended while he stood by us.

"This is piracy!" cried Dick. "You'll pay for this! You'll do years in jail over this!"

"No more," replied the captain quietly. "Maybe you do jail. You steal our goods!"

Dick raved at him. He was winded, but was still full of fight. It was hopeless, though, even if we could have writhed free of our bonds, which we couldn't. It was only just beginning to dawn on me that the Japs were taking our precious treasure, our trochus shell that was going to mean so much to us. But I was too bewildered to understand it all.

When the dinghies were filled, six Japs stepped into them and rowed out to the lugger, where two jumped aboard. With quick efficiency they lifted the bags to the deck. And this time they returned with the three dinghies, leaving one man aboard to heave the bags below. At this rate they would very soon clear out our fifteen tons of precious trochus shell.

And they did.

When the last bag was loaded, the Jap skipper just looked at each of us in turn a moment.

"Suppose blackboy throw another spear," he quietly threatened, "we shoot you!"

Then he walked to a dinghy. Slinker followed, walking backwards, with revolver pointing threateningly lest he stop a spear in the back. Fortunately no little black head appeared. We learnt presently that Little Paddy on escaping had managed to snatch up only the one spear.

The Japs rowed away with the last load. There was silence, except for the diminishing music of the rowlocks, and the insects buzzing round our ears.

Then Little Paddy leapt up from the grass and came running to Dick, frantically trying to undo his bonds.

"Cut him!" snapped Dick. "Get him knife!"

Quickly Little Paddy cut our bonds. I was surprised to find how stiff my wrists were; it seemed quite a time before the blood flowed again through the numbed arms.

"Look out father belonga you," ordered Dick. "Billy, too."

Little Paddy hurried into the tent, and we heard him sawing at Big Paddy's bonds. Then a gurgle like a turtle breaking water as Big Paddy gasped for breath, and spat the loosened gag from his mouth.

They came hobbling out of the tent, glaring furiously.

Especially Big Paddy. The Jap skipper had given him two black eyes, and a flattened nose into the bargain. That is, if it is possible to blacken an aboriginal's eyes and flatten his nose. But Big Paddy's eyes were almost closed up, and his nose looked as if a sledge-hammer had hit it. I suppose the Jap skipper was getting even for his purloined dinghy.

Big Paddy's story was soon told. Sound asleep, they awoke to find themselves already half bound up. Immediately they opened their mouths, gags were thrust in. They were trussed immovably to the bunks, then treated to a few sound thumps from fist and foot.

They didn't seem pleased about it.

Goro Nagita, the last Japanese Consul in Townsville, 1906 with his wife.

32

THE PLOT UNFOLDS

"PUT billy on," muttered Dick.

Little Paddy hastened to obey. We sat down and unhappily rolled cigarettes, looking out at the activity aboard the black lugger.

"Surely they can't get away with this!" I protested.

"What's to stop them?" inquired Dick.

The stack of bags on the deck was rapidly disappearing.

They gave us a display of efficient teamwork, these brown pirates, as they stowed our precious shell below, then hauled aboard the dinghies and manned the winch. The chain came clanking up. As they lashed the anchor aboard, others hauled up the jib. The skipper stood by the tiller, and there came a sputter and throb of a powerful engine. She forged ahead as the foresail went creaking up. As she gathered speed, up billowed the mainsail, and away she sped, heading south.

"So that's that!" said Dick slowly. "We may as well see the last of her."

And, rising, he commenced to walk towards the Hill.

"You boys catch 'em pish," he called.

When we climbed to the Look-out she was in full view, heading south fast under sail and engine.

"They're not short of petrol," murmured Dick.

"What on earth are they using petrol for, when there's a good breeze?"

"Speed," answered Dick, "and because the money doesn't count. It's our money anyway."

"It's a shame, Dick, and I can't understand why you seem resigned to it. After all our wonderful luck, to see our good trochus shell pirated like this! Serves Cross-eyed Joe right for leaving us here so long. But surely they can't get away with it?"

"I'm afraid they can," replied Dick in cheerless voice, and sat down.

"But do you mean to say they can take that trochus into Cooktown, sell it, and just clear out and no one do anything?"

"I'm afraid so."

'What nonsense! It isn't done these days. The *Nancy Bell* must return at any time and Cross-eyed Joe will race to Cooktown. The police will get the wires going-they must be caught somewhere."

"Where?" asked Dick. "Those Japs can easily disappear, Jack. They sell the shell in Cooktown, Cairns, Townsville, even Thursday island, should they double back north. And everyone would believe it was their own. They could paint the lugger a different colour, and cut off Slinker's moustache, or could tranship to another lugger if they wished; they could sail to the Dutch East Indies; they could vanish in a dozen ways. But they won't bother even to hide their tracks, Jack, for they know we won't dare to do a thing."

"What on earth do you mean?"

"Sit down. I'll explain. A dozen times," he went on, "I've been on the point of telling you. You've no idea how glad I am I didn't. Do you remember, way back, we realized that Slinker must have lain outside our camp at night and listened in to our conversation? And we knew that if he understood English, then he must have learnt all about our trochus shell, all about our plans?"

"Yes."

"Well, if I'd told you before what I'm going to tell you now, then we certainly would often have discussed it, and he would have known that *we* knew. At the time it was only vague suspicion to me, but gradually my suspicions grew stronger, but I could never be quite sure, and I didn't want to upset us both unless I was certain."

"Blessed if I know what you're talking about." "Remember that pie-faced Jap skipper? He insisted we had stolen goods that belonged to him."

"Yes. I puzzled over that silly statement and meant to ask you about it. But everything happened so quickly!"

"You remember, he wanted to know where those goods were buried."

"Yes, the silly goat."

"Well, Jack, if I had told you my suspicions, Slinker would have heard, and nothing then would have convinced them that we did not know all about it – that we did not know of those stolen goods, and where they were. Goodness knows what they would have done to us to make us talk!"

"But we didn't steal any of their goods, Dick!"

"No. But Cross-eyed Joe did. And Alor San and Ah Matt."

"What on earth do you mean? And what are these goods? You've got me puzzled."

"Opium!"

I stared at Dick. He puffed his cigarette. "What was it you said, Dick?"

"Opium. Cross-eyed Joe and his mates have stolen a parcel of opium belonging to, or rather relayed to, those Japs."

I stared at Dick a moment, then gazed to the south where the black lugger was rapidly growing smaller. That fly-by-night, elusive lugger took on quite a new significance now. No longer was she just an ordinary poacher, muscling in to seize advantage of om lucky find of trochus. I thought again of the strong throb of those engines, the bushmanship of Slinker, the Jap skipper-the teamwork, the efficiency of the crew.

"The black lugger is exceptionally speedy," I said slowly.

"She doesn't depend only on wind, either. She can sail in any direction she likes-even in a dead calm. Petrol isn't precious to her, like it is to all other boats."

"That's so," murmured Dick.

We smoked quietly a little while, our eyes on the distant lugger.

"It is just as well you didn't mention your suspicions," I said. "Otherwise that Jap skipper would have forced us to talk. I didn't like the look in his eyes, as I remember it. I suppose Slinker rowed aboard when they arrived and reported everything. He'd tell them, too, that we knew absolutely nothing about this opium, and that the *Nancy Bell* had not returned here, so that their precious opium could not be hidden on this island.

"That's so. And there's this, too – just another reason for Slinker cracking Big Paddy on the head when he landed in the dinghy – he couldn't have known, at the time, that his own lugger had picked up Big Paddy. At least, until he recognized their own dinghy, he probably thought the *Nancy Bell* was lying off shore, while Big Paddy was quietly landing the opium by dinghy. So he cracked him on the head."

"H'm. It's working out."

"Yes."

"Well then, tell me all about it. I'm not convinced yet. When did you first get this idea?"

"Quite a time back. Do you remember, on those early nights when we formed a station on the island, occasionally we'd come up here. Strangely enough, I was curious to get a sight of the *Changte* or *Taiping* passing by night."

"Yes."

'Well, do you remember that we found that someone else was up here on look-out?"

"Heavens, yes! Those cigarettes – and Alor San!"

"Yes. And when the black lugger first came, do you remember that we saw the glow of two cigarettes!"

"Yes, that's right."

"And one night we saw the passing of either the *Changte* or *Taiping*. Those other watchers saw them, too, that's what they were waiting for. And then the *Nancy Bell* and the black lugger cleared out."

"By Jove! So that's how it works out."

"Yes. I became very suspicious then. It seemed silly, though. But I'm jolly glad I didn't say anything."

"So am I – now. But go on. What do you think happened afterwards?"

"Well, the passing of the China boat going north told them fairly accurately when her sister ship from China would be coming down the coast, south. So both the *Nancy Bell* and black lugger set out to be in a position to intercept her, to hide behind some handy island where she would pass close by at night. It probably would be a hilly island where they could keep a look-out; but it must be an island where the passage-way for steamers goes close-by. They might have sailed for Number One Howick, but I think they'd go further north; they'd probably round Cape Melville to the Flinders group. Anyway, both vessels knew the rendezvous where the steamer must pass at night. And both knew the signals."

"Go on," I said. "But I'm a bit puzzled, again."

"But you know, Jack, about the opium smugglers? You've often heard of them in Cooktown. Don't you remember I pointed out some of them to you one day in Chinatown?"

"Yes, I'm beginning to see it all now. They meet the China steamer away up north, flash some sort of signal from a certain spot, and those aboard in the know throw the opium overboard in a tin, or a hollowed-out lifebelt."

"Yes, in a kerosene tin, or watertight drum. But it's a clever little arrangement, I've seen half a dozen of them in Chinatown. The airtight tin or drum is very buoyant, and has a little anchor hanging from its bottom to keep it upright in the waves. Some of them have four strong wires, a foot or more long, soldered to each corner of the bottom. The four ends meet dead centre under the tin, fixed into a ball of lead. Makes a great anchor, or rather, steadier. It would take a nasty cress-sea to capsize such a tin. Then again, each tin has its own little 'lighthouse'." Dick grinned.

"Lighthouse?"

"Yes, of wire – a little gridiron of a tower, sticking up nearly two feet above the top of the tin, with dead-centre a little light. It flashes and flashes. When they throw the tin overboard it just sails away, there is no sign of the light till the tin is too far astern for anyone on the steamer bridge to notice it. Then it flashes; it's worked by clockwork. But some are worked by putting water on a powdered chemical, which liberates a gas in ten minutes or so. They don't wet the chemical in the lamp till they throw the tin overboard."

"Sounds jolly clever!"

"It is clever, all the arrangements and organization, let alone little details like the tin or lamp. . . ."

"And when the lamp flashes, the smugglers who are waiting see it, and sail to it?"

"Yes. They see the steamer coming – you saw how plainly we saw the Taiping, miles away, that night – then they creep out from their island hide-out under engine power. They'd be helpless in a calm without an engine. Old Cross-eyed Joe got a little engine put in the *Nancy Bell* not long ago – to help him in calms when fishing for trochus," added Dick surlily.

"Never mind that cunning old Filipino – this is too interesting. Go on."

"Well," resumed Dick, "the boat creeps out and into the passage-way along which the steamer must go. They wait close to where she must pass. The steamer passes in a blaze of lights, but the little vessel lies quietly, as dark as the pit, away out in the night. Guess how difficult it would be to detect the black lugger under bare poles on a dark night!"

I nodded.

"When the steamer passes, the waiting vessel flashes a single light, low down, probably against her side, in such a position that only a watcher on the stern of the vessel could see it. A single light is flashed back from low down on the steamer's stern, or from a porthole, in reply. Then the tin is thrown overboard. The steamer passes on.

"The smugglers wait, they know how the tide is running, and of course they wait in that position where the tin must be carried towards them. Even if it is rough weather and a strong tide running the tin cannot be carried out of their sight, for the little anchor steadies the pace of the tin. When the light flashes they chug towards it, and lift the tin inboard."

"And everyone is happy."

"Yes. But not in this case."

33

STOLEN TREASURE

WE gazed again away out southward, where the black lugger was fading away. For the time being I'd forgotten our heart-breaking loss, it was all so jolly interesting, and so full of possibilities dimly looming ahead. I remembered, now, listening in to many a yarn of the old hands at their. home and in the quiet Cooktown street of an evening. Now and again there'd be comments on opium smuggling as coloured men in bare feet went noiselessly by. And I'd hear of the constant. war between the opium smugglers and Customs men in the port of Cairns, further south, and at Townsville, further south still. The larger steamers by-passed little Cooktown. But to defeat the Customs net in the larger ports south it was known locally that opium came into Cooktown's Chinatown, to be shipped in smaller vessels to the south, or even, it was rumoured, to be taken over the wild ranges inland by horse, and delivered where required on the Atherton Tableland, far from the ken of Customs officers. And here were Dick and I unwittingly mixed up with opium smuggling!

"I say, Dick," I exclaimed, "we may be in a mess!" "You're telling me," replied Dick.

"Anyway, I'm not sure of it all yet, though *you* seem certain. If Cross-eyed Joe and the Japs aboard the lugger met at their rendezvous to collect their parcels of opium, then what went wrong?"

"Cross-eyed Joe should not have been there. And there was only *one* parcel. And Cross-eyed Joe got that parcel and it did not belong to him."

"I'm becoming a bit puzzled again."

"This is the way I've thought it out," said Dick slowly.

"And I've done plenty of thinking about it. On some previous trip, before charming old Joe invited you and me to cruise with him seeking trochus shell, he and Alor San and Ah Matt were fishing round the Flinders Islands, or wherever their rendezvous may be. By some coincidence they must have been on the very spot, when the black lugger lifted a parcel of opium. They saw it all – it could happen on a dark night – they saw the signals, saw the lugger pick up the tin, then steam away. They put their heads together. It was simple. They knew now the exact rendezvous, knew the signals. Easy to guess that other parcels would come. They could guess when, for they knew even better than we when the China boats are due. They could easily enough work out the date when the next dark night was due, and the returning *Changte* or *Taiping* must pass that very spot again...

They planned to be there, but a little further along the passage, just a shade further to the north. The black lugger would be waiting in the same spot as usual. But Cross-eyed Joe would signal just a little sooner than the black lugger. The tin would be dropped overboard, the *Nancy Bell* would pick it up and steal away, which she apparently did. The black lugger stayed there and signalled – and must have been stone mad when they found out something was wrong."

"Ah! And they've been playing hide-and-seek ever since."

"Yes."

"But why didn't Cross-eyed Joe run back here, load up with trochus, and carry straight on to Cooktown?"

"That was his plan, of course, but the plan went wrong. In the first case he never dreamed the Japs would use Lizard Island as a look-out station; he thought they would keep their look-out from the Flinders Group, away nor'west. That's where he and Alor San and Ah Matt must first have seen them pick up the opium. But the Japs are cunning, too – as we know to our sorrow. They reasoned out that if they hung round there waiting each time for the coming of the China boat, then pearling luggers or trochus vessels must sooner or later see them. They'd start fishing, too, of course, and when they found nothing to keep the black lugger hanging about, they'd become suspicious. So after they'd delivered their parcel, probably the very parcel Cross-eyed Joe saw them pick up, the Jap skipper must have planned to wait at Lizard Island on the next trip. It's rarely that anyone ever sets a foot ashore here. But it is an ideal look-out. And it's many miles south of wherever they pick up the opium. From here they would see the China boat steaming north. They'd know then when to expect her sister ship steaming south. They would then sail north at their leisure and wait at the rendezvous. And they wouldn't have to wait long."

"I see. And when. the black lugger did arrive here, it was to find old Cross-eye in possession."

"Yes. And I'll bet he squinted from the other eye when he saw that black lugger. And the Jap must have become suspicious. He'd be sure when his own man, up here on look-out at night, saw Alor San's cigarette – saw us, too, when we came strolling up here two or three times just because I was curious to see the *Changte* pass by."

"That's why, when the Jap captain sailed, he sent Slinker ashore to hide and keep an eye on us."

"Of course. A wise old bird is Slinker, but a shrewd devil is that Jap skipper. When the China boat steamed by and the *Nancy Bell* stole away he must have been pretty mad; he guessed the race was on. He sent Slinker ashore not only to watch us but also to signal the black lugger, should the

Nancy Bell return. We don't know what he was to signal."

"So that when both vessels left here they knew they were at one another's throats – either to take delivery of, or to steal a parcel of opium."

"That's it."

"Well, I'm blessed! And all the time we thought it was only cunning old Cross-eyed Joe trying to outwit poachers to keep them away from our trochus find – or at least I did. But you worked it out pretty well, Dick."

"Yes, but I was never sure. You see, Jack, I was born in Cooktown. And I know the coloured people as well as the whites, and every Chinaman in Chinatown. I've known lots of things that have been going on that the whites don't take much interest in. So that when we came up here and found Alor San keeping a nightly watch when there was no need to, and then found a Jap keeping a watch, then both vessels clearing out when the China boat steamed by – well, it was easy to put two and two together."

"But where on earth do we come in? You and I. We're not concerned in this opium, knew nothing whatever about it. I thought we sailed with Cross-eyed Joe to look for trochus shell."

"So we did. We were to have nothing to do with the opium, we were to have known nothing about it."

"It seems we've learned too jolly much."

"So we have," answered Dick slowly.

"Oh well, don't get gloomy, nothing worse can happen to us than having lost our share of the trochus, though that's heart-breaking enough. If Joe and his Malay mates were after that opium, then why on earth did they take you and me aboard at all?"

"That puzzled me for a while," replied Dick, "but I reckon I've worked it out. We were signed on only as a cloak – two white lads known to everyone in Cooktown, going on a half-holiday, half-working cruise with old Joe the Filipino. The boys would enjoy themselves. Good experience, too. They might even make a few pounds out of it. It was decent of the old Filipino to take the two lads. That's what everyone would say, and *did* say. Old Cross-eye guessed that, and he knew, *too,* that with us aboard he could return to Cooktown and not a soul would dream the *Nancy Bell* was returning to port with thousands of pounds' worth of opium aboard."

"Heavens! Thousands of pounds?"

"It's worth £20 and more a tin," said Dick. "A tin only about the size of a mustard tin. It doesn't take many of those tins to run into a few thousand pounds. And you can see that those trained Japs with their big lugger and powerful engine are part of a big organization. They don't waste time with chicken feed."

"H'm, I'm beginning to wake up now. Just fancy old Cross-eyed Joe and Alor San and Ah Matt with that loot aboard the *Nancy Bell*! It would be worth risking a lot for."

"Of course. And they did risk it – and have won. If those Japs had caught them, Jack, we would never have seen them or the *Nancy Bell* again. But Cross-eyed Joe is just as cunning as that Jap skipper. He planned well beforehand."

"He did."

"Do you remember that when the folks saw us off, the old Sergeant with the bank manager strolled across from the police station? And the Customs Officer was there, too. Half Cooktown was there – in a way of speaking."

"A wonderful blind for old Cross-eyed Joe."

"Of course. Could anyone dream that we were really sailing on a desperate opium-stealing cruise! When we returned, would anyone ever dream that there was opium hidden aboard the *Nancy Bell*?"

"Of course not."

"Joe and his mates could have brought a million pounds' worth ashore and not a soul would have dreamt it."

"That's so. What about Little Paddy?"

"That was just a lucky touch on Joe's part. It all fitted in. There was Little Paddy carrying my things with his eyes bulging out of his head trying to stop from howling. The folk all around were grinning and murmuring, Poor little blighter! He'll miss his mate Dick: If you remember, he got a lot of sympathy. Well, Little Paddy's father was one of the crew, What more natural then than at the last moment the kindly, cunning old Cross-eyed Joe could find some corner on his ship for the poor little nigger boy? Little Paddy would have fitted into a cockroach hole, anywhere, so long as he was offered a job aboard. So everything was natural again, everyone was happy. And all hands ashore knew that Little Paddy would more than earn his tucker."

"I see. A shrewd old bird is Cross-eyed Joe."

"You bet," agreed Dick heartily. "A shrewd old bird is Cross-eyed Joe – blast him!"

34

TEMPTATION

"BUT, Dick, we really did go fishing for trochus."

"We had to. Neither you nor I nor the aboriginals were ever to know anything about the opium. We arrived here a few weeks before the China boat was due, plenty of time to start a station and commence fishing. We'd surely find a few hundredweight of trochus somewhere or other to take back into port. When the China boat should pass, Joe would leave us here with plenty of tucker while he cruised north seeking 'more profitable' fishing-grounds. A reasonable excuse, as you know. He'd return with the opium. We'd continue fishing until we'd got a few hundred-weight of shell, with luck a ton or two – then return to Cooktown after a jolly interesting cruise, and with a few pounds in our pockets. Joe would sell the opium after we left the boat; there'd be plenty of time."

"I see. But we found a patch of trochus."

"Yes. But whoever would have thought it? It was like a prospector on his first trip striking a patch of gold. And that trochus was right beside the very island they'd picked out as a hide-out base. I'll bet the most surprised men in the Coral Sea when we located that trochus were Cross-eyed Joe and his poker-faced pirate mates."

"Oh, well," I said, laughing, "it was all to the good especially for us."

"Yes," mused Dick. "Remember how everyone was pleased? Particularly Joe and Company. Because it was not only the unexpected money we would make, but our return to Cooktown. On the boys' first cruise – sailing back to town with fifteen tons of shell! We'd be the talk of the town, and the envy of the waterfront. Every boat would want us to sail with them – we'd be lucky mascots."

"Yes," I agreed regretfully, "and now our trochus has gone – to the Japs."

Dick frowned. He was feeling very sore.

"You must have had a job, keeping all this to yourself," I said curiously.

"I didn't know, Jack," he answered, "not for certain, not until the Japs came this morning and took our trochus. It was only when the Jap skipper accused us of stealing his goods that I felt sure,"

"Still, you'd thought a lot of it out before."

"Yes. But we'd had such luck, everything had gone so well and we were having such a grand time that I didn't like to spoil it by mentioning silly suspicions. I thought I might make a fool of myself as well, because, to tell you the truth, it was only when climbing up here a couple of hours ago that I took a tumble as to why Joe took you and me on this cruise. If he really had set out to steal the Japs' opium, then why should he take two white boys aboard? Two witnesses? For a long time I couldn't make it out. But I see it all plainly now. Silly ass!" he added, disgustedly. "I should have seen through it long ago."

"I'm not so Sure of that; it was a jolly clever plan. If everything had gone all right, then we would have landed back in Cooktown pleased as punch with our trochus, never ever dreaming that we'd sailed back with thousands of pounds' worth of stolen opium."

"That's so," admitted Dick grudgingly.

"Well then, the big shock for Cross-eyed Joe and his merry men was when we woke up and found the black lugger at anchor."

"Yes," agreed Dick, with a grin, "and for the Jap skipper and his cut-throats, too."

"Well Dick, Joe and Alor San and Ah Matt must be game men when they decided to carry on against *those* odds."

"They're game all right," admitted Dick. "They knew what was coming to them if they were caught in the act. And with the Jap at their heels they knew it would be touch and go."

What did they leave Big Paddy on Howick Island for?" I asked.

"So that he wouldn't be a witness," answered Dick. "Only Joe and Alor San and Ah Matt would ever know. It was quite an ordinary excuse to leave Big Paddy on the island for a day or two's fishing. No one would ever have thought anything about that. When they returned and found him gone they must have guessed the Japs had got him."

"Finding Paddy gone would make Joe doubly cautious."

"Yes."

"And when Paddy slipped away in the dinghy, then those aboard the black lugger would not be feeling too pleased, either."

"No," Dick grinned. "Both vessels then knew that the crews aboard each were well and truly warned one against the other. Neither dared return here until she received an 'all clear' signal. Neither could be certain what was happening here. I reckon for a good while past both of them have been hiding away nor-west there with their glasses on the island, waiting for the other to break cover."

"Then why did the Jap do it first and thus put himself away?"

"Because he probably came to the conclusion that the Filipino had got frightened and sailed across to the mainland, and buried the opium there. He could then pick it up again in six months' time – any time at all. If

Joe did that then the Jap knew he could carry on with trochus fishing; it wouldn't matter who might board his craft, there'd be no opium there."

"H'm"

"Or," continued Dick, "when Big Paddy escaped in the dinghy it might have occurred to the Jap skipper that Joe could keep him on a wild goose chase while one of the crew brought the opium ashore here by dinghy. It would be a long pull, but the weather was calm then and a dinghy could go a long way between sunset and sunrise."

"Oh well, he came here anyway – as we know to our cost."

"Yes. And Slinker boarded him and told him we knew nothing at all about the opium – luckily for us. So the Jap decided to take our fifteen tons of trochus as part payment, and he's sailed back to Cooktown with it."

"And he sneered when you threatened him with jail because he knew we daren't say anything when we arrive back in Cooktown."

"Yes," Dick agreed miserably. 'We've lost our trochus and now we daren't say anything about it. There'd be a nice how-de-do at home if they knew we were mixed up with opium smuggling and, worse still, opium stealing."

"But we had nothing to do with it."

"Who'd believe it? We've lost our trochus and daren't say a word, and that's a fact."

"I suppose there would be some who'd think we knew a bit about it."

"Plenty," replied Dick abruptly. "They'd be suspicious for years, no one would ever be certain."

"H'm, Looks as if we're out of luck. Oh well, when Cross-eyed Joe buries his opium on the mainland you reckon he'll return here?"

"He'll return before that now," answered Dick. "I expect a signal from him any time. And – he hasn't buried his opium on the mainland."

"Why not?"

"For one thing, because it would be too risky. Joe knows how clever the aboriginals are at finding and digging up things, and he knows the *Nancy Bell* would be watched all along the coast by the aboriginals – all the fishing vessels are. No, Joe and his bright boys have got that rich haul aboard and they mean to stick to it through thick and thin. And another and important reason why they won't bury it on the mainland or anywhere else is – us!"

"Us? How?"

"Because with us aboard they can sail into Cooktown without the slightest trouble or suspicion, land the opium when they wish, and sell it without suspicion – either then or afterwards."

"I see. But – they don't know about the black lugger pirating our trochus and taking it to Cooktown."

"No, but they soon will," said Dick grimly. "I expect them at any time."

We had been sitting there and talking a long time, the afternoon shadows were coming. The black lugger, even from our height, was almost out of sight. But through the glasses she was still visible speeding south-with our trochus and our hopes, I thought dismally.

Then I gazed at Dick, wondering how to put the thought that flashed into my mind.

"Dick," I said hesitantly, "if all you say is right, then when the *Nancy Bell* returns she'll still have that opium aboard."

"Yes," answered Dick, and stared down at the sea. "What are we going to do about it?"

"I don't know."

We both stared down at the sea. Here was a new puzzle.

If trochus shell was worth £ 100 a ton then we had lost £1500 – a lot more if it was selling at over £100 a ton – Dick's share and mine was very small, but it meant a fortune to us. We could have bought a complete prospecting outfit with it. Well, we had lost all the trochus, but through no fault of ours. It had really been the fault of Cross-eyed Joe and his Malay mates. Meanwhile the *Nancy Bell* supposedly had some thousands of pounds' worth of opium hidden aboard her. But we had no share in that, were not supposed even to know of it. But – we did know of it.

"When he returns," said Dick slowly, "he'll take in all that's happened. Then he'll make us an offer. He'll propose to give us just the same amount as would have been ours from the trochus – if the Japs had not taken the trochus. Then he'll suggest we get busy quickly and fish for more trochus. We must get some trochus, for to return to town without any at all would look too bad."

"The trochus may have moved on," I ventured.

"Of course," said Dick. "It's not likely the patch will still be there."

"And what are you going to say to the offer?" I asked curiously.

'We can't accept, Jack," answered Dick miserably. "I know we've lost what would have been a fortune to us, we could have bought a bonzer team, could have loaded up with twelve months' tucker and gone out through the Starcke and had a look round there, then travelled right up the Peninsula to Ebagoolah and the Coen, right to the Batavia. We would have been made –

I'm sure we would have found gold – we'd never have looked back." He Sighed.

Silently I rolled a cigarette. The black lugger was out of sight. Away below, Little Paddy was lighting the fire to put the billy on, staring up at the Hill.

I lit up. "So you're not going to accept the offer."

"We can't, Jack," he answered slowly. "I've got nothing much against opium smugglers or the people who want to buy the stuff. But it's not in our line. I suppose I'd do lots of things that are not considered to be quite right, but I don't think we'd ever feel comfortable if we bought our first team of horses from money we made out of opium – and stolen opium at that."

"Oh well," I said slowly, "if that's the way you think about it, then I'm with you."

Dick stood up, with his old smile.

"Good-oh, Jack! I didn't know how you'd feel about it, it's been such a bitter disappointment. I had to work my hardest to down the idea. I'm sure Cross-eyed Joe will make that offer, and I couldn't blame anyone for accepting it."

"Oh well," I growled, "we've turned it down. Are we going below for a feed?"

"You bet," replied Dick, and we started down the Hill. "We'll get those horses, Jack," he said enthusiastically. "Nothing can stop us. And when we do get them then when we camp out of nights under the stars we'll have no regrets."

His prophecy was to be fully realized in the wonderful years to come.

35

A BATTLE OF WITS

AT dawn the mists came floating up the Hill as Dick and I rolled our blankets. But a steady breeze caught the mists and breathed them in, and there was the sea, all clear and sparkling and capped with white horses. We gazed all around. Not a sail in sight. For some strange reason smoke was coiling up from the camp-fire below. Little Paddy, looking like a black puppy bending, was putting the billy on.

"He must have woke up proper-feller hungry," I remarked, smiling, "to crawl out of the blankets at this hour.

"Not on your life," answered Dick. "It's instinct."

"In what way?"

"I don't know, and neither does he. But in some way he realizes our days and nights of watching up here are over. So he won't have this tedious duty to do any more. In some dim way he feels he is nearer home, and that instinct wakes up any blackfellow."

"How on earth. would he know or feel all that – if it is true?"

"I don't know. But mark my words, Cross-eyed Joe will anchor here before sundown."

"You must possess a jolly lot of instinct yourself," I retorted.

"Not so much in my case. It's only that I'm used to the aboriginals and the coloured people and to the conditions and life of this country." Dick meant of his beloved Cape York Peninsula, and its wild coast. He settled himself comfortably to face the north, and put the glasses to his eye.

"It's an empty sea," I said.

"Yes." Slowly he swept the glasses to the nor'-west. "A lonely sea. By jove," he exclaimed, "don't you realize it? We're lonely, too."

"How?" I asked.

"Don't you miss anything?"

"No."

"Slinker?"

"Can't say I miss him," I said, "and yet – it does make a difference."

"Look at all our thoughts and time that he took up. And now he's gone – bad cess to him and all his gang!"

"Aren't you glad we'll never see him again?"

"I'd like to give him a thump in the eye," answered Dick vindictively.

"But I don't know – he didn't hurt Little Paddy."

"Only tanned his hide." Dick laughed.

Ten minutes later he exclaimed, "Ah, what did I tell you! Here, take a be-peep at this!" And he handed me the glasses and pointed.

I took the glasses and steadied them on a distant islet agreed on long ago by Cross-eyed Joe and us. From its highest point a smoke column was rising, only to be blown away by the breeze. Concentrating on a point near the base of the smoke I saw a tiny flag, obviously on a flag-pole.

"We'll run up the 'all clear'," said Dick. "I felt certain that that wall-eyed Filipino would signal today."

We lashed a blanket to the bamboo flagpole and hoisted it in the cairn. The blanket flapped out, a signal to be seen for many miles on a clear day, many miles further through the glasses.

"He'll be here before sundown;' said Dick. "He's got a fair breeze. Here goes for breakfast!' And in cheerier mood we clambered down the Hill.

Our aboriginal henchmen greeted news of the coming of the *Nancy Bell* with grins that spread from ear to ear. Not that they were in love with Cross-eyed Joe, oh dear, no; it was belly-love with them. They would soon have plenty to eat, plenty of damper and "Cocky's joy" and tinned meat, and plenty tea and "tugar". Above all, there would be tobacco, for our supply was done.

"There's one thing," growled Dick at the aboriginals, as he cooked the very last of the johnny-cakes. "Cross-eyed Joe will make you work for your tucker. For of all the loafers I've ever seen, you three take the bun!"

But Big Paddy and Billy and Man Friday only licked their chops and gazed hungrily on the browning johnnies. We were tired of fish with only a rationed bite of johnny to help them down.

The *Nancy Bell* came gliding into anchorage about mid-afternoon. We stood on the little beach to greet her, they waved cheerily as the sails tumbled down. Down splashed the anchor, they made all snug aboard, then lifted the dinghy overboard. The three of them stepped into her, cast off, and rowed to the beach.

"We been long time, Dicky." Joe beamed. Somehow, it was good to see his weather-beaten, cross-eyed face again.

"Yes," answered Dick, "you've been a long time coming. We thought the Japs had got you."

Joe's grin broadened. "They no wake up in time," he smirked.

"No?" Dick raised his eyebrows, and gestured towards where our stack of trochus once had lain.

The three men looked, gazed in puzzlement, and slowly their

grins disappeared. Joe glanced at Dick, then me, then back to the vacant spot.

"You move him shell, Dicky?" He asked quietly.

"No."

Cross-eyed Joe's wrinkled brown face was quaintly puzzled.

"Where shell?" he asked softly.

"In the black lugger – if it's not sold by this time."

"What you say?"

The eyes of the Filipino narrowed to slits. I noticed Alor San's mouth drawn in a straight line. And the face of Ah Matt became a mask.

"The Japs took the shell!" said Dick.

"What for?" demanded Cross-eyed Joe.

"You should know," shrugged Dick, and glanced at the listening aboriginals. "But we're hungry – nothing to eat but fish. How about sending Ah Matt aboard with the boys to bring some tucker ashore? Then we can talk."

Joe turned to Ah Matt, and nodded. Eagerly Big Paddy and Billy and Man Friday followed Ah Matt to the dinghy. We walked slowly into the shed, sat down, and commenced to roll a cigarette.

"The black lugger came in the night," Dick explained to the skipper as he lit up. "They took us by surprise. Tied us up. Took our trochus aboard. Their skipper told us he took the trochus because you stole goods belonging to him."

For a startled second their eyes met. Then the Filipino calmly puffed his cigarette.

'What goods he say I steal?" he asked softly.

"He didn't tell."

We puffed for a while, then Dick said, "I threatened him with the police. He sneered. He said you'd be too frightened to go to the police."

"That Jap skipper one -- liar," said Cross-eyed Joe calmly.

"He didn't sound like it!" declared Dick explosively. "Anyway, he got away with our shell. What are you going to do about it?"

For quite a time there was silence in the shed. Cross-eyed Joe's eyes had not left Dick's face, nor had Alor San's, their wits working their hardest to guess how much Dick knew.

It certainly must have been a puzzler for them. Puffing at my. cigarette, I tried to work it out. Supposing they really did have a valuable parcel of stolen opium aboard? Then they'd returned to camp when certain the coast was clear, only to find that our trochus shell worth £ 1500 was gone. That was a severe loss. But they mIght be working out that they had thousands of pounds' worth of opium aboard, which would ease their loss.

But Dick and I had lost everything. And now what was their position if Dick and I knew they had stolen opium aboard – let alone the Japs in the black lugger!

Several times Cross-eyed Joe opened his lips to speak, then shut them tight again. With his mind swiftly working, he still could keep control over his tongue. Silence was golden.

Presently, we heard rowlocks as the dinghy neared shore.

Cross-eyed Joe stood up and threw away the butt of his cigarette.

"Sorry we so long away, Dicky," he said quietly. 'We no more can help it. What say all you feller have good feed? Me an' Alor San an' Ah Matt go aboard talk this thing over. This serious. We think what we do. We come ashore tonight, tell you, Jacky."

"Right," agreed Dick grimly. "Better think out some plan. Jack and I feel very angry."

The Filipino nodded as the dinghy grated on the beach.

They walked outside and stood by while our delighted abos carried the tucker up to the shed. Then the three men stepped into the dinghy and rowed quietly out to the *Nancy Bell*.

As Little Paddy put the billy on, Dick turned to me with a satisfied grin.

"Given them something to think about," he said. "I'll bet that wall-eyed Filipino's brains are running a banker with sweat. And I'm going to get something out of the wreck, Jack. They're all right, they've got their loot, but you and I are not going to sail back from here with our tails between our legs."

"What can we do now?" I asked.

"Make them fish for trochus by hook or by crook. We've got the upper hand now and they know it. They'll have to go out on the fishing grounds again, Billy is nearly quite all right now. We can't expect to find trochus thickly as we found it before. But we must find some. Then we'll sail for Cooktown, and Cross-eyed Joe will have to stock up again with tucker – at their expense. Then we'll sail out again, but this time you and I will demand a bigger share of the trochus won. And they'll have to keep on fishing till we get enough money for a few horses, anyway."

"That sounds good to me," I agreed, relievedly. "It would be awful to go back to the old town dead broke."

"We're not going to do that," said Dick with determination. "They can keep their opium, but we're going to have our horses."

"I'm all for it," I agreed. And we turned to the good tucker with ravenous appetites and cheery peace of mind.

It was early evening when Cross-eyed Joe and Alor San rowed ashore. Out of earshot of Big Paddy and Billy and Little Paddy we sat down under the stars, and lit cigarettes. The water of the anchorage was murmurous with ripples.

"We been think him, Dicky," said Cross-eyed Joe.

"Yes?" inquired Dick.

"More better we look for trochus again - catch Jap man later. You, Jacky, share trochus same share, Alor San, Ah Matt. We not got much tucker left, but enough. What you, Jacky say?'

"We agree."

The Filipino stood up quietly and stifled a yawn. "Arright," he said. "We start early morning time. Good night, Dicky, good night, Jacky."

"Good night," we replied.

On bare feet they stepped into the dinghy and rowed away, phosphorus sparkling from their paddle blades.

"That was short and sweet," I murmured.

"Yes," agreed Dick. "They're going to say little as possible until they're certain how much we know. We've won already – they've come across with a bigger share of trochus. Meanwhile they simply must get one cargo of trochus to take back to Cooktown. It would all come out if we returned without any."

"And when we do scratch up that trochus and return to town, you think they'll come across with an offer to keep our mouths shut?"

"Yes," replied Dick, "but I'll be the dumb one then. They'll simply have to come straight back on another cruise until we get enough trochus to buy some horses."

We sat there a long while yarning under the beautiful night sky, dreaming those dreams of adventure that all boys dream.

36

THE JAPS CATCH UP WITH CROSS-EYED JOE

NEAR dawn I was awake – asleep – awake – asleep, tossing as I tried to work out this queer dream-the soft thudding of heavy bodies with little, glass-like creaks in them. Then a stuttering, hysterical hissing and pulling of blankets, and I awoke to see Little Paddy, his eyes like doorknobs as he tugged at Dick. We both sat up. Little Paddy couldn't speak, open-mouthed he pointed out the shed with trembling arm. We jumped up and hurried outside.

In the grey light of coming dawn three dinghies were at the water's edge. Japs were unloading bags of trochus shell and throwing them on the beach. We blinked at the Jap captain; he gazed impassively back. I was positive I was dreaming. I gazed out over the lightening water and, yes, there was the outline of the Nancy Bell and – heavens, yes – not far away there lay the black lugger!

Not a word had been spoken, not a sound, just the thump-thump as the bags of shell were dumped on the sand. I must be dreaming. I knew that Dick felt he was dreaming. The Jap captain walked towards us; his voice broke the spell.

"We bring back shell," he said impassively.

"Wah-wah?" gurgled Dick.

"We bring back shell."

"What for?" muttered Dick sillily.

"You no want?"

"My word, yes!" exclaimed Dick decisively, We were awake now.

"We bring back shell," said the captain, "because we find our goods – aboard your cutter!"

We gazed across at the *Nancy Bell* growing more distinct every minute. I was too astounded to think clearly.

"You and your goods?" echoed Dick.

"Yes."

"And bring back shell?"

"Yes."

"Then you'd better have a cup of tea!"

It sounded so silly that I burst out laughing. And now the spell was really broken. For the first time I saw the Jap skipper smile, while the Japs, unloading the bags of trochus, grinned broadly. Dick grinned bashfully.

"Thank you," replied the skipper. "We too much hurry to advantage offer – very late appointment – men aboard your ship blame. We got what we want now – our property. We return yours. No harm done – only much less convenience against us. Suppose you send your two men aboard we unload quicker-advantage both sides."

"Right-oh," agreed Dick, cheerfully. "Here Big Paddy, Billy, you two feller go along Jap man skipper help him unload shell."

Not too enthusiastically, Big Paddy and Billy stepped towards the dinghies.

"What did you do to them?" grinned Dick with a wave towards the Nancy Bell. "I hope you haven't killed them."

"No," answered the skipper. "Not convenient to kill. We not hurt them – much."

"Much?" said Dick, inquiringly. "I suppose you would have killed them if we had not been here."

"Maybe," answered the skipper quietly. And with a nod he stepped towards the dinghies. Swiftly they pulled out to the black lugger.

"We've got our trochus back," laughed Dick. "Oh Jack, what luck! Come on!"

We stepped to the beach and, each lifting a bag, carried the shell up above high-water mark. Dick eager as a schoolboy to get that precious trochus as far back from the Japs as possible. As we stepped down to the beach for another load we saw two of the Japs returning to the black lugger with two of the *Nancy Bell*'s dinghies. With five dinghies they'd quickly unload the shell. Big Paddy and Billy apparently were down below hoisting up the bags.

"Those two little blackboys will earn their breakfast today, anyway," said Dick grimly. "I bet that Jap skipper is a nigger-driver."

"You don't think they've scuttled Cross-eye and Alar San and Ah Matt?" I asked anxiously, as we picked up another bag.

"No, If they'd caught them on the open sea with no witnesses I'm certain they would have. But there's too many ashore here; it would leak out for certain."

"Why on earth are they returning our shell? It's very valuable. They could have got away with the shell and their wretched opium, too."

"And spoilt their little game for the future," replied Dick. "Now they've got their opium back we've got nothing to hide, but we could squeal if they stole our shell. And you can bet that old Cross-eye and Alar San and Ah Matt would talk in the right quarters, for revenge. But by giving us back our shell they reckon we'll keep quiet – you and I because we've got our shell back and wouldn't want the townspeople; let alone our own people, to ever have suspicions that we were mixed up with opium smuggling; Cross-eyed Joe and Alar San and Ah Matt, not only because they've got their shell back, but because we know it was *they* who stole the opium. And they wouldn't like the Customs Officer and the old Sergeant to know that!" and Dick chuckled.

"You've worked it out right again. And now everything in the garden is lovely."

"It is," said Dick exultantly. "Isn't it a bonzer sunrise?" And old Sol bounded up out of the sea, a ball of molten gold. The five laden dinghies were pulling to shore all rosy upon rosy water. The brown bodies of the rowers shone like burnished bronze.

"Dick," I said suddenly, "how on earth did they time it so well? What a lucky fluke – for them! And what on earth made them come back here at all? How did they manage to arrive before the dawn, only a few hours after the Nancy Bell arrived here? Before Cross-eyed Joe had recovered from the shock of their taking our trochus? Before he had time to form new plans? Even before he had time to hide the opium ashore? How did they work it out to the very minute? Or was it just a fluke?"

"I hadn't thought of that," said Dick, thoughtfully, as the dinghies grated on the beach. "We'll keep on stacking the shell while they unload; and try to think it out."

We did so. But when they pulled away for another load Dick still hadn't solved the problem. With a bag on his shoulder he gazed thoughtfully up at the Hill, suddenly stopped, then laughed and, walking to the forming stack, threw the bag in place. 1 threw mine beside his.

"There is the answer!" he said and pointed up the Hill. On the Look-out cairn there was our flag lazily floating in a light breeze. 1 stared a moment, but could not make it out.

"I don't savvy."

"Don't you see," said Dick, smiling, "there's our 'all clear' signal to Cross-eyed Joe? When those Japs sailed south to Cooktown or elsewhere to sell our shell, they actually did nothing of the sort. They simply sailed out of sight. Then came about in the night and hid within spy-glass sight of the Look-out. Our signal to Cross-eyed Joe in the nor-west was the signal to the Japs hiding in the south. We actually Ssgnalled them ourselves that the *Nancy Bell* was coming – no need for old Slinker at all."

"Ah! That was shrewd."

"It was. Old Slinker was a wise old bird, but that pie-faced Jap skipper is the goods. The whole crowd of pirates are shrewd birds – highly trained men, as i should have realized long ago. They put it over us, but we've learnt a lot. If we've any sense the knowledge will come handy in the future. Anyway," he laughed at me, "I'm glad they put it over Cross-eyed Joe, too."

"So am I. Otherwise we'd never have got our trochus back."

"We would not. Neither would we have got our horses."

"I suppose they worked it this way. When they saw our signal they gave Cross-eye time to sail here. Then they started out about sunset-they'd have the engine, so wind wouldn't matter. They'd steam through the night and get here before dawn."

"Yes. And silently board the *Nancy Bell* from their dinghies. I'll bet they caught those three innocent birds sound asleep!"

"And if we hadn't been here they would have wrung their necks."

"Yes. And they'd twist the whereabouts of the opium out of them, then cut their throats and heave them overboard for the sharks."

"I'm glad they didn't do that."

"So am I, real glad. I've known the three blighters for years and always liked them. But this cunning little trick nearly landed us in an awful fix,"

Morning was well advanced, but it was in a surprisingly short time that the last bag of shell was thrown upon the beach. Little Paddy was staring out towards the black lugger, his eyes wide with apprehension. We could now see the figures of Big Paddy and Billy standing upon the deck. Dick was tempted, but he couldn't bring himself to say, "Jap man he sail away now,"

"Put 'im on billy," he said instead. "We have 'im breakfus soon now. He's scared they're going to run away with Big Paddy and Billy," he murmured to me, "He's afraid he's seeing the last of Pop."

Fancy calling Big Paddy "Pop"! It did seem funny – to us. But to little Man Friday Big Paddy was the most wonderful pop in the world.

They manned the winch out there, the clanking of the anchor chain was startlingly clear. Up went the jib, the engine murmured, then rose into a steady hum. Big Paddy and Billy stepped into our own two – dinghies and cast off as she forged ahead, the fore-sail rolled up. Up went the main-sail and the black lugger was away. Big Paddy and Billy were pulling swiftly to shore.

We jumped into the dinghy, rowed straight to the *Nancy Bell*, and leapt aboard. With hurried glance at the empty deck, we dropped down into the tiny cabin.

Three agonized eyes were the first thing I saw, one slowly being closed by blood. The other three were already closed. Cruel wooden gags forced the men's jaws apart. Their twisted limbs were lashed to the bunks and each other's limbs in such a way that, if one man strained tortured arm or leg, he racked the limb of another. Their faces looked awful through the blood.

We undid the gags, cut the lashings to groans and splutterings, then gasping Malay curses as they rolled to straighten their twisted limbs. Presently they were huddled there on the cabin floor, tenderly massaging limbs and muscles. Alor San gasped in a deep breath, spat out several teeth, then sputtered into furious wrath in Malay. They all appeared to be in urgent need of a dentist.

"How about coming up on deck and washing that blood off?" suggested Dick. "You might feel better then. Can you manage it?"

"Where Jap man go?" growled Cross-eyed Joe.

"He sail away."

"Ah!!" The Filipino spat our some furious malediction against the vanishing Japs. I had never seen him so stirred before.

They dragged themselves up to the deck where Dick slung a bucket overside and deftly hauled it up. Cross-eyed Joe bathed first. The sting of the salt in his open wounds did not improve his temper, while I thought Alor San was going to chew the bucket in his gasping rage. Ah Matt put up a good show, too. If his swear-words had been dynamite they would have blown the bucket and himself to smithereens. But they looked like human beings afterwards, very sore, very angry humans with the salt biting into their bruised wounds. Obviously the Japs had knocked them about badly, either in revenge, or to make them tell quickly where the opium was hidden. I suppose they smashed their faces and twisted their arms and punched their kidneys to invite them to tell; then gave them a good hiding just to get properly square.

"I don't like your mates, skipper," I ventured.

He stared both ways at once at me with queerly twitching face.

"The Japs, I mean," I explained.

I thought he was going to explode. Then he grinned wryly at me."

"Me wish Jap men fry in white-man hell," he gritted out. "Me give *Nancy Bell* to stoke up fire."

A growl from Alor San and a deep curse from Ah Matt agreed with these amiable sentiments. Then old Cross-eye grinned funnily at me, for the other side of his face now seemed all cross-eyed too.

"You help me sew up Billy when shark bit him, Jacky," he mumbled.

"Yes, skipper."

"More interesting job now Jacky – you watch me sew up myself."

"Sort your tools out then," suggested Dick. "And we'll go ashore. You'll all feel better after a bucket of tea and a lining to your insides."

Which suggestion brightened them up quite a lot.

Endeavour Tree, Cooktown, N. Queensland

37

OUR HAPPY HOME-COMING

AND they did enjoy that tea. No wonder. They'd been severely handled, then tied in very painful positions for some time. They gulped that hot tea with a grateful, "Ah, tha's good!" and tried to grin. But their faces were too cut about, their feelings too sour. They ate a good breakfast, though a slow and painful. one. In the middle of a bite Ah Matt howled and, thrusting fingers into open mouth, lugged out a loosened tooth. Dick chuckled; Ah Matt swore awfully. Alor San, too, for sauce used Malay swear-words most of which sounded hot – very hot.

Cross-eyed Joe suffered his troubles more quietly, though a scowl on his saturnine face betrayed a brooding, very angry man.

"Well, skipper," said Dick when they'd finished and lit up for a smoke, "what about it?"

Cross-eyed Joe gazed thoughtfully at Dick's challenging face. Then he grinned wryly, shrugged, and murmured, "Kismet, Dicky". And Alor San and Ah Matt shrugged agreement to that Eastern philosophy.

"Maybe," smiled Dick meaningly, "but Fate has not been as hard as you believe. Come outside."

With one curious look they followed Dick. He pointed to the stack of trochus shell. They stared uncomprehendingly.

They had been so worried at their loss of the wretched opium, not to mention their pain, that they had not noticed the bags when we rowed ashore. Now they stared in comical amazement.

"The Japs brought all our trochus back," explained Dick, and gazed straight at Cross-eyed Joe. "The Jap skipper said they had taken their own goods back, so they returned our trochus."

Joe stared silently, reading Dick's face. Then he grinned and murmured once again, "Kismet!"

Alor San exclaimed something in Malay, 11 twisted grin causing fresh blood to well from his cut face. Ah Matt answered with some amazed Malay oath. It was a magical right-about-turn to nearly cheerful good humour.

"So," grinned Dick, "you haven't lost everything, while Jack and I have recovered all we ever had. So what about it now?"

"Kismet!" murmured Cross-eye Joe, grinning back at Dick. "We talk later." He glanced meaningly at the grinning aboriginals. "Better be doctor now."

"Right-oh," agreed Dick. "You heathen little wretch," he called to Man Friday, "boil bucket quick-feller-plenty hot water."

Cheerfully we all trooped into the shed where, after he had washed his hands in hot Condy water, Cross-eyed Joe carefully laid out and prepared his "tools".

Alor San, squatting on a box, was the first case – not a willing one, either. We stood round, all eyes, Billy with a reminiscent grin. And Alor San gave us a show. He stood it like a Briton, but an angry one, as his screwed-up face and occasional cuss words plainly showed. He had some nasty cuts on face and head and he did not like the feeling of Cross-eyed Joe's needle at all. As each cut was stitched up he'd draw' deep breaths, while his hands clenched and his dark eyes smouldered. Then he'd curse deep down in bitter Malay, while Joe calmly threaded another needle. Alor did not seem the least bit grateful and was obviously pleased when it came Ah Matt's turn.

Ah Matt "took it" too, but he also put on a show in between the threadings of the needle, the occasional snip of the scissors. I did not blame them. What they were going through was not a pretty picture. I would have been scared to go through the same thing myself, and I'll bet I would have told where that opium was hidden quicker than they had. As the operation had proceeded Billy had grown into one huge grin, his appreciative eyes did not miss one prick of the needle, one push through tough skin, nor one horrid pulling through of the thread.

"Me feel 'im that one plenty time," he murmured, "when shark bite 'im me."

"Me like 'im bite 'im them-Japs!" grinned Alor sourly. Billy's wounds had been ever so much worse than these, and he had stood it without a whimper. But then he had not been worried by the furious anger of losing some thousands of pounds worth of opium, followed by a smashing at the hands of the angry Japanese.

Finally came the "doctor's" own turn, and we wondered how he would manage it. Quietly he prepared. Then he sat down by his tools and arranged our two small looking-glasses before him, one low down, the other high up. He was really arranging a periscope. In the lower he could see his face, while the top one threw the reflection of the top of his head down into the lower. Then calmly he began to stitch his own cuts, his tough old brown face first, then some nasty gashes across his head, and a chew out of his ear. He might have been carefully sewing a patch in the seat of his Sunday trousers for all the fuss he made. We watched in a silence so tense that the occasional twittering of a bird outside sounded urgently businesslike and shrill.

When he had finished the last stitch Dick could not help exclaiming,

"Bravo, skipper! You've made a wonderful job of it. Here, drink this."

Old Cross-eye took the drink with a steady hand, and he needed it .. The shadow of a pleased grin twitched across his stitched face.

"Better take it easy for the day," suggested Dick. "Stretch out here while Big Paddy rows to the cutter for your blankets. Here, you little black monkey! Put 'im on billy· quick-feller!" And Little Paddy again darted out to the fire.

They took it easy for a couple of days. On the second evening Dick and I were fishing from the beach when the skipper came along and quietly said, "What you think, Dicky?"

"We'd better take a load of shell into town quick as we can," answered Dick. 'We've no idea what the price is now."

"Me think that way, too. We load up tomorrow morning time."

"Right," agreed Dick enthusiastically. "But you three spell. Jack and I and the boys will load the cutter and get all shipshape."

Joe nodded, and puffed his cigarette while I quietly noted that our skipper had deferred to Dick. No word or suggestion of opium had yet been mentioned between us.

"Who will man the cutter?" asked Dick after a while. "You an' me an' Jacky," answered Cross-eye dreamily.

"Weather good, petrol still left, we manage easy. Others mind camp, we soon be back."

"Right-oh," agreed Dick.

When we went back to bunk that night Dick winked at me as he said, "Old Cross-eye is taking no chances, even now. And his shrewd old head is still busy working it out. He leaves Alar San and Ah Matt ashore here, for if the three of them landed in Cooktown looking as if they'd just tumbled out of a mincing machine, then there'd have to be explanations. He can easily make an excuse for himself – an accident. Anyway, we'll only be in town a few hours. He leaves the abos here, too, so they can't talk."

"And we won't."

"He's not so' sure of that," grinned Dick. "I bet he comes across with a better proposition before we hit Cooktown."

And he did. It was after midday, only two days later.

The *Nancy Bell* was singing her way over a playful sea.

Grassy Hill rose over the bows with the white signal station sparkling in the sunlight, and the little town nestling along the waterfront at the foot of the hills. Dick's face was alight with pleasure as he gazed longingly at his beloved home town. Old Cross-eyed Joe quietly smoked by the tiller.

"You glad be home, Dick?" he asked softly. "You're telling me," laughed Dick.

"We have good cruise?"

"Very good."

Cross-eye rolled another cigarette, and lit up. "We make plenty money this voyage, Dicky."

"Yes, skipper. We've made a little fortune."

"Shell good price. Alor San, Ah Matt an' me, we talk back there. You and Jacky work very hard. We agree I give bigger share you an' Jacky."

"That's jolly good of you, skipper," answered Dick enthusiastically. "Thanks a lot."

"Same with me, skipper," I agreed. "That's real good of you."

The old Filipino smilingly nodded, puffed his cigarette.

Then, as an afterthought, lifted his brow in a puzzled way and gazed at Dick.

"Dicky," he said softly, "those Jap men – they worry me. P'raps it better not say anything about Jap man in town. People maybe think wrong way," he added apologetically.

"Forget it, skipper," said Dick with a laugh and a wave of his hand. "Jack and 1 are so glad to be coming home with a good cargo of shell that we've forgotten all about the Japs. We won't mention them."

Cross-eyed Joe nodded and smiled in pleased relief. "Good," he said. "Much better we all forget."

And so we came into the mouth of the old Endeavour, and gently steamed to the little wharf used for the unloading of shell. The skipper already was dolled out in his shore-going togs, and away he went up the street to the Chinese merchant to arrange the sale.

"It's some time since. old Cross-eye stepped out so smartly," grinned Dick.

"Yes." I smiled. "He's as anxious now to find out the price of shell as we are."

Someone shouted from across the street. Dick waved in reply. Soon a little group had gathered, all hearty congratulations at our wonderful catch of shell. The whole town would know almost in a matter of minutes. Dick arranged with a couple of the local wharfies to unload the shell. There was only five tons of it, it wouldn't take long.

Presently, Cross-eyed Joe came striding back along the footpath past Mrs Watson's monument, and despite his patched face we saw he was fairly bubbling with pleasure.

Trochus shell was £ 120 a ton! And he'd sold the whole fifteen tons!

"Oh, Jack," laughed Dick, "what a great team we'll buy now!"

The unloading of the shell went on quickly, and the dray came clanking down the street to cart it away to the store. Cross-eyed Joe hurried back to town to order stores and petrol; we'd have them aboard by nightfall and be away again by the dawn tide. Dick and I hurried up the main street, for Dick was anxious to get home and tell his family our good fortune. We could not hurry much, though; everyone knew Dick and we had to stop and yarn all the way along the street.

The first one to greet Dick at home came bounding out with a roar like a young lion. A clumsy, half-grown puppy that would grow into a huge dog of some sort, a fearsome one. This was Dick's "Bully", and he was training him to go with us on our trips through the wild north, our watch-dog-to-be when travelling through "bad native" country. Bully tried to knock Dick down, tried, in fact, to eat both of us! In the commotion Dick's mother and sisters and brothers came bustling out on to the veranda. A happy home-coming.

There's very little more to tell, and what there is is cheery. We returned to Lizard Island and soon were back in town with another cargo.

Then again back to the island, where we spent a day diving for trochus. But the "patch" had moved on, and there were only a few trochus every here and there. I feel certain we were all secretly glad; we had made a wonderful catch and were looking forward to a spell and "spend-up" in the old home town.

What presents all of us could now afford to buy wives and mothers, brothers and sisters and friends! Big Paddy and Billy spent their time excitedly talking and dreaming about their pay, and a good bonus was to be added, making it far and away above anything they had ever earned before. As to Little Paddy, his eyes popped so far out of his head we thought they would never roll back when old Cross-eyed Joe told him what wealth was to be his share. He was going to have enough to buy not only a whole "bullick", but three cases of Nigger Twist tobacco as well! And a new print dress for his "mumma". What a hero he would be to his tribe!

We loaded up for the last trip, pulled down the tent, took all aboard, then "Up anchor!" and away. Never were orders so cheerily obeyed.

As the *Nancy Bell* turned her perky nose south the spray seemed to sing of our home-coming. Dick and I gazed back at the island, the bamboo flagpole stood straight up towards the sky from the cairn on the Look-out. Bright sunlight bathed the Hill and the ridge, the granite rocks and shrubs and little beaches.

"Well?" inquired Dick at last.

"I was thinking," I replied, "of how we played hide-and-seek with Slinker."

"Yes," said Dick reminiscently. "It's been a wonderful cruise, Jack. But what a lot happened to us on that little island! In a way it's just a little bit hard to leave it. But how very nearly again and again our cruise came to a tragic end. It's been like magic, the way it has ended so wonderfully."

"Yes, a wonderful cruise."

"Only the start of many cruises, Jack," said Dick, smiling delightedly. "And the next one by land. What a great team we'll buy, we can pick the very best horses. And then away to the Peninsula and the land of gold."

We both laughed. And all hands, and the sea and the sky and the sea-birds laughed with us.

Printed in Australia
AUHW021049110122
358057AU00006B/6

9 781922 698070